Healthcare Management

(Concept and Cases)

Dr. Ruchi Singh
MBA, Ph.D (Management),
Head, Department of Management,
National P.G. College, Lucknow

Ms. Deeksha Sharma
MBA
Lecturer, Department of Management,
National P.G. College, Lucknow

Himalaya Publishing House
ISO 9001:2015 CERTIFIED

First Edition : 2011
Reprint : 2023

Published by : Mrs. Meena Pandey
for **HIMALAYA PUBLISHING HOUSE PVT. LTD.,**
"Ramdoot", Dr. Bhalerao Marg, Girgaon, Mumbai - 400 004.
Phone: 022-23860170, 23863863; **Fax:** 022-23877178
E-mail: himpub@bharatmail.co.in; **Website:** www.himpub.com

Branch Offices :

New Delhi : "Pooja Apartments", 4-B, Murari Lal Street, Ansari Road, Darya Ganj, New Delhi - 110 002. Phone: 011-23270392, 23278631; Fax: 011-23256286

Nagpur : Kundanlal Chandak Industrial Estate, Ghat Road, Nagpur - 440 018. Phone: 0712-2721215, 2721216

Bengaluru : Plot No. 91-33, 2nd Main Road, Seshadripuram, Behind Nataraja Theatre, Bengaluru - 560 020. Phone: 080-41138821; Mobile: 09379847017, 09379847005

Hyderabad : No. 3-4-184, Lingampally, Besides Raghavendra Swamy Matham, Kachiguda, Hyderabad - 500 027. Phone: 040-27560041, 27550139

Chennai : No. 34/44, Motilal Street, T. Nagar, Chennai - 600 017. Mobile: 09380460419

Pune : "Laksha" Apartment, First Floor, No. 527, Mehunpura, Shaniwarpeth (Near Prabhat Theatre), Pune - 411 030. Phone: 020-24496323, 24496333; Mobile: 09370579333

Cuttack : Plot No 5F-755/4, Sector-9, CDA Market Nagar, Cuttack - 753 014, Odisha. Mobile: 09338746007

Kolkata : 3, S.M. Bose Road, Near Gate No. 5, Agarpara Railway Station, North 24 Parganas, West Bengal - 700109. Mobile: 09674536325

DTP by : Bright Computer Systems

Printed at : Infinity Imaging System, New Delhi. On behalf of HPH.

Dedicated to
Our Parents
and Family
with
Love and Affection

PREFACE

The book Healthcare Management is based on the need and requirement of students pursuing various degree courses in management. Due to difficulties faced by the students. We decided to write a book having all the relevant topics in a single book. The syllabus is vast and there are diversified topics. So, it was a dream came true when all the topics were summed up.

The book has been organised into fair section. Section one deal with Healthcare and Social development, section two deals with Healthcare System. Section three comprises of Healthcare economics and finance section four deals with the Hospital functions, organisation, classification and components. The book also comprises of relevant cases studies according to the topic of syllabus and also last three years question papers and a model question paper. We do not claim that much of the material in the book represent new or original thinking on our part. The material was developed from various sources and from the works of well-known authorities. References were taken from well known literature, books, journals and websites. Possibly, we have cited the reference at appropriate places. If inadvertently, we could not cite the reference, it is deeply regretted.

All possible efforts have gone into preparing this book, but if there is any mistakes, the readers are requested to bring it into our notice, so that rectification can be made. Without active involvement of readers we won't be able to improve and update the book.

We wish to 'thank' all our well wishers and friends. We are grateful to Dr. S.P. Singh,

Mr. M.C. Pandey, Mr. Bachan Singh, Mr. Vibhav Singh for their constant support and encouragement.

We are indebted to our parents & family members for their support.

Authors

ACKNOWLEDGEMENTS

"In the midst of a land without silence you have to make a place for yourself. Those who have worn out their shows many times know where to step. It is not only their shoes you can wear their footsteps you may follow, if you let it happen."

M. Cotter

For us to write this book, an inspiring force has been students of Management Colleges since introduction of the paper on Healthcare Management. They have always complained that they could not find a comprehensive book on Healthcare Management. Their persistent demand had heightened semester after semester.

Their request has turned into a fruitful compliance. We will feel delighted if this book quenches the thirst of student's knowledge on this subject.

We record my appreciation to our Dynamic Principal Dr. S.P. Singh whose support and encouragement had always been there.

The mention of support of our families should not go unnoticed.

Our special thanks are due to Mr. M.C. Pandey, Mr. Bachhan Singh and Mr. Vibhav Singh of Himalaya Publishing House for providing us the publishing support.

Authors

CONTENTS

Unit-III

Unit IV

1

HEALTHCARE MANAGEMENT: THE BASIC FRAMEWORK AND THE CURRENT STATE OF AFFAIRS

Learning Objectives

After studying this Chapter you should be able to :

- Understand the framework for Healthcare Management in India.
- Understand the current state of affairs of Healthcare Management in India.
- Have an Industry overview of Healthcare Services.
- Understand the Micro and the Macro Environment playing crucial role in Healthcare Services in India.
- Understand the demographic challenges and how vital is to satisfy customers.

"Management is efficiency in climbing the ladder of success; leadership determines whether the ladder is leaning against the right wall."

— Stephen R. Covey

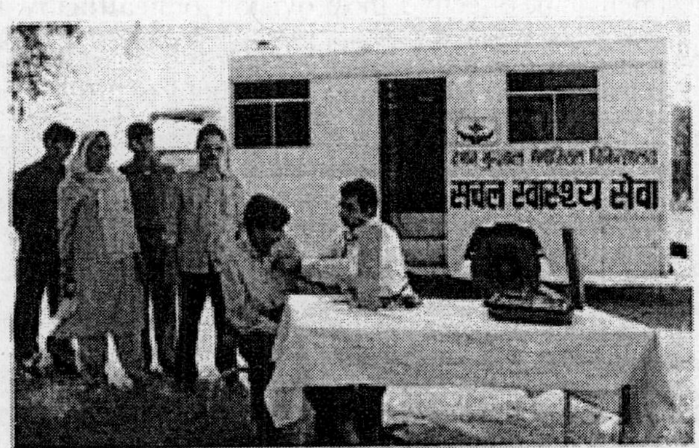

The book is aimed at **practitioners of healthcare** to make them understand the role of management studies in Healthcare and at students studying post-graduate programs in healthcare management and allied areas. This book brings forth not only academic learning but experiential learning as well to both managers and managers-to-be. It is true that management cannot be taught through a book so we have made an effort, make this book as practical as possible replete with case studies and examples from real life.

But the best and most successful managers are reflective practitioners profoundly aware of their own behaviours, attitudes and actions and their impact on others and their organisation, and able to analyse and critically review their own practice and set it in a wider context framed by appropriate theories, models and concepts. (Peck 2004)The future leaders of the healthcare sector need to amalgamate their theories successfully with their experiences.

This chapter sets the base for the book by explaining the current environment in which the sector is being placed. We will thoroughly look into the various environments affecting healthcare sector viz., the political environment, the social environment and how that environment is changing. Then we shall discuss the various challenges faced by this sector and what makes it so novice and interesting to work in. we then will lay out the entire structure of the book and explain how each unit contributes towards better understanding of the subject.

Healthcare Services: Industry Overview

The 2009 KPMG report on *Global Infrastructure: Trend Monitor* says that Indian Healthcare industry is estimated to double in value by 2012 and more than quadruple by 2017. The main factors propelling this growth are rising income levels, changing demographics and illness profiles with a shift from chronic to lifestyle diseases. This is likely to result in considerable infrastructure challenges and opportunities.

There is growing appreciation in the role. Private involvement may have in meeting public demand and governments are assessing the utility of **public private partnership (PPP) models** to help improve infrastructure and healthcare provisions. The government is also exploring setting up state-funded healthcare insurance schemes to support healthcare delivery to poorer sections of the society. For investment to be effective, the provision for **healthcare infrastructure** and insurance should be strategically coordinated. Unlike in developed markets, where there is a focus on generating specialized healthcare facilities and innovations to drive improvements in health services, the Indian healthcare delivery model (including the use of PPP) has to date only had success in the provision of more healthcare services in relatively small segments. The challenge remains to develop scalable and sustainable healthcare delivery models to deal with India's diversity and challenging socio-economic profiles. The major innovations in Indian healthcare delivery models need to be focused on developing and delivering affordable healthcare services.

Healthcare Systems: Micro and Macro-Environment

In most developed countries, the healthcare sector is anything from 8% to 15% of the economy, making it one of the largest industries in any state bigger generally than education, agriculture, IT, tourism or telecommunications and a crucial component of wider economic performance. In most countries, one out of 10 workers is employed in the healthcare sector-as doctors, nurses, scientists, therapists, cleaners, cooks, engineers, administrators, clerks, finance controllers- and of course as managers. This means that almost anyone has a relative or knows someone who works in healthcare, and the healthcare workforce can be a politically powerful group with a considerable influence over public opinion. Almost everyone uses health services, or has member of their family or friends who are significant healthcare users, and everyone has a view to express about their local healthcare system.

In many countries, the history of the healthcare system is intertwined with the development of communities and social structure. Religious groups, charities, voluntary organisations, trade unions and local municipalities have all played important roles in building the healthcare organisations and systems we have today, and people in those communities often feel viscerally connected to those hospitals, community clinics, ambulance service and other parts of the healthcare system. They fundraise to support new facilities or equipment, and volunteer to work in a wide range of roles which augment or support the employed healthcare workforce. That connection with the community also comes to the force with anyone-especially govern-ment-suggests changing or reconfiguring healthcare provision. Proposals to close much loved community hospitals or to reorganize district hospital services or to change maternity services are often professionally driven by a laudable policy imperative to make health services more effective, safe and efficient. But when evidence of clinical effectiveness and technocratic appraisals of service options collide with popular sentiments and public opinion, what matters is usually not 'what works' but 'what people want'.

For many local and national politicians, health policy and healthcare system offer not only the opportunity to shine in the eyes of the electorate when things are going well, but also threats to future electoral success when there are problems with **healthcare funding or service provision** and people look for someone to hold account. Many of the problems that constituents bring to politicians in their local office concern healthcare services, and politicians are closely in touch with and aware of the attitudes and beliefs of the public about their local health service. While they will happily gain political benefit from the opening of a new facility, or the expansion of clinical services, they will equally happily secure benefit by criticizing the plans of 'faceless bureaucrats' in the local healthcare organisations for changes in healthcare services, argue that there are too many managers and pen pushers, and wax nostalgically about times past when hospitals were run by doctors and nurses and matrons were in charge.

Finally, for the press, TV and radio media, both locally and nationally, the healthcare system is an endless source of news stories, debates and current affair topics. From patient safety to bird flu, from dangerous doctors to hospital closures, from waiting lists to celebrity illnesses, the healthcare system is news. Big healthcare stories can command coverage in national dailies and repeated presentations on TV news bulletins, while at local level it will be hard to find a local newspaper which did not have some content about local hospitals, clinics or other healthcare services in each issue. Healthcare organizations can use the level of media interest to their advantage, to raise public awareness of health issues and to communicate with the community, but they can also find themselves on the receiving end of intense media scrutiny when things go wrong.

In other words, healthcare organisations exist in a turbulent political and social environment, in which their actions and behaviours are highly vulnerable and much scrutinized. Leadership and management take place in his 'goldfish bowl', where their performance and process can be just as important as their outcomes. But if that were not enough, in every developed country the healthcare system is subject to four challenging social trends:

- The demographic shift
- The pace of technological innovation
- Changing user and consumer expectations
- Rising costs

The only certainty is that if it is difficult to make the sums add up for the healthcare system today, these pressures mean it will be even harder to do it tomorrow.

The demographic challenge is because people are living longer, the number of elderly and very elderly people are rising fast-and those people make much heavier use of healthcare system. People may live longer, but they cost more to keep alive, they are more likely to have complex, chronic health conditions and their last few months of life tend to be more expensive. A further dimension to this demographic challenge is the rising incidences of chronic diseases in the wider population of developed countries. The World Health Organization suggests that this is the direct result of risk factors such as tobacco use, physical inactivity and unhealthy diets. (WHO 2005).

The second challenge is related to the first in that it reflects an increasing ability to control chronic disease and thus extend life-the pace of technological innovation. Most obviously in pharmaceuticals, but also in surgery, diagnostics and other areas, we keep finding new ways to cure or mange disease. Sometimes that means new treatments which are more effective than (and usually more expensive than) the existing ones. But it also means new treatments for diseases or problems which we simply could not treat before. Previously fatal conditions become treatable.

Satisfying customers is vital to organizational health and well-being. Successful organiza-tions focus on the customer to create **sustainable competitive advantage.** By adopting a customer orientation, the organization seeks to understand consumer needs and expectations, then develop offerings they need. This creates a corporate culture in which continuous improvements in quality, customer service and cost and ultimately customer-perceived value becomes the norm.

These dynamics are especially relevant in the context of healthcare services. Recent hos-pital satisfaction studies have shown that most patients are either 'delighted' or 'pleased'. On the surface, this research seems positive unless reviewed with recent data. Several studies have shown that just satisfying or pleasing the customer does not result in brand loyalty. Furthermore it has been proved that many satisfied customers have been prone to **'switching behaviour'.** Therefore, in the context of healthcare almost 70% of the customers are prone to 'switching'.

Despite expectations that employers would be forced to rein in the rising cost of Healthcare by radically reducing benefit plan coverage, this has not occurred. In fact, benefit plans have tended to remain stable, with employers being relatively slow to adopt the innovative Healthcare benefit strategies and major benefit design changes proposed by benefit plan providers to control costs (e.g. consumer-driven health plans, health reimbursement accounts, health savings accounts, etc.). Instead, recent practices reported by HR professionals to partially offset the rapid rise in premiums have included cost shifting of premium increases to employees, higher deductibles, mail-order and **generic prescription programs**, and increased patient cost sharing. Because Healthcare costs and therefore premiums are expected to continue to outstrip the overall Indian economy by a significant margin for the foreseeable future, these strategies cannot continue unabated indefinitely without having a negative impact on total employee compensation. This includes the plight of the uninsured and makes recommendations on how HR practice leaders can provide a framework for employers and employees to partner together as consumers to facilitate appropriate Healthcare selections on the basis of cost and quality factors for their organizations.

Keywords : Healthcare practitioners, PPP models, Healthcare funding service provisions, demographic challenges, sustainable competitive advantage, switching beha-viour, generic prescription programmes.

Summary : KPMG survey predicted that the share of Healthcare Services will double by the year 2012. Increased emphasis has been seen on the role of PPP (public private partnership) in the growing era.

In most developing countries, healthcare constitutes one of the major section of the economy.

Thus, Healthcare Sector provides advantages to many social and political environment verities and others like demographic, technological rising cost and consumer expectation pose a challenge today.

Questions :

1. Briefly state an overview on the current and failure status of Healthcare in India. Also describe the system.
2. List out the various advantages, disadvantages of Healthcare Sector. Give a SWOT analysis to the same effect.

Short Notes :

- Demographic Challenges
- Customer Satisfaction
- Switching behaviour

2

HEALTHCARE IN SOCIAL DEVELOPMENT CONTEXT-INDIGENOUS, PARTICIPATORY AND EMPOWERING APPROACHES

Learning Objectives

After studying this Chapter you should be able to understand :

- The various approaches in social development of Healthcare Industry.
- The various responsibilities listed by Ministry of Healthcare and Family Welfare as related to social development.
- The development of strategy of rural primary Healthcare.
- The various measures adopted by Ministry of Healthcare and Family Welfare for improving health condition of people.
- The commitment made by Indian government.

"Health is the foundation for overall development of human society."

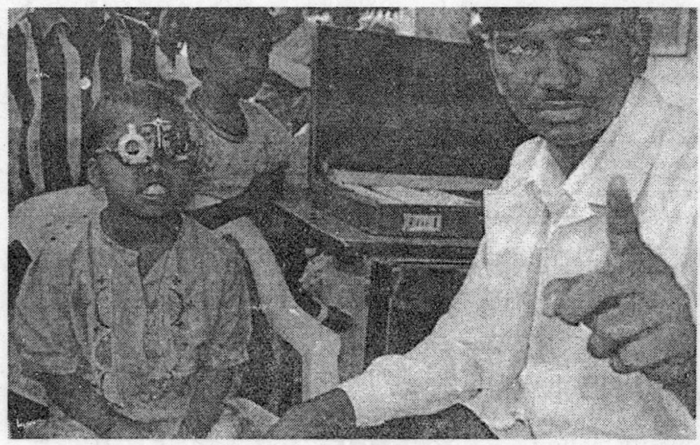

Social development scholars and practitioners have long advocated and important role for indigenization and grassroots participation in designing and implementing social development programs. Because of the recognized connection between health and social development, they have increasingly advocated for more indigenous and participatory approaches in conducting health assessments and in the delivery of health programs of relevance to individuals, families and communities.

The Ministry of Healthcare and Family Welfare has the following responsibilities as related to social development:

Drafting and implementing national policy and legal regulation for:

- healthcare
- social development
- labour and consumer rights protection
- regular health checks to control the spread of infectious diseases and AIDS
- medical aid and **medical rehabilitation**
- the pharmaceutical industry, including quality control and the effectiveness and safety of medical products
- sanitation and **epidemiological safety**
- living standards and personal income
- demographic policy
- health services for professionals employed in hazardous industries
- medical-biological evaluation of the effects of physical and chemical hazards on the human body
- the spa and health resort services
- labour compensation
- pension benefits, including non-government pension funds
- social insurance
- labour conditions and safety
- social partnership and labour relations
- employment and unemployment
- labour migration
- alternative to military service
- government civil services (excluding labour compensation issues)
- social protection (especially for families, women and children).

Providing state services and managing state property in:

- healthcare and social development, medical aid (including high medical technologies such as human tissue and organ transplantation)
- development and implementation of new medical technology, new diagnostic and treatment methods
- the spa and health resort services
- forensic medical and psychiatric examination
- social services
- prosthetic and orthopaedic services
- rehabilitation services for people with disabilities
- medical and social examination
- professional training and retraining
- professional growth of individuals working in medicine, pharmaceuticals and sanitary-epidemiological services, social development and health resorts and in the sphere of labour safety.

The development strategy of **rural primary healthcare** in the 21st century has reached consensus that primary Healthcare is the best approach to achieving health for all and a reliable guarantee for sustainable improvement in people's health. The idea of primary Healthcare advocated by WHO is an important guidance for achieving the UN Millennium Development Goals (MDGs).

Decades of practices in primary Healthcare in India has proved that it is the unshakable responsibility of the government to put people first and safeguard their rights to health; that promoting accessible Healthcare for everyone, protecting and improving people's health constitute an important cornerstone for the sustainable social and economic development; that achieving a balanced development of urban and rural health by putting rural and remote areas in priority and empowering the people of all walks of life to share the development outcomes, provide a strong guarantee for the enhancement of social harmony; and that emphasizing prevention and giving full play to the traditional medicine during the course of introducing modern medical technologies is an effective approach to bringing down the health cost and leveraging the benefits of Healthcare. The cause of global health in the 21st century is facing a lot of opportunities as well as challenges. The tasks specified in the Millennium Development Goals require us to assume due responsibilities. Both developed and developing countries need to overcome a series of emerging problems such as unbalanced social and economic development, changes in disease spectrum, shortage and irrational allocation of health resources, increased population migration. Working out the solutions to these difficult problems is a test of the vision and wisdom of the governments of individual countries.

The health condition of the people in a specific country brings direct impact on its overall economic development and represents the level of its overall social advancement. Transforming the ideas into actions and giving priority to promoting health of the people in the rural and remote areas is the key to the realization of "health for all". Therefore, we the Ministry of Health and Family Welfare, on behalf of Chinese government propose the following measures be adopted:

- Government's responsibilities in promoting primary Healthcare shall be clearly defined. Government shall incorporate the primary Healthcare into their work objectives and social and economic development planning, with government's responsibilities stressed and the health policy improved. An inter-jurisdictionally coordinated primary Healthcare work mechanism participated by the whole society shall also be established.
- Greater importance shall be attached to the development of the Healthcare in rural and remote areas. The government shall include the rural areas as a whole and promote an **equity-oriented health policy.** A health funding mechanism with preference being given to the rural and remote areas shall be set up to provide guarantees for the sustainable development of the primary Healthcare.
- A sound primary Healthcare service network shall be built. A primary Healthcare service network targeted at the rural and remote areas in line with the actual conditions of each individual country shall be constructed in order to provide safe, efficient and accessible medical and Healthcare services.
- Priorities shall be given to the development of human resources for the rural and remote areas. Investment in human resources shall be increased to develop a sizable pool of talents. And an effective mechanism to attract and retain quality health workers in rural areas shall be established.
- The rural medical insurance system shall be improved. A medical insurance system that covers all rural residents shall be established to effectively reduce the farmers' burden of medical expenses and secure their access to the basic medical and health services.
- Feasible health technologies shall be extended and applied. Reliable, cost-effective and popular health technologies shall be promoted in the rural and remote areas, while giving full play to the advantages and roles of the traditional medicine in the primary Healthcare.
- Prevention shall be stressed. Strengthen **health promotion** and advocate a healthy philosophy of life through enhancing the health awareness and self Healthcare capabilities of the residents.
- International exchanges and cooperation shall be strengthened. A closer partnership shall be established among the member states to share the success experience and technologies in primary Healthcare.

The Indian government has made the following commitments:

- To formulate national development program for rural primary Healthcare and incorporate it into the government work plan and the objectives for social and economic development.
- To increase government input to health development in rural and remote areas and ensure the increased health expenditures be mainly utilized for rural and remote areas. Transfer payment to the poor areas shall be strengthened in order to provide adequate funds for the operation of rural public health institutions and the prevention and treatment of major infectious diseases.
- To establish rural health service system covering all rural and remote areas in the country. Efforts shall also be made to strengthen the construction of rural Healthcare facilities, enhance service capacity and provide safe and effective public health services and basic medical services for the rural residents.
- To be dedicated to the development of human resources for health for the rural and remote areas. Dedications shall also be made to establish a long-term mechanism to promote urban support to rural Healthcare and to support the applied research and extend feasible health technologies while giving full play to the role of the traditional medicine in the primary Healthcare.
- To push forward in an all-round way the development of rural medical security system. A fund-raising mechanism shall be established with government leadership, public funding and individual's participation. The standards of this system shall be gradually upgraded with the economic development. By year 2010, to reach the goal that the rural medical security system basically covers all rural residents. At the same time, a **Medicaid system** targeted at the rural poor people shall be set up to improve their basic Healthcare.

Health is an eternal pursuit of human being. Serving as the driving force for social development, health itself is the goal of social development.

Keywords : Medical Rehabilitation, epidemiological safety, equity – oriented health policy.

Summary : For Social Development of Healthcare sector, there is a due requirement of grass root participation. The Ministry of Healthcare and amity welfare has taken the responsibilities of Drafting in Implementing National Policy & legal regulations, and providing state services and managing state property.

The health of people of a country contribute to its overall social and economic development. Research and experience says success is with 'Primary Healthcare' and it is the onus of the government to provide primary Healthcare.

Questions :

1. How can grass root participation promote Healthcare?
2. List out the responsibilities of Ministry of Health & Family Welfare, Government of India as related to social development.

Short Notes:

- Implementation of National Policy
- Primary Healthcare
- PHC service network
- Government inputs to promote social development

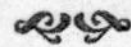

3

NATIONAL HEALTH POLICY

Learning Objectives

After studying this chapter you should be able to understand :

- The progress India has achieved in promotion of health status of our people.
- The existing picture of health status of our people.
- The 20-point programme.
- How population stabilisation has been brought as out?
- How delivery of Healthcare improves with Medical & Health Education?
- How is the Re-Orientation of existing health personnel done?
- How is practice produce done by government functionaries?
- Highlight problems requiring urgent attention.
- Discuss briefly on Health Education and on MIS, Health Insurance, Health Legislation. Medical Research, Inter-Sectoral Cooperation, Monitoring and review of progress.
- An Introduction to National Health Policy-2002.
- The current scenario of NHP-2002.
- The delivery of National Public Health Programmes.

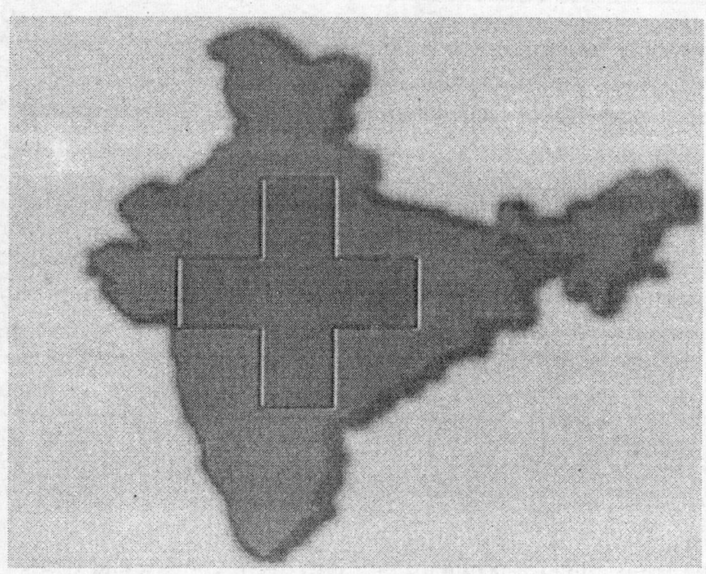

Introduction

The Constitution of India envisages the establishment of a new social order based on equality, freedom, justice and the dignity of the individual. It aims at the elimination of poverty, ignorance and ill-health and directs the State to regard the raising of the level of nutrition and the standard of living of its people and the improvement of public health as among its primary duties, securing the health and strength of workers, men and women, specially ensuring that children are given opportunities and facilities to develop in a healthy manner.

Since the inception of the planning process in the country, the successive Five Year Plans have been providing the framework within which the States may develop their health services infrastructure, facilities for medical education, research, etc. Similar guidance has sought to be provided through the discussions and conclusions arrived at in the Joint Conferences of the Central Councils of Health and Family Welfare and the National Development Council. Besides, Central legislation has been enacted to regulate standards of medical education, prevention of food adulteration, maintenance of standards in the manufacture and sale of certified drugs, etc.

While the broad approaches contained in the successive Plan documents and discussion in the forums referred to in Para 1.2, may have generally served the needs of the situation in the past, it is felt that an integrated, comprehensive approach towards the future development of medical education, research and health services requires to be established to serve the actual health needs and priorities of the country. It is in this context that the need has been felt to evolve a National Health Policy.

Our Heritage

India has a rich, centuries-old heritage of medical and health sciences. The **philosophy of Ayurveda** and the surgical skills enunciated by Charaka and Shushruta bear testimony to our ancient tradition in the scientific Healthcare of our people. The approach of our ancient medical systems was of a holistic nature, which took into account all aspects of human health and disease. Over the centuries, with the intrusion of foreign influences and mingling of cultures, various systems of medicine evolved and have continued to be practiced widely. However, the **allopathic system of medicine** has, in a relatively short period of time, made a major impact on the entire approach to Healthcare and pattern of development of the health services infrastructure in the country.

Progress Achieved

During the last three decades and more, since the attainment of Independence, considerable progress has been achieved in the promotion of the health status of our people. Smallpox has been eliminated; plague is no longer a problem; mortality from cholera and related diseases has decreased and malaria brought under control to a considerable extent. The mortality rate per thousand of population has been reduced from 27.4 to 14.8 and the life expectancy at birth has increased from 32.7 to over 52. A fairly extensive network of dispensaries, hospitals and institutions providing specialized curative care has developed and a large stock of medical and health personnel of various levels has become available. Significant indigenous capacity has been established for the production of drugs and pharmaceuticals, vaccines, sera, hospital equipments, etc.

The Existing Picture

In spite of such impressive progress, the demographic and health picture of the country still constitutes a cause for serious and urgent concern. The high rate of population growth continues to have an adverse effect on the health of our people and the quality of their lives. The mortality rates for women and children are still distressingly high; almost one third of the total deaths occur among children below the age of 5 years; infant mortality is around 129 per thousand live births. Efforts at raising the nutritional levels of our people have still to bear fruit and the extent and severity of malnutrition continues to be exceptionally high. Communicable and non- communicable diseases have still to be brought under effective control and eradicated. Blindness, Leprosy and T.B. continue to have a high incidence. Only 31% of the rural population has access to potable water supply and 0.5% enjoys basic sanitation.

High incidence of diarrheal diseases and other preventive and infectious diseases, especially amongst infants and children, lack of safe drinking water and poor environmental sanitation, poverty and ignorance are among the major contributory causes of the high incidence of disease and mortality.

The existing situation has been largely by the almost wholesale adoption of health manpower development policies and the establishment of curative centers based on the Western models, which are inappropriate and irrelevant to the real needs of our people and the socio-economic conditions obtaining in the country. The hospital-based disease and cure-oriented approach towards the establishment of medical services has provided benefits to the upper crusts, of society, especially those residing in the urban areas. The proliferation of this approach has been at the cost of providing **comprehensive primary Healthcare services** to the entire population, whether residing in the urban or the rural areas. Furthermore, the continued high emphasis on the curative approach has led to the neglect of the preventive, promotive, public health and rehabilitative aspects of Healthcare. The existing approach, instead of improving awareness and building up self-reliance, has tended to enhance dependency and weaken the community's capacity to cope with its problems. The prevailing policies in regard to the education and training of medical and health personnel, at various levels, has resulted in the development of a cultural gap between the people and the personnel providing care. The various health programs have, by and large, failed to involve individuals and families in establishing a self-reliant community. Also, over the years, the planning process has become largely oblivious of the fact that the ultimate goal of achieving a satisfactory health status for all our people cannot be secured without involving the community in the identification of their health needs and priorities as well as in the implementation and management of the various health.

Need for Evolving a Health Policy - the Revised 20-Point Programme

India is committed to attaining the goal of "**Health for All** by the Year 2000 A.D." through the universal provision of comprehensive primary Healthcare services. The attainment of this goal requires a thorough overhaul of the existing approaches to the education and training of medical and health personnel and the reorganization of the health services infrastructure. Furthermore, considering the large variety of inputs into health, it is necessary to secure the complete integration of all plans for health and **human development** with the overall national socio-economic development process, especially in the more closely health related sectors, e.g. drugs and pharmaceuticals, agriculture and food production, rural development, education and social welfare, housing, water supply and sanitation, prevention of food adulteration, maintenance of prescribed standards in the manufacture and sale of drugs and the conservation of the environment. In sum, the contours of the **National Health Policy** have to be evolved within a fully integrated planning framework which seeks to provide universal, comprehensive primary Healthcare services, relevant to the actual needs and priorities of the community at a cost which the people can afford, ensuring that the planning and implementation of the various health programs is through the organized involvement and participation of the community, adequately utilizing the services being rendered by **private voluntary organisations active in the Health sector.**

It is also necessary to ensure that the pattern of development of the health services infrastructure in the future fully takes into account the revised 20-Point Programme. The said Programme attributes very high priority to the promotion of family planning as a people's programme, on a voluntary basis; substantial augmentation and provision of primary Healthcare facilities on a universal basis; control of Leprosy, T.B. and Blindness; acceleration of welfare programs for women and children; nutrition programs for pregnant women, nursing mothers and children, especially in the tribal, hill and backward areas. The Programme also places high emphasis on the supply of drinking water to all problem villages, improvements in the housing and environments of the weaker sections of society; increased production of essential food items; integrated rural developments; spread of universal elementary education; expansion of the public distribution system, etc.

Population Stabilization

Irrespective of the changes, no matter how fundamental, that may be brought about in the over-all approach to Healthcare and the restructuring of the health services, not much headway is likely to be achieved in improving the health status of the people unless success is achieved in securing the small family norm, through voluntary efforts and moving towards the goal of population stabilization. In view of the vital importance of securing the balanced growth of the population, it is necessary to enunciate separately a National Population Policy.

Medical and Health Education

It is also necessary to appreciate that the effective delivery of Healthcare services would depend very largely on the nature of education, training and appropriate orientation towards community health of all categories of medical and health personnel and their capacity to function as an integrated team, each of its members performing given tasks within a coordinated action programme. It is, therefore, of crucial importance that the entire basis and approach towards medical and health education, at all levels, is reviewed in terms of national needs and priorities and the curricular and training programs restructured to produce personnel of various grades of skill and competence, who are professionally equipped and socially motivated to effectively deal with day-to-day problems, within the existing constraints.

Towards this end, it is necessary to formulate, separately, a National Medical and Health Education Policy which (i) sets out the changes required to be brought about in the curricular contents and training programme of **medical and health personnel**, at various levels of functioning; (ii) takes into account the need for establishing the extremely essential inter-relations between functionaries of various grades; (iii) provides guidelines for the production of health personnel on the basis of realistically assessed manpower requirements; (iv) seeks to resolve the existing sharp regional imbalances in their availability; and (v) ensures that personnel at all levels are socially motivated towards the rendering of community health services.

Need for providing primary Healthcare: Special emphasis on the preventive, promotive and rehabilitative aspects

Presently, despite the constraint of resources, there is disproportionate emphasis on the establishment of curative centers—dispensaries, hospitals, institutions for specialist treatment—the large majority of which are located in the urban areas of the country. The vast majority of those seeking medical relief have to travel long distance to the nearest curative centre, seeking relief for ailments which could have been readily and effectively handled at the community level. Also, for want of a well established **referral system**, those seeking curative care have the tendency to visit various specialist centers, thus further contributing to congestions, duplication of efforts and consequential waste of resources. To put an end to the existing all-round unsatisfactory situation, it is urgently necessary to restructure the health services within the following broad approach:

To provide, within a phased, time-bound programme a well dispersed network of comprehensive primary Healthcare services, integrally linked with the extension and health education approach which takes into account the fact that a large majority of health functions can be effectively handled and resolved by the people themselves, with the organized support of volunteers, auxiliaries, **Para-medics** and adequately trained multi-purpose workers of various grades of skill and competence, of both sexes. There are a large number of private, voluntary organisations active in the health field, all over the country. Their services and support would require be utilizing and intermeshing with the governmental efforts, in an integrated manner.

To be effective, the establishment of the primary Healthcare approach would involve large scale transfer of knowledge, simple skill and technologies to Health Volunteers, selected by the communities and enjoying their confidence. The functioning of the front line workers, selected by the community would require to be related to definitive action plans for the translation of medical and health knowledge into practical action, involving the use of simple and inexpensive interventions which can be readily implemented by persons who have undergone short periods of training. The quality of training of these health guides/workers would be of crucial importance to the success of this approach.

The success of the **decentralized primary Healthcare system** would depend vitally on the organized building up of individual self-reliance and effective community participation; on the provision of organized, back-up support of the secondary and tertiary levels of the Healthcare services, providing adequate logistical and technical assistance.

The decentralization of services would require the establishment of a well worked out referral system to provide adequate expertise at the various levels of the organisational set-up nearest to the community, depending upon the actual needs and problems of the area, and thus ensure against the continuation of the existing rush towards the curative centers in the urban areas. The effective establishment of the referral system would also ensure the optimal utilization of expertise at the higher levels of the hierarchical structure. This approach would not only lead to the progressive improvement of comprehensive Healthcare services at the primary level but also provide for timely attention being available to those in need of urgent specialist care, whether they live in the rural or the urban areas.

To ensure that the approach to Healthcare does not merely constitute a collection of **disparate health interventions** but consists of an integrated package of services seeking to tackle the entire range of poor health conditions, on a broad front, it is necessary to establish a nation-wide chain of sanitary-cum-epidemiological stations. The location and functioning of these stations may be between the primary and secondary levels of the hierarchical structure, depending upon the local situations and other relevant considerations. Each such station would require to have suitably trained staff equipped to identify, plan and provide preventive, promotive and mental Healthcare services. It would be beneficial, depending upon the local situations, to establish such stations at the Primary Health Centers. The district health organisation should have, as an integral part of its set-up, a well organized epidemiological unit to coordinate and superintend the functioning of the field stations. These stations would participate in the integrated action plans to eradicate and control diseases, besides tackling specific local environmental health problems.

In the **urban agglomerations,** the municipal and local authorities should be equipped to perform similar functions, being supported with adequate resources and expertise, to effectively deal with the local preventable public health problems. The aforesaid approach should be implemented and extended through community participation and contributions, in whatever form possible, to achieve meaningful results within a time-bound programme.

The location of curative centers should be related to the populations they serve, keeping in view the densities of population, distances, topography, and transport connections. These centers should function within the recommended **referral system**, the gamut of the general specialties required to deal with the local disease patterns being provided as near to the community as possible, at the secondary level of the hierarchical organisation. The concept of domiciliary care and the field-camps approach should be utilized to the fullest extent, to reduce the pressures on these centers, especially in efforts relating to the control and eradication of Blindness, Tuberculosis, Leprosy, etc. To maximize the utilization of available resources, new and additional curative centers should be established only in exceptional cases, the basic attempt being towards the upgradation of existing facilities, at selected locations, the guiding principle being to provide specialist services as near to the beneficiaries as may be possible, within a well-planned network. Expenditure should be reduced through the fullest possible use of cheap locally available building materials, resort to appropriate architectural designs and engineering concepts and by economical investment in the purchase of machineries and equipments, ensuring against avoidable duplication of such acquisitions. It is also necessary to devise effective mechanisms for the repair, maintenance and proper upkeep of all bio-medical equipments to secure their maximum utilization.

With a view to reducing governmental expenditure and fully utilizing untapped resources, planned programs may be devised, related to the local requirements and potentials, to encourage the establishment of practice by private medical professional, increased investment by non- governmental agencies in establishing curative centers and by offering organized logistical, financial and technical support to voluntary agencies active in the health field.

While the major focus of attention in restructuring the existing govern- mental health organisations would relate to establishing comprehensive primary Healthcare and public health services, within an integrated referral system, planned attention would also require to be devoted to the establishment of centers equipped to provide specialty and super-specialty services, through a well dispersed network of centers, to ensure that the present and future requirements of **specialist treatment** are adequately available within the country. To reduce governmental expenditures involved in the establishment of such centers, planned efforts should be made to encourage private investments in such fields so that the majority of such centers, within the governmental set-up, can provide adequate care and treatment to those entitled to free care, the affluent sectors being looked after by the paying clinics. Care would also require to be taken to ensure the appropriate dispersal of such centers, to remove the existing **regional imbalances** and to provide services within the reach of all, whether residing in the rural or the urban areas.

Special, well-coordinated programs should be launched to provide mental Healthcare as well as medical care and the physical and social rehabilitation of those who are mentally retarded, deaf, dumb, blind, physically disabled, and infirm and the aged. Also, suitably organized of various disabilities.

In the establishment of the re-organized services, the first priority should be accorded to provide services to those residing in the tribal; hill and backward areas as well as to **endemic disease** affected populations and the vulnerable sections of the society.

In the re-organized health services scheme, efforts should be made to ensure adequate mobility of personnel, at all level of functioning.

In the various approaches, set out in (1) to (12) above, organized efforts would require to be made to fully utilize and assist in the enlargement of the services being provided by private voluntary organisations active in the health field. In this context, planning encouragement and support would also require to be afforded to fresh voluntary efforts, especially those which seek to serve the needs of the rural areas and the urban slums.

Re-orientation of the Existing Health Personnel

A dynamic process of changes and innovation is required to be brought about in the entire approach to **health manpower development,** ensuring the emergence of fully integrated bands of workers functioning within the "Health Team" approach.

Private Practice by Governmental Functionaries

It is desirable for the States to take steps to phase out of system of private practice by medical personnel in government service, providing at the same time for payment of appropriate compensatory no-practicing allowance. The States would require carefully reviewing the existing situation, with special reference to the availability and dispersal of private practitioners and taking timely decisions in regard to this vital issue.

Practitioners of indigenous and other systems of medicine and their role in Health-care: The country has a large stock of health manpower comprising of private practitioners in various systems, for example, Ayurveda, Homeopathy, yoga, Naturopathy, etc. This resource has not so for been adequately utilized. The practitioners of these various systems enjoy high local acceptance and respect and consequently exert considerable influence on health beliefs and practice. It is, therefore, necessary to initiate organized measures to enable each of these various systems of medicine and Healthcare to develop in accordance with its genius. Simultaneously, planned efforts should be made to dovetail the functioning of the practitioners of these various systems and integrate their service, at the appropriate levels, within specified areas of responsibility and functioning, in the over-all Healthcare delivery system, especially in regard to the preventive, primitive and public health objectives. Well considered steps would also require to be launched to move towards a meaningful phased integration of the indigenous and the modern systems.

Problems Requiring Urgent Attention

Besides the recommended restructuring of the health services infrastructure, precision of the medical and health manpower, community involvement and exploiting of the services of private medical practitioners, especially those of the traditional and other system, involvement and utilization of the services of the voluntary agencies active in the health field, etc., it would be necessary to devote planned, time-bound attention to some of the more important inputs required for improved Healthcare. Of these, priority attention would require to be devoted to:

Nutrition: National and regional strategies should be evolved and implemented, on a time-bound basis, to ensure adequate nutrition for all segments of the population through a well developed distribution system, especially in the rural areas and urban slums. Food of acceptable quality must be available to every person in accordance with his physical needs. Low cost, processed and ready-to-eat foods should be produced and made readily available. The over-all strategy would necessarily involve organized efforts at improving the purchasing power of the poorer sections of the society. Schemes like employment guarantee scheme, to which the government is committed, could yield optimal results if these are suitably linked to the objective of providing adequate nutrition and health cover to the rural and the urban poor. The achievement of this objective is dependent on integrated socio-economic development leading to the generation of productive employment for all those constituting the labour force. **Employment guarantee scheme** and similar efforts would require to be specially enforced to provide social security for identified vulnerable sections of the society. Measures aimed of improving eating habits, inculcation of desirable nutritional practices, improved and scientific utilization of available food material and the effective popularization of improved cooking practices would require to be implemented. Besides, a nation-wide programme to promote breast feeding of infants and eradication of various social taboos detrimental to the promotion of health would need to be initiated. Simultaneously, the problems of communities afflicted by chronic nutritional disorders should be tackled through special schemes including the organisation of supplementary feeding programs directed to the vulnerable sections of the population. The force and effect of such programs should be ensured by delivering them within the setting of **fully integrated Healthcare activities**, to ensure the inculcation of the educational aspects, in the over-all strategy.

Prevention of food adulteration and maintenance of the quality of drugs: Stringent measures are required to be taken to check and prevent the adulteration and contamination of foods at the various stages of their production, processing, storage, transport, distribution, etc. To ensure uniformity of approach, the existing laws would require being reviewed and effective legislation enacted by the Centre. Similarly, the most urgent measures require to be taken to ensure against the manufacture and sale of **spurious and sub-standard drugs.**

Water supply and sanitation: The provision of safe drinking water and the sanitary disposal of wastewaters, human and animal wastes, both in urban and rural areas, must constitute an integrated package. The enormous backlog in the provision of these services to the rural population and in the urban agglomerations must be made up on the most urgent basis. The provision of water supply and basic sanitation facilities would not automatically improve health. The availability of such facilities should be accompanied by intensive health education campaigns for the improvement of personal hygiene, the economical use of water and the sanitary disposal of waste in manner that will improve individual and community health. All water-supply schemes must be fully integrated with efforts at proper water management, including the drainage and disposal efforts of proper water management, including the drainage and disposal of waste waters. To reduce expenditures and for achieving a quick headway, it would be necessary to devise appropriate technologies in the planning and management of the delivery systems. Besides, the involvement of the community in the implementation and management of the systems would be of crucial importance, both for reducing costs as well as to see that the beneficiaries value and protect the services provided to them.

Environmental protection: While preventive, promotive, public health services are established and the **curative services** re-organized to prevent, control and treat diseases, it would be equally necessary to ensure against the haphazard exploitation of resources which cause ecological disturbances leading to fresh health hazards. It is, therefore, necessary that economic developed plans in the various sectors, are devised in adequate consultation with to Central and the State Health authorities. It is also vitally essential to ensure that the present and future industrial and urban development plans are centrally reviewed to ensure against congestion, the unchecked release of noxious emissions and the pollution of air water. In this context, it is vital to ensure that the sitting and location of all manufacturing units is strictly regulated, through legal measures, if necessary. Central and State Health authorities must necessarily be consulted in establishing locational policies for industrial development and urbanization programs. Environmental appraisal procedures must be developed and strictly applied in according clearance to the various developmental projects.

Immunization programme: It is necessary to launch and organized, nation- wide immunization programme, aimed at cent percent coverage of targeted population groups with vaccines against preventable and communicable diseases. Such an approach would not only prevent and reduce disease and disability but also bring down the existing high infant and child mortality rate.

Maternal and Child Health Services: A vicious relationship exists between high birth rates and high infant mortality, contributing to the desire for more children. The highest priority would, therefore, require to be devoted to efforts at launching special programs for the improvement of maternal and child heath with + special focus on the less privileged sections of society. Such programs would require to be decentralised to the maximum possible extent, their delivery being at the primary level, nearest to doorsteps of the beneficiaries. While efforts should continue at providing refresher training and orientation to the traditional birth attendants, schemes and programs should be launched to ensure that progressively all deliveries are conducted by competently trained persons so that complicated cases receive timely and expert attention, within a comprehensive programme providing ante-natal, **intra-natal and post- natal care.**

School health programme: Organized school health services, integrally linked with the general, preventive and curative services, would require to be established within time-limited programs.

Occupational health services: There is urgent need for launching well- considered schemes to prevent and treat diseases and injuries arising from occupational hazards, not only in the various industries but also in the comparatively un-organized sectors like agriculture. For this purpose, the extended ensuring adequate coordination of efforts with general health services. In their respective spheres of responsibility, the Centre and the States must introduce organized occupational health services to reduce morbidity, disabilities and mortality and thus promote better health and increased welfare and productivity on all fronts.

Health Education

The recommended efforts, on various fronts, would bear only marginal results unless nationwide health education programs, backed by appropriate communication strategies are launched to provide health information in easily understandable form, to motivate the development of an attitude for healthy living. The public health education programs should be supplemented by health, nutrition and population education programs in all educational institutions, at various levels. Simultaneously, efforts would require to be made to promote universal education specially adult and family education without which the various efforts to organise preventive and promotive health activities, family planning and improved material and child health cannot bear fruit.

Management Information System

Appropriate decision making and programme planning in the health and related fields are not possible without establishing an effective health information system. A nation-wide organisational set-up should be established to procure essential health information. Such information is required not only for assisting in planning and decision making but to also provide timely warnings about emerging health problems and for reviewing, monitoring and evaluating the various on-going health programs. The building up of a well conceived health information system is also necessary for assessing medical and health manpower requirements and taking timely decisions, on a continuing basis, regarding the manpower requirements in the future medical industry.

The country has built up sound technological and manufacturing capability in the field of drugs, vaccines, bio-medical equipments, etc. The available know-how requires to be adequately exploited to increase the production of essential and life saving drugs and vaccines of proven quality to fully meet the national requirements, especially in regard to the national programs to combat Malaria, TB, Leprosy Blindness, Diarrheal diseases etc. The production of the essential life saving drugs under their generic names and the adoption of econbmical packaging practices would considerable reduce the unit cost of medicines bringing them within the reach of the poorer sections of society, besides significantly reducing the expenditure being incurred by the governmental organisation on the purchase of drugs. In view of the low cost of indigenous and herbal medicines, organized efforts may be launched to establish herbal gardens, producing drugs of certified quality and making them easily available.

The practitioners of the modern medical system rely heavily on diagnostic aids involving extensive use of costly, sophisticated biomedical equipment. Effective extensive use and to promote and enlarge their indigenous manufacture, for such devices being readily available, at reasonable process, for use at the Healthcare centers.

Health Insurance

Besides monishing the community resources, through its active participation in the implementation and management of national health and related programs, it would be necessary to device well considered health insurance schemes, an a State- wise basis, for mobilizing additional resources for health promotion and ensuring that the community shares the cost of the services, in keeping with its paying capacity.

Health Legislation

It is necessary to urgently review all existing legislation and work towards a unified, comprehensive legislation in the health field, enforceable all over the country.

Medical Research

The frontiers of the medical sciences are expanding of a phenomenal pace. To maintain the country's lead in this field as well as to ensure self-sufficiency and generation of the requisite competence in the future, it is necessary to have an organized programme for the building up and extension of fundamental and basic research in the field of bio-medical and allied sciences. Priority attention would require to be devoted to the resolution of problems relating to the containment and eradication of the existing, widely prevalent diseases as well as to deal with emerging health problems. The basic objective of medical research and the ultimate test of its utility would involve the translation of available know-how into simple, low-cost, easily applicable appropriate technologies, devices and interventions suiting local conditions, thus placing the latest technological achievements within the reach of health personal, and to the front line health workers, in the remotest corners of the country. Therefore, besides devotion to basic, fundamental research, high priority should be accorded to applied, operational research including action research for continuously improving the cost effective delivery of health services. Priorities would require be indemnifying and laying down in collaboration with social scientists, planners and decision makers and the public. Basic research efforts should devote high priority to the discovery and development of more effective treatment and preventive procedures in regard to communicable and tropical diseases—Blindness, Leprosy, T.B., etc. Very high priority would also have to be devoted to **contraception research,** to urgently improve the effectiveness and acceptability of existing methods as well as to discover more effective and acceptable devices. Equally high attention would require to devoted to nutrition research, to improve the health status of the community. The overall effort should aim at the **blanched development** of basic clinical and problem-oriented operational research.

Inter-Sectoral Cooperation

All health and human development must ultimately constitute on integral component of the overall socio-economic developmental process in the country. It is thus of vital importance to ensure effective coordination between the health and its more intimately related sectors. It is, therefore, necessary to set up standing mechanisms, of the Centre and in the States, for securing **inter-sectoral coordination** of the various efforts in the fields of health and family planning, medical education and research, drugs and pharmaceutical, agriculture and food, water supply and drainage, housing, education and social welfare and rural development. The coordination and review committees, to be up, should review progress, resolve bottlenecks and bring about such shifts in the contents and priorities of programs as may appear necessary, to achieve the overall objectives. At the community level, it would be desirable to devise arrangements for health and all other developmental activities being coordinated under an integrated programme of rural development.

Monitoring and Review of Progress

It would of crucial importance to monitor and periodically review the success of the efforts made and the results achieved. For this purpose, it is necessary to urgently identify the base line situation and to evolve a phased programme for the achievement of certain basic health and family welfare goods are set out in the **annexed tabular statement.** These goals, as well as other allied objectives, would require too be further worked upon and specific targets for achievement established by the Central and the state governments in regard to the various areas of functioning.

Goals for Health and Family Welfare Programs

SL.	Number of Indicator	Current level	Goal 1985	1990	2000
1	2	3	4	5	6
1.	Infant mortality rate	Rural 136 (1978) 122			
		Urban 70 (1978) 60			
		Total 125 (1978)106			
		87	below 60		
	Perinatal mortality	67	(1976) 30-35		
2.	Crude death rate	around 14	12	10.4	9.0
3.	Pre-school child (1-5yrs.) mortality	24	(1976)20-24	15-20	10
4.	Maternal mortality rate (4-5yrs)		(1976)3-4	2-3	>2
5.	Life expectancy of birth (yrs.) male	52.6	(1976)55.1	57.6	64
6.	Babies with birth weight >2500 gms. (%)	30	25	18	10
7.	Crude birth rate	around 35	31	27.0	21.0
8.	Effective couple protection (Percentage)		37.0	42.0	60.0
9.	Net Reproduction Rate (NRR)	1.48	1.13	1.17	1.00
10.	Growth rate (annual)	2.24	1.90	1.66	1.20
11.	Family size		4.4	3.8	2.3
12.	Pregnant mothers RCVG Ante-natal		50-60	60-75	100

13.	Deliveries by trained birth attendants (%)		50	80	100
14.	Immunizations status (% coverage)				
	TT (for Pregnant women)		60	100	100
	TT (for school children)	10years	40	100	100
		16years	40	100	100
	DPT (children below 3 years)		70	85	85
	Polio (infants)		50	70	85
	BCG (infants)		70	80	85
	DT (new school entrants (5-6 years)		80	85	85
	Typhoid (new school entrants 5-6 years)		70	85	85
15.	Leprosy (%age of disease arrested cases)		40	60	80
16.	TB (%age of disease arrested cases)		60	75	90
17.	Blindness (Incidence of (%)		1	0.7	0.3

National Health Policy - 2002

Introductory

A National Health Policy was last formulated in 1983, and since then there have been marked changes in the determinant factors relating to the health sector. Some of the policy initiatives outlined in the NHP-1983 have yielded results, while, in several other areas, the outcome has not been as expected.

The NHP-1983 gave a general exposition of the policies which required recommendation in the circumstances then prevailing in the health sector. The noteworthy initiatives under that policy were:-

- A phased, time-bound programme for setting up a well-dispersed network of comprehensive primary Healthcare services, linked with extension and health education, designed in the context of the ground reality that elementary health problems can be resolved by the people themselves;

- Intermediation through 'Health volunteers' having appropriate knowledge, simple skills and requisite technologies;
- Establishment of a well-worked out referral system to ensure that patient load at the higher levels of the hierarchy is not needlessly burdened by those who can be treated at the decentralized level;
- An integrated network of evenly spread specialty and super-specialty services; encouragement of such facilities through private investments for patients who can pay, so that the draw on the Government's facilities is limited to those entitled to free use.

Government initiatives in the public health sector have recorded some noteworthy successes over time. Smallpox and Guinea Worm Disease have been eradicated from the country; Polio is on the verge of being eradicated; Leprosy, Kala Azar, and Filariasis can be expected to be eliminated in the foreseeable future. There has been a substantial drop in the Total Fertility Rate and Infant Mortality Rate. The success of the initiatives taken in the public health field are reflected in the progressive improvement of many demographic / **epidemiological / infrastructural indicators** over time – (Box-I).

Box-1: Achievements through the Years - 1951-2000

Indicator	1951	1981	2000
Demographic Changes			
Life Expectancy	36.7	54	64.6(RGI)
Crude Birth Rate	40.8	33.9(SRS)	26.1(99 SRS)
Crude Death Rate	25	12.5(SRS)	8.7(99 SRS)
IMR	146	110	70 (99 SRS)
Epidemiological Shifts			
Malaria (cases in million)	75	2.7	2.2
Leprosy cases per 10,000 population	38.1	57.3	3.74
Small Pox (no of cases)	>44,887	Eradicated	
Guinea worm (no. of cases)		>39,792	Eradicated
Polio		29709	265
Infrastructure			
SC/PHC/CHC	725	57,363	1,63,181 (99-RHS)
Dispensaries &Hospitals (all)	9209	23,555	43,322 (95–96-CBHI)

Beds (Pvt & Public)	117,198	569,495	8,70,161 (95-96-CBHI)
Doctors (Allopathy)	61,800	2,68,700	5,03,900 (98-99-MCI)
Nursing Personnel	18,054	1,43,887	7,37,000 (99-INC)

While noting that the public health initiatives over the years have contributed significantly to the improvement of these health indicators, it is to be acknowledged that public health indicators / disease-burden statistics are the outcome of several complementary initiatives under the wider umbrella of the developmental sector, covering Rural Development, Agriculture, Food Production, Sanitation, Drinking Water Supply, Education, etc. Despite the impressive public health gains as revealed in the statistics in Box-I, there is no gainsaying the fact that the morbidity and mortality levels in the country are still unacceptably high. These unsatisfactory health indices are, in turn, an indication of the limited success of the public health system in meeting the preventive and curative requirements of the general population.

Out of the communicable diseases which have persisted over time, the incidence of Malaria staged resurgence in the1980s before stabilizing at a fairly high prevalence level during the 1990s. Over the years, an increasing level of insecticide-resistance has developed in the malarial vectors in many parts of the country, while the incidence of the more deadly P-Falciparum Malaria has risen to about 50 percent in the country as a whole. In respect of TB, the public health scenario has not shown any significant decline in the pool of infection amongst the community, and there has been a distressing trend in the increase of drug resistance to the type of infection prevailing in the country. A new and extremely virulent communicable disease – HIV/AIDS - has emerged on the health scene since the declaration of the NHP-1983. As there is no existing therapeutic cure or vaccine for this infection, the disease constitutes a serious threat, not merely to public health but to economic development in the country. The common water-borne infections – Gastroenteritis, Cholera and some forms of Hepatitis – continue to contribute to a high level of morbidity in the population, even though the mortality rate may have been somewhat moderated.

The period after the announcement of **NHP-83** has also seen an increase in mortality through 'life-style' diseases- diabetes, cancer and cardiovascular diseases. The increase in life expectancy has increased the requirement for geriatric care. Similarly, the increasing burden of trauma cases is also a significant public health problem.

Another area of grave concern in the public health domain is the persistent incidence of macro and micro nutrient deficiencies, especially among women and children. In the vulnerable sub-category of women and the girl child, this has the multiplier effect through the birth of low birth weight babies and serious ramifications of the consequential mental and physical retarded growth.

NHP-1983, in a spirit of optimistic empathy for the health needs of the people, particularly the poor and under-privileged, had hoped to provide 'Health for All by the year 2000 AD', through the universal provision of comprehensive primary Healthcare services. In retrospect, it is observed that the financial resources and public health administrative capacity which it was possible to marshal, was far short of that necessary to achieve such an ambitious and holistic goal. Against this backdrop, it is felt that it would be appropriate to pitch NHP-2002 at a level consistent with our realistic expectations about financial resources, and about the likely increase in Public Health administrative capacity. The recommendations of NHP-2002 will, therefore, attempt to maximize the broad-based availability of health services to the citizenry of the country on the basis of realistic considerations of capacity. The changed circumstances relating to the health sector of the country since 1983 have generated a situation in which it is now necessary to review the field, and to formulate a new policy framework as the National Health Policy-2002. **NHP-2002** will attempt to set out a new policy framework for the accelerated achievement of Public health goals in the socio-economic circumstances currently prevailing in the country.

Current Scenario

Financial Resources

The public health investment in the country over the years has been comparatively low, and as a percentage of GDP has declined from 1.3 percent in 1990 to 0.9 percent in 1999. The aggregate expenditure in the Health sector is 5.2 percent of the GDP. Out of this, about 17 percent of the aggregate expenditure is public health spending, the balance being out-of-pocket expenditure. The central **budgetary allocation** for health over this period, as a percentage of the total Central Budget, has been stagnant at 1.3 percent, while that in the States has declined from 7.0 percent to 5 percent. The current annual per capita public health expenditure in the country is no more than Rs. 200. Given these statistics, it is no surprise that the reach and quality of public health services has been below the desirable standard. Under the constitutional structure, public health is the responsibility of the States. In this framework, it has been the expectation that the principal contribution for the funding of public health services will be from the resources of the States, with some supplementary input from Central resources. In this backdrop, the contribution of Central resources to the overall public health funding has been limited to about 15 percent. The fiscal resources of the State Governments are known to be very inelastic. This is reflected in the declining percentage of State resources allocated to the health sector out of the State Budget. If the decentralized public health services in the country are to improve significantly, there is a need for the injection of substantial resources into the health sector from the Central Government Budget. This approach is a necessity – despite the formal Constitutional provision in regard to public health, if the State public health services, which are a major component of the initiatives in the social sector, are not to become entirely moribund. The NHP-2002 has been formulated taking into consideration these ground realities in regard to the availability of resources.

Equity

In the period when centralized planning was accepted as a key instrument of development in the country, the attainment of an equitable regional distribution was considered one of its major objectives. Despite this conscious focus in the development process, the statistics given in Box-II clearly indicate that the attainment of health indices has been very uneven across the rural – urban divide.

Box II: Differentials in Health Status among States

Sector	Population BPL (%)	IMR/ Per 1000 Live Births (1999-SRS)	<5Mortality per 1000 (NFHS II)	Weight For Age-% of Children Under 3 years (<-2SD)	MMR/ Lakh (Annual Report 2000)	Leprosy cases per 10000 population	Malaria +ve Cases in year 2000 (in thousands)
India	26.1	70	94.9	47	408	3.7	2200
Rural	27.09	75	103.7	49.6	-	-	-
Urban	23.62	44	63.1	38.4	-	-	-
Better Performing States							
Kerala	12.72	14	18.8	27	87	0.9	5.1
Maharashtra	25.02	48	58.1	50	135	3.1	138
TN	21.12	52	63.3	37	79	4.1	56
Low Performing States							
Orissa	47.15	97	104.4	54	498	7.05	483
Bihar	42.60	63	105.1	54	707	11.83	132
Rajasthan	15.28	81	114.9	51	607	0.8	53
UP	31.15	84	122.5	52	707	4.3	99
MP	37.43	90	137.6	55	498	3.83	528

Also, the statistics bring out the wide differences between the attainments of **health goals** in the better- performing States as compared to the low-performing States. It is clear that national averages of **health indices** hide wide disparities in public health facilities and health standards in different parts of the country. Given a situation in which national averages in respect of most indices are themselves at unacceptably low levels, the wide **inter-State disparity** implies that, for vulnerable sections of society in several States, access to public health services is nominal and health standards are grossly inadequate. Despite a thrust in the NHP-1983 for making good the unmet needs of public health services by establishing more public health institutions at a decentralized level, a large gap in facilities still persists. Applying current norms to the population projected for the year 2000, it is estimated that the shortfall in the number of SCs/PHCs/CHCs is of the order of 16 percent. However, this shortage is as high as 58 percent when disaggregated for CHCs only. The NHP-2002 will need to address itself to making good these deficiencies so as to narrow the gap between the various States, as also the gap across the rural-urban divide.

Access to, and benefits from, the public health system have been very uneven between the better-endowed and the more vulnerable sections of society. This is particularly true for women, children and the socially disadvantaged sections of society. The statistics given in Box-III highlight the handicap suffered in the health sector on account of socio-economic inequity.

Box-III: Differentials in Health status Among Socio-Economic Groups

Indicator	Infant Mortality/1000	Under 5 Mortality/1000	% Children Underweight
India	70	94.9	47
Social Inequity			
Scheduled Castes	83	119.3	53.5
Scheduled Tribes	84.2	126.6	55.9
Other Disadvantaged	76	103.1	47.3
Others	61.8	82.6	41.1

It is a principal objective of NHP-2002 to evolve a policy structure which reduces these inequities and allows the disadvantaged sections of society a fairer access to public health services.

Delivery of National Public Health Programmes

It is self-evident that in a country as large as India, which has a wide variety of socio-economic settings, national health programs have to be designed with enough flexibility to permit the State public health administrations to craft their own programme package according to their needs. Also, the implementation of the national health programme can only be carried out through the

State Governments' decentralized public health machinery. Since, for various reasons, the responsibility of the Central Government in funding additional public health services will continue over a period of time, the role of the Central Government in designing broad-based public health initiatives will inevitably continue. Moreover, it has been observed that the technical and managerial expertise for designing large-span public health programs exists with the Central Government in a considerable degree; this expertise can be gainfully utilized in designing national health programs for implementation in varying socio-economic settings in the States. With this background, the NHP-2002 attempts to define the role of the Central Government and the State Governments in the public health sector of the country.

Over the last decade or so, the Government has relied upon a **'vertical' implementation** structure for the major disease control programs. Through this, the system has been able to make a substantial dent in reducing the burden of specific diseases. However, such an organizational structure, which requires independent manpower for each disease programme, is extremely expensive and difficult to sustain. Over a long time-range, 'vertical' structures may only be affordable for those diseases which offer a reasonable possibility of elimination or eradication in a foreseeable time-span.

It is a widespread perception that, over the last decade and a half, the rural health staff has become a vertical structure exclusively for the implementation of family welfare activities. As a result, for those public health programs where there is no separate vertical structure, there is no identifiable service delivery system at all. The Policy will address this distortion in the public health system.

Keywords : Ayurveda; Allopathy; National Health Policy; Health For All; Population stabilization; Preventive Healthcare Promotion; Healthcare and Rehabilitative aspects; Health Interventions; Maternal & Child Health Services; Health Education; Health Insurance, Health Legislation; Medical Research; Inter-sectoral cooperation; Equity.

Summary : India is committed to attaining 'Health for All'. A policy is required to cater to the following:

(*a*) Population stabilization.

(*b*) Health Education

(*c*) Orientation of existing and new Health personnel

(*d*) Improve government Functionaries.

(*e*) Special question on nutrition, food adulteration, quality of drugs, sanitation, environmental protection, immunization, maternal and child health, etc. is required.

(*f*) Developing a request Management Information System.

(*g*) Health Insurance & Legislation.

(*h*) Medical Research.

And to monitor and review programme. A National Heath Policy was formulated in 1983 and we have seen some noteworthy success over times.

Though the budgetary allocation is still low but centralised planning has contributed a development.

National Public Health Programmes have been formulated & successfully implemented.

Questions :

1. Give a brief on the current Indian Healthcare Sciences briefly mentioning the progress achieved from 1983.
2. Briefly discuss the various factors that contributed to the development of the National Health Policy.
3. List out certain programmes which require urgent attention.
4. What do you mean by Health Education?
5. Why was NHP-1983 envisaged? How is NHP-2002 an improvement over the earlier policy?
6. List out the achievements of the National Health Policy.
7. Elucidate how the followers factors are changing the invent scenario :

   (*a*) Financial Resources

   (*b*) Equity
8. How does the delivery of National Health Programs take place?

Short Notes:

- 20 Point Programme
- Health Education
- Food Adulteration
- Immunization Programme
- Occupational Health Services.
- Health Insurance.

4

DISTRIBUTION OF HEALTH SERVICES IN INDIA

Learning Objectives

After studying this Chapter you should be able to understand:

- How the distribution of Health Services in India takes place?
- What is the National Disease surveillance Network?
- What are the various apprehensions related to Health Sector?
- A brief on Healthcare Infrastructure and how it assists in distribution of Health Services to India.
- Role of Central Government in distribution of Health Services.
- The expenditure pattern and how primary health services are the comerstone of Healthcare distribution.
- What are the traditional practices in Healthcare delivery?
- A note on Healthcare insurance.

In principle, this Policy welcomes the participation of the private sector in all areas of health activities – primary, secondary or tertiary. However, looking to past experience of the private sector, it can reasonably be expected that its contribution would be substantial in the urban primary sector and the tertiary sector, and moderate in the secondary sector. This Policy envisages the enactment of suitable legislation for regulating minimum infrastructure and quality standards in clinical establishments/medical institutions by 2003. Also, statutory guidelines for the conduct of clinical practice and delivery of medical services are targeted to be developed over the same period. With the acquiring of experience in the setting and enforcing of minimum quality standards, he Policy envisages graduation to a scheme of **quality accreditation** of clinical establishments/ nedical institutions, for the information of the citizenry. The regulatory/accreditation mechanisms will no doubt also cover public health institutions. The Policy also encourages the setting up of rivate insurance instruments for increasing the scope of the coverage of the secondary and ertiary sector under private health insurance packages.

In the context of the very large number of poor in the country, it would be difficult to conceive f an **exclusive Government mechanism** to provide health services to this category. It has ometimes been felt that a social health insurance scheme, funded by the Government, and with ervice delivery through the private sector, would be the appropriate solution. The administrative nd financial implications of such an initiative are still unknown. As a first step, this policy envisges the introduction of a pilot scheme in a limited number of representative districts, to determine e administrative features of such an arrangement, as also the requirement of resources for it. he results obtained from these pilot projects would provide material on which future public health olicy can be based.

NHP-2002 envisages the co-option of the non-governmental practitioners in the **national disse control programmes** so as to ensure that standard treatment protocols are followed in their y-to-day practice.

This Policy recognizes the immense potential of information technology applications in the ea of **tele-medicine** in the tertiary Healthcare sector. The use of this technical aid will greatly hance the capacity for the professionals to pool their clinical experience.

istribution of Health Services in India

Healthcare in India features a universal Healthcare system run by the constituent states d territories of India. The Constitution charges every state with "raising of the level of nutrition and standard of living of its people and the improvement of public health as among its primary ties". The National Health Policy was endorsed by the Parliament of India in 1983 and updated 2002. However, the government sector is understaffed and underfinanced; poor services at te-run hospitals force many people to visit private medical practitioners.

Government hospitals, some of which are among the best hospitals in India, provide treatment taxpayer expense. Most essential drugs are offered free of charge in these hospitals. Govern-nt hospitals provide treatment either free or at minimal charges. For example, an outpatient card at AIIMS (one of the best hospitals in India) costs a onetime fee of rupees 10 (around 20 cents US) and thereafter outpatient medical advice is free. In-hospital treatment costs depend on financial condition of the patient and facilities utilized by him but are usually much less than the private sector. For instance, a patient is waived treatment costs if he is below poverty line. Another patient may seek for an air-conditioned room if he is willing to pay extra for it. The charges for basic in-hospital treatment and investigations are much less compared to the private sector. The cost for these subsidies comes from annual allocations from the central and state governments.

Primary Healthcare is provided by city and district hospitals and rural **primary health centres (PHCs).** These hospitals provide treatment free of cost. Primary care is focused on immunization, prevention of malnutrition, pregnancy, child birth, postnatal care and treatment of common illnesses. Patients who receive specialized care or have complicated illnesses are referred to secondary (often located in district and taluk headquarters) and tertiary care hospitals (located in district and state headquarters or those that are teaching hospitals).

In recent times, India has eradicated mass famines, however the country still suffers from high levels of malnutrition and disease especially in rural areas. Water supply and sanitation in India is also a major issue in the country and many Indians in rural areas lack access to proper sanitation facilities and safe drinking water. However, at the same time, India's Healthcare system also includes entities that meet or exceed international quality standards. The **medical tourism** business in India has been growing in recent years and as such India is a popular destination for medical tourists who receive effective medical treatment at lower costs than in developed countries.

NHP-2002 recognizes the significant contribution made by NGOs and other institutions of the civil society in making available health services to the community. In order to utilize their high motivational skills on an increasing scale, this Policy envisages that the disease control programme should earmark not less than 10% of the budget in respect of identified programme components, to be exclusively implemented through these institutions. The policy also emphasizes the need to simplify procedures for government – civil society interfacing in order to enhance the involvement of civil society in public health programmes. In principle, the state would encourage the handing over of public health service outlets at any level for management by NGOs and other institutions of civil society, on an 'as-is-where-is' basis, along with the **normative funds** earmarked for such institutions.

National Disease Surveillance Network

This Policy envisages the full operationalization of an integrated disease control network from the lowest rung of public health administration to the Central Government, by 2005. The programme for setting up this network will include components relating to the installation of database handling hardware; IT inter-connectivity between different tiers of the network; and in-house training for data collection and interpretation for undertaking timely and effective response. This **public hea**

surveillance network will also encompass information from private Healthcare institutions and practitioners. It is expected that real-time information from outside the government system will greatly strengthen the capacity of the public health system to counter focal outbreaks of seasonal diseases.

Apprehensions: Health Sector

The Policy takes into account the serious apprehension, expressed by several health experts, of the possible threat to health security in the post-TRIPS era, as a result of a sharp increase in the prices of drugs and vaccines. To protect the citizens of the country from such a threat, this policy envisages a national patent regime for the future, which, while being consistent with TRIPS, avails of all opportunities to secure for the country, under its patent laws, affordable access to the latest medical and other therapeutic discoveries. The policy also sets out that the Government will bring to bear its full influence in all international flora – UN, WHO, WTO, etc. – to secure commitments on the part of the Nations of the Globe, to lighten the restrictive features of TRIPS in its application to the Healthcare sector.

Summation

The crafting of a National Health Policy is a rare occasion in public affairs when it would be legitimate, indeed valuable, to allow our dreams to mingle with our understanding of ground realities. Based purely on the clinical facts defining the current status of the health sector, we would have arrived at a certain policy formulation; but, buoyed by our dreams, we have ventured slightly beyond that in the shape of NHP-2002, which, in fact, defines a vision for the future.

The health needs of the country are enormous and the financial resources and managerial capacity available to meet them, even on the most optimistic projections, fall somewhat short. In this situation, NHP-2002 has had to make hard choices between various priorities and operational options. NHP-2002 does not claim to be a road-map for meeting all the health needs of the populace of the country. Further, it has to be recognized that such health needs are also dynamic, as threats in the area of public health keep changing over time. The Policy, while being holistic, undertakes the necessary risk of recommending differing emphasis on different policy components. Broadly speaking, NHP – 2002 focuses on the need for enhanced funding and an organizational restructuring of the **national public health initiatives** in order to facilitate more equitable access to the health facilities. Also, the Policy is focused on those diseases which are principally contributing to the disease burden – TB, Malaria and Blindness from the category of historical diseases; and HIV/AIDS from the category of 'newly emerging diseases'. This is not to say that other items contributing to the disease burden of the country will be ignored; but only that the resources, as also the principal focus of the public health administration, will recognize certain relative priorities. It is unnecessary to labour the point that under the umbrella of the macro-policy prescriptions in this document, governments and private sector programme planners will have to design separate schemes, tailor-made to the health needs of women, children, geriatrics, tribals and other socio-economically under-served sections. An adequately robust disaster management plan has to be in place to effectively cope with situations arising from natural and man-made calamities.

One nagging imperative, which has influenced every aspect of this Policy, is the need to ensure that 'equity' in the health sector stands as an independent goal. In any future evaluation of its success or failure, NHP-2002 would wish to be measured against this equity norm, rather than any other aggregated financial norm for the health sector. Consistent with the primacy given to 'equity', a marked emphasis has been provided in the policy for expanding and improving the primary health facilities, including the new concept of the provisioning of essential drugs through Central funding. The Policy also commits the Central Government to an increased **under-writing of the resources** for meeting the minimum health needs of the people. Thus, the Policy attempts to provide guidance for prioritizing expenditure, thereby facilitating rational resource allocation.

This Policy broadly envisages a greater contribution from the Central Budget for the delivery of Public Health services at the State level. Adequate appropriations, steadily rising over the years, would need to be ensured. The possibility of ensuring this by imposing an **earmarked health cess** has been carefully examined. While it is recognized that the annual budget must accommodate the increasing resource needs of the social sectors, particularly in the health sector, this Policy does not specifically recommend an earmarked health cess, as that would have a tendency of reducing the space available to Parliament in making appropriations looking to the circumstances prevailing from time to time.

The Policy highlights the expected roles of different participating groups in the health sector. Further, it recognizes the fact that despite all that may be guaranteed by the Central Government for assisting public health programmes, public health services would actually need to be delivered by the State administration, NGOs and other institutions of civil society. The attainment of improved health levels would be significantly dependent on population stabilisation, as also on complementary efforts from other areas of the social sectors – like improved drinking water supply, basic sanitation, minimum nutrition, etc. - to ensure that the exposure of the populace to health risks is minimized.

Any expectation of a significant improvement in the quality of health services, and the consequential improved health status of the citizenry, would depend not only on increased financial and material inputs, but also on a more empathetic and committed attitude in the service providers, whether in the private or public sectors. In some measure, this optimistic policy document is based on the understanding that the citizenry is increasingly demanding more by way of quality in health services, and the health delivery system, particularly in the public sector, is being pressed to respond. In this backdrop, it needs to be recognized that any policy in the social sector is critically dependent on the service providers treating their responsibility not as a commercial activity, but as a service, albeit a paid one. In the area of public health, an improved standard of governance is a prerequisite for the success of any health policy.

Healthcare Infrastructure

The Indian healthcare industry is seen to be growing at a rapid pace and is expected to become a US$280 billion industry by 2020. The Indian healthcare market was estimated at US$35 billion in 2007 and is expected to reach over US$70 billion by 2012 and US$145 billion by 2017. According to the Investment Commission of India, the healthcare sector has experienced phenomenal growth of 12 percent per annum in the last 4 years. Rising income levels and a growing elderly population are all factors that are driving this growth. In addition, changing demographics, disease profiles and the shift from chronic to lifestyle diseases in the country has led to increased spending on healthcare delivery.

Even so, the vast majority of the country suffers from a poor standard of healthcare infrastructure which has not kept up with the growing economy. Despite having centres of excellence in **healthcare delivery**, these facilities are limited and are inadequate in meeting the current healthcare demands. Nearly one million Indians die every year due to inadequate healthcare facilities and 700 million people have no access to specialist care and 80% of specialists live in urban areas.

In order to meet manpower shortages and reach world standards, India would require investments of up to $20 billion over the next 5 years. Forty percent of the primary health centres in India are understaffed. According to WHO statistics, there are over 250 medical colleges in the modern system of medicine and over 400 in the Indian system of medicine and homeopathy (ISM&H). India produces over 250,000 doctors annually in the modern system of medicine and a similar number of ISM&H practitioners, nurses and **para professionals**. Better policy regulations and the establishment of public private partnerships are possible solutions to the problem of manpower shortage.

India faces a huge need gap in terms of availability of number of hospital beds per 1000 population. With a world average of 3.96 hospital beds per 1000 population India stands just a little over 0.7 hospital beds per 1000 population. Moreover, India faces a shortage of doctors, nurses and paramedics that are needed to propel the growing healthcare industry. India is now looking at establishing **academic medical centres (AMCs)** for the delivery of higher quality care with leading examples of The Manipal Group & All India Institute of Medical Sciences (AIIMS) already in place.

As incomes rise and the number of available financing options in terms of health insurance policies increase, consumers become more and more engaged in making informed decisions about their health and are well aware of the costs associated with those decisions. In order to remain competitive, healthcare providers are now not only looking at improving operational efficiency but are also looking at ways of enhancing patient experience overall.

India has approximately 600,000 allopathic doctors registered to practice medicine. This number however, is higher than the actual number practicing because it includes doctors who have immigrated to other countries as well as doctors who have died. India licenses 18,000 new doctors a year.

Central Government's Role

Critics say that the national policy lacks specific measures to achieve broad stated goals. Particular problems include the failure to integrate health services with wider economic and social development, the lack of nutritional support and sanitation and the poor participatory involvement at the local level.

Central government efforts at influencing public health have focused on the five-year plans, on coordinated planning with the states, and on sponsoring major health programs. Government expenditures are jointly shared by the central and state governments. Goals and strategies are set through central-state government consultations of the Central Council of Health and Family Welfare. Central government efforts are administered by the Ministry of Health and Family Welfare, which provides both administrative and technical services and manages medical education. States provide public services and health education.

The 1983 National Health Policy is committed to providing health services to all by 2000. In 1983, Healthcare expenditures varied greatly among the states and union territories, from Rs 13 per capita in Bihar to Rs 60 per capita in Himachal Pradesh and Indian per capita expenditure was low when compared with other Asian countries outside of South Asia. Although government Healthcare spending progressively grew throughout the 1980s, such spending as a percentage of the gross national product (GNP) remained fairly constant. In the meantime, Healthcare spending as a share of total government spending decreased. During the same period, private-sector spending on Healthcare was about 1.5 times as much as government spending.

Expenditure

In the mid-1990s, health spending amounted to 6% of GDP, one of the highest levels among developing nations. The established per capita spending is around Rs 320 per year with the major input from private households (75%). State governments contribute 15.2%, the central government 5.2%, third-party insurance and employers 3.3%, and municipal government and foreign donors about 1.3, according to a 1995 World Bank study. Of these proportions, 58.7% goes toward primary Healthcare (curative, preventive, and promotive) and 38.8% is spent on secondary and tertiary inpatient care. The rest goes for **non-service costs.**

The fifth and sixth five-year plans (FY 1974-78 and FY 1980-84, respectively) included programs to assist delivery of preventive medicine and improve the health status of the rural population. **Supplemental nutrition programs** and increasing the supply of safe drinking water were high priorities. The sixth plan aimed at training more community health workers and increasing efforts to control communicable diseases. There were also efforts to improve regional imbalances in the distribution of Healthcare resources.

The Seventh Five-Year Plan (FY 1985-89) budgeted Rs 33.9 billion for health, an amount roughly double the outlay of the sixth plan. Health spending as a portion of total plan outlays, however, had declined over the years since the first plan in 1951, from a high of 3.3% of the total plan spending in FY 1951-55 to 1.9% of the total for the seventh plan. Mid-way through the Eighth Five-Year Plan (FY 1992-96), however, health and family welfare was budgeted at Rs 20 billion, or 4.3% of the total plan spending for FY 1994, with an additional Rs 3.6 billion in the non-plan budget.

Primary Services

Healthcare facilities and personnel increased substantially between the early 1950s and early 1980s, but because of fast population growth, the number of **licensed medical practi-tioners** per 10,000 individuals had fallen by the late 1980s to three per 10,000 from the 1981 level of four per 10,000. In 1991, there were approximately ten hospital beds per 10,000 individuals. For comparison, in China there are 1.4 doctors per 1000 people.

Primary health centres are the cornerstone of the rural Healthcare system. By 1991, India had about 22,400 primary health centers, 11,200 hospitals, and 27,400 clinics. These facilities are part of a tiered Healthcare system that funnels more difficult cases into urban hospitals while attempting to provide routine medical care to the vast majority in the countryside. Primary health centers and subcenters rely on trained paramedics to meet most of their needs. The main problems affecting the success of primary health centers are the predominance of clinical and curative concerns over the intended emphasis on preventive work and the reluctance of staff to work in rural areas. In addition, the integration of health services with family planning programs often causes the local population to perceive the primary health centers as hostile to their traditional preference for large families. Therefore, primary health centers often play an adversarial role in local efforts to implement national health policies.

According to data provided in 1989 by the Ministry of Health and Family Welfare, the total number of **civilian hospitals** for all states and union territories combined was 10,157. In 1991, there was a total of 811,000 hospitals and Healthcare facilities beds. The geographical distribution of hospitals varied according to local socio-economic conditions. In India's most populous state, Uttar Pradesh, with a 1991 population of more than 139 million, there were 735 hospitals as of 1990. In Kerala, with a 1991 population of 29 million occupying an area only one-seventh the size of Uttar Pradesh, there were 2,053 hospitals.

Although central government has set a goal of Healthcare for all by 2000, hospitals are distributed unevenly. Private studies of India's total number of hospitals in the early 1990s were more conservative than official Indian data, estimating that in 1992 there were 7,300 hospitals. Of this total, nearly 4,000 were owned and managed by central, state, or local governments. Another 2,000, owned and managed by charitable trusts, received partial support from the government, and the remaining 1,300 hospitals, many of which were relatively small facilities, were owned and managed by the private sector. The use of state-of-the-art medical equipment was primarily limited to urban centers in the early 1990s. A network of regional cancer diagnostic and treatment facilities was being established in the early 1990s in major hospitals that were part of government medical colleges. By 1992 twenty-two such centers were in operation. Most of the 1,300 private hospitals lacked sophisticated medical facilities, although in 1992 approximately 12% possessed state-of-the-art equipment for diagnosis and treatment of all major diseases, including cancer. The fast pace of development of the private medical sector and the burgeoning middle class in the 1990s have led to the emergence of the new concept in India of establishing hospitals and Healthcare facilities on a for-profit basis.

By the late 1980s, there were approximately 128 medical colleges - roughly three times more than in 1950. These medical colleges in 1987 accepted a combined annual class of 14,166 students. Data for 1987 show that there were 320,000 registered medical practitioners and 219,300 registered nurses. Various studies have shown that in both urban and rural areas people preferred to pay and seek the more sophisticated services provided by private physicians rather than use free treatment at public health centers.

Traditional Practices

Indigenous or traditional medical practitioners continue to practice throughout the country. The two main forms of traditional medicine practised are the **ayurvedic system**, which deals with mental and spiritual as well as physical well-being, and the **unani (or Galenic) herbal medical practice**. A vaidya is a practitioner of the ayurvedic tradition, and a hakim is a practitioner of the unani or Greek tradition. These professions are frequently hereditary. A variety of institutions offer training in indigenous medical practice. Only in the late 1970s did official health policy refer to any form of integration between European-trained medical personnel and indigenous medical practitioners. In the early 1990s, there were ninety-eight ayurvedic colleges and seventeen unani colleges operating in both the governmental and non-governmental sectors.

Health Insurance

The majority of the Indian population is unable to access high quality healthcare provided by private players as a result of high costs. Many are now looking towards insurance companies for providing alternative financing options so that they too may seek better quality healthcare. The opportunity remains huge for insurance providers entering into the Indian healthcare market since 75% of expenditure on healthcare in India is still being met by 'out-of-pocket' consumers. Even though only 10% of the Indian population today has health insurance coverage, this industry is expected to face tremendous growth over the next few years as a result of several private players that have entered into the market. Health insurance coverage among urban, middle and upper-class Indians, however, is significantly higher and stands at approximately 50% .

The Insurance Regulatory and Development Authority (IRDA) is the governing body responsible for promoting insurance business and introducing insurance regulations in India. The share of public sector companies in health insurance premiums was 76% and that of private sector companies was 24% for the period 2005-06. Health insurance premiums collected over 2005-06 registered a growth of 35% over the previous year. In 2001, the IRDA introduced provisions for Third Party Administrators (TPAs) to support the administration and management of health insurance products offered by insurance companies. TPAs are facilitators in the coordination process between the health insurance provider and the hospital. Currently there are 27 TPAs registered under the IRDA.

Health insurance has a way of increasing accessibility to quality healthcare delivery especially for private healthcare providers for whom high cost remains a barrier. In order to encourage foreign health insurers to enter the Indian market the government has recently proposed to raise the foreign direct investment (FDI) limit in insurance from 26% to 49%. Increasing health insurance penetration and ensuring affordable premium rates are necessary to drive the health insurance market in India.

Keywords : Quality Acereditation; Tele-medicine; Primary Health Centres (PHC); Medical Tourism; National Disease Surveillance Network; Healthcare Infrastructure; Academic Medical Centres (AMC); Unani Herbal Medical Practice.

Summary : Be it the primary, secondary or literacy sector of the country, private practice alone can improve distribution of Health Services in India. The model of healthcare delivery is robust and constitutes multi-level distribution including centre and state, govt. of India, Significant contribution has been made by NGOs and other agencies and together the delivery model has achieved success. The National Disease Surveillance Network has operationalized healthcare from top to bottom. the demand and supply in this sector is crucial. The apprehensions of a poor healthcare infrastructure which requires investments financing option. The Government has achieved much through 5 year plans.

Questions:

1. Explain the Healthcare Delivery Model in India. What role does various agencies play in delivering healthcare?
2. How does 'National Disease Surveillance Network' cater to the various apprehensions of the healthcare sector?
3. What is the requirement in the following areas for improving healthcare delivery in India:
   - Infrastructure
   - Public Private Partnership
   - 5 year plans
   - Insurance

Short Note :

- National Disease Surveillance Network
- Healthcare Infrastructure.
- Traditional practices.

5

HEALTH SECTOR- THE ROLE OF PRIVATE, PUBLIC AND OTHER AGENCIES

Learning Objectives

After studying this Chapter you should be able to understand:

- The impact of globalisation on Healthcare.
- How various sectors contribute to Health?
- The role of Local Self-Government Institute in Healthcare.
- Impact of populations growth on Health Standards.
- A brief on Ayush Alternative system of medicine.

Introduction: Impact of Globalisation on Healthcare

There are some apprehensions about the possible adverse impact of economic globalization on the health sector. Pharmaceutical drugs and other health services have always been available in the country at extremely inexpensive prices. India has established a reputation around the globe for the innovative development of **original process patents** for the manufacture of a wide-range of drugs and vaccines within the ambit of the existing patent laws. With the adoption of **Trade Related Intellectual Property Rights (TRIPS),** and the subsequent alignment of **domestic patent laws** consistent with the commitments under TRIPS, there will be a significant shift in the scope of the parameters regulating the manufacture of new drugs/vaccines. Global experience has shown that the introduction of a TRIPS-consistent patent regime for drugs in a developing country results in an across-the-board increase in the cost of drugs and medical services. NHP-2002 will address itself to the future imperatives of health security in the country, in the post-TRIPS era.

Inter-Sectoral Contribution to Health

It is well recognized that the overall well-being of the citizenry depends on the synergistic functioning of the various sectors in the socio-economy. The health status of the citizenry would, inter alia, be dependent on adequate nutrition, safe drinking water, basic sanitation, a clean environment and primary education, especially for the girl child. The policies and the mode of functioning in these independent areas would necessarily overlap each other to contribute to the health status of the community. From the policy perspective, it is therefore imperative that the independent policies of each of these inter-connected sectors, be in tandem, and that the interface between the policies of the two connected sectors, be smooth.

Sectoral policy documents are meant to serve as a guide to action for institutions and individual participants operating in that sector. Consistent with this role, NHP-2002 limits itself to making recommendations for the participants operating within the health sector. The policy aspects relating to inter-connected sectors, which, while crucial, fall outside the domain of the health sector, will not be covered by specific recommendations in this Policy document. Needless to say, the future attainment of the various goals set out in this policy assumes a reasonable complementary performance in these inter-connected sectors.

Role of Local Self-Government Institutions

NHP-2002 lays great emphasis upon the implementation of public health programmes through local self-government institutions. The structure of the **national disease control programmes** will have specific components for implementation through such entities. The Policy urges all State Governments to consider decentralizing to the implementation of the programmes to such Institutions by 2005. In order to achieve this, financial incentives, over and above the resources normatively allocated for disease control programs, will be provided by the Central Government.

Population Growth and Health Standards

Efforts made over the years for improving health standards have been partially neutralized by the rapid growth of the population. It is well recognized that population stabilization measures and general health initiatives, when effectively synchronized, synergistically maximize the socio-economic well-being of the people. Government has separately announced the **'National Population Policy – 2000'.** The principal common features covered under the National Population Policy-2000 and NHP-2002, relate to the prevention and control of communicable diseases; giving priority to the containment of HIV/AIDS infection; the universal immunization of children against all major preventable diseases; addressing the unmet needs for basic and reproductive health services, and supplementation of infrastructure. The synchronized implementation of these two Policies – National Population Policy – 2000 and National Health Policy-2002 – will be the very cornerstone of any national structural plan to improve the health standards in the country.

Alternative Systems of Medicine

Under the overarching umbrella of the national health frame work, the alternative systems of medicine – Ayurveda, Unani, Siddha and Homoeopathy – have a substantial role. Because of inherent advantages, such as diversity, modest cost, low level of technological input and the growing popularity of natural plant-based products, these systems are attractive, particularly in the underserved, remote and tribal areas. The alternative systems will draw upon the substantial untapped potential of India as one of the eight important global centers for plant diversity in medicinal and aromatic plants. The Policy focuses on building up credibility for the alternative systems, by encouraging evidence-based research to determine their efficacy, safety and dosage, and also encourages certification and quality-marking of products to enable a wider popular acceptance of these systems of medicine. The Policy also envisages the **consolidation of documentary knowledge** contained in these systems to protect it against attack from foreign commercial entities by way of malafide action under patent laws in other countries. The main components of NHP-2002 apply equally to the alternative systems of medicines. However, the Policy features specific to the alternative systems of medicine will be presented as a separate document.

Box-IV: Goals to be achieved by 2000-2015

Eradicate Polio and Yaws	2005
Eliminate Leprosy	2005
Eliminate Kala Azar	2010
Eliminate Lymphatic Filariasis	2015
Achieve Zero level growth of HIV/AIDS	2007
Reduce Mortality by 50% on account of TB, Malaria and Other Vector and Water Borne diseases	2010
Reduce Prevalence of Blindness to 0.5%	2010
Reduce IMR to 30/1000 And MMR to 100/Lakh	2010

Increase utilization of public health facilities from current Level of <20 to >75%	2010
Establish an integrated system of surveillance,, National Health Accounts and Health Statistics.	2005
Increase health expenditure by Government as a % of GDP from the existing 0.9 % to 2.0%	2010
Increase share of Central grants to Constitute at least 25% of total health spending	2010
Increase State Sector Health spending from 5.5% to 7% of the budget	2005
Further increase to 8%	2010

Keywords : Patents; TRIPS; Inter-Sectoral Contribution; Alternative Systems of Medicine.

Summary : Globalisation has had more adverse impact on healthcare than positive. The objective is 'Health for all' which requires Inter – Sectoral Competition NHP-2002 lays great emphasis on implementation of Public Health Programmes through local self-government institutions. But populations growth has kept Health Standards at bay.

Question :

1. How has globalisation affected Healthcare in India?
2. Which are the various government & non-government institutions delivering healthcare & how?

Short Notes :

- TRIPs
- Inter-Sectoral Contributism.
- Population growth : Impact on Health Standards.

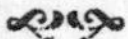

6

OUTPUT-BASED PERFORMANCE

Learning Objectives

After studying this chapter you should be able to understand:

- What is output based Healthcare?
- Performance based payment system and how it leads to efficient delivery of high quality services.

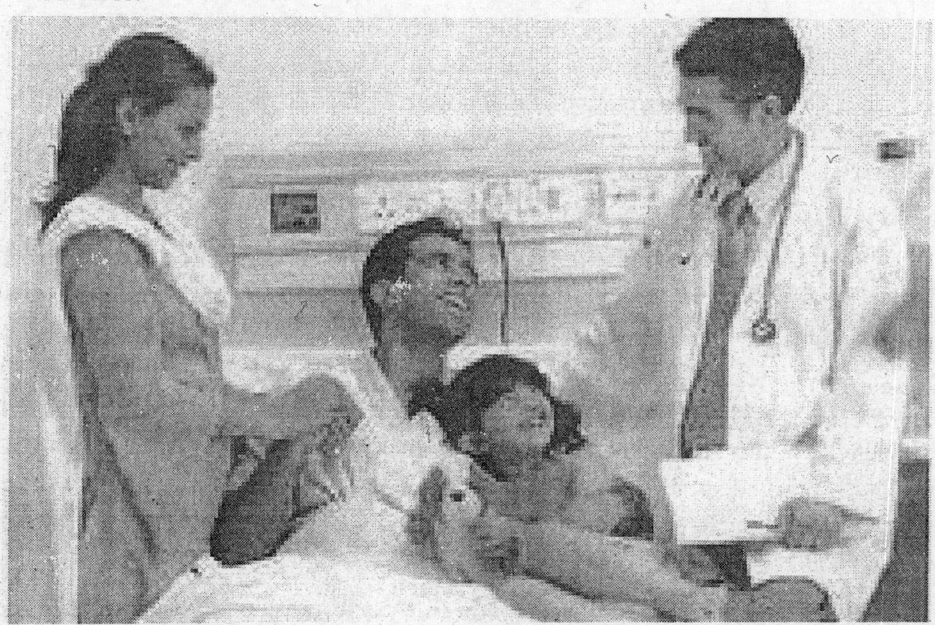

Output Based Healthcare

Those paying for Healthcare services in developing countries typically have not required the providers to guarantee their performance. Public payers tend to fund public institutions to maintain capacity (paying salaries and recurrent costs) rather than to ensure that consumers receive high-quality services. Any contracts with private providers generally have not held them accountable for performance. Donors have tended to adopt similar practices, providing lump sum grants or reimbursing public providers and nongovernmental organizations (NGOs) for documented expenditures. As a result, providers tend to focus on securing funds rather than improving efficiency or the quality of care.

In this context, in 1995 the U.S. Agency for International Development (USAID) launched a 10-year project in Haiti aimed at strengthening the capacity of NGOs to deliver primary Healthcare services. A key part of this effort was the introduction of a performance-based payment system. The challenge was to develop a system based on attainment of goals without imposing an excessive burden of monitoring and reporting requirements.

Following competitive tenders, USAID awarded funding for the two-phase, US$92 million project to Management Sciences for Health (MSH), a U.S. based NGO operating in developing countries. MSH manages and disburses the funds. During the first five-year phase, beginning in 1995, the project provided funding to 23 NGOs, an established group that had received USAID support in the past. For the second five-year phase, beginning in 2000, the number of NGOs increased to 33.

When the project began, the immediate need was to develop rapid mechanisms for funding NGOs so that they could provide **critical basic health services,** including maternal and child health and **family planning services**. Initially, and in line with general practice, NGOs were reimbursed for expenses up to a ceiling that was essentially a negotiated budget. Under this expenditure-based financing, NGOs submit a proposed annual budget and a plan showing how they intend to ensure the delivery of a basic package of services. Then each month they submit cost reports with detailed documentation of their expenditures for reimbursement. NGOs are free to set their own fees for services. Most charge patients for drugs and some for consultations.

A 1997 **population-based survey** to review the existing system found that NGO performance was extremely uneven. In vaccinations a good performer reached 70 percent of the target population while the worst performer reached only 7 percent. One NGO made sure that 80 percent of women knew how to prepare an oral rehydration solution; another educated only 44 percent. Some NGOs provided the minimum two prenatal visits to 43 percent of pregnant women; others reached only 21 percent. These wide ranging results were not correlated with costs (average costs per patient visit ranged from US$1.35 to US$51.93).

So in 1999 MSH decided to test a new approach—**performance-based payment**. The new payment system was expected to lead to efficient delivery of high-quality services in several ways:

- Because institutions receive a bonus if they achieve performance targets, they feel strong incentives to attain those targets.

- Because institutions assume financial risk for improving performance, they feel strong incentives to use resources efficiently and effectively.
- Because institutions are paid on the basis of results, they face strong incentives to improve management, motivate staff, and innovate.

Three NGOs, serving about 534,000 people, participated in a one-year pilot study. Under the performance-based system NGOs receive an upfront payment and then a quarterly sum rather than submitting their expenditures every month.

At the end of a defined period—one year in this case—performance is measured and the size of the bonus determined.

To ensure that the NGOs viewed the change as advantageous, MSH used a collabourative approach in designing the new system. NGOs demonstrating the leadership and institutional capacity to respond to the system were invited to meetings to express their views about the pilot. Because these meetings occurred after NGOs had signed contracts for fiscal 1999 (October 1998–September 1999), they were willing to renegotiate only if the new contract could make them better off.

The meetings led to agreement on a new contract that would pay 95 percent of the budget under the expenditure-based contract—but would also pay a bonus of as much as 10 percent of that budget. The NGOs thus assumed a financial risk: if they failed to attain performance targets, they would lose 5 percent of the budget under the original contract. But they were willing to do so because they also had the possibility of earning 5 percent more than the budget. Seven **performance indicators** were chosen, and a target was negotiated for each indicator and linked to a share of the bonus.

(Negotiating with MSH, each NGO then translated the general targets into specific targets.)

Five indicators related to improving health impact, one to increasing consumer satisfaction by reducing waiting time, and one to improving community participation and coordination with the Ministry of Health.

Another goal of the project was to improve **institutional sustainability**. To facilitate learning and sharing, the project helped create a network of local NGOs. Regular meetings encouraged NGOs to share strategies that have succeeded or failed in the challenging Haitian environment. The project also provided technical assistance, to help NGOs review their pricing policies and develop a plan to generate revenue through sources unrelated to health services. CORE, a cost and revenue analysis tool, was used to help NGOs identify unit costs, revenues, and staff utilization (MSH 1998).

Keywords : Output Based Healthcare; population based survey; performance based payment.

Summary : Healthcare delivery requires guarantee of performance. Many projects have been undertaken to maintain quality on the basis of outcome, i.e. relative outcome to performance & payment. 'Performance Based Payment'.

Question :

1. How can healthcare be improved through output based performance?
2. Explain the concept of Healthcare Management.
3. What do you mean by social development?
4. What is National Health Policy and what are the need for providing primary Healthcare?
5. What are the current state of public health distribution?
6. Explain the role of private group in Healthcare services.
7. Discuss the importance of national & International agencies in Healthcare services?
8. Write an essay on Healthcare and social development with specific reference to India.
9. Explain the output based performance of Healthcare System.

Short Notes :

- Performance based payment.

7

HEALTHCARE SYSTEM

Learning Objective

- This chapter deals with the detailed analysis of Healthcare System.
- It provides learner goals & functions of Healthcare System.

Healthcare systems are designed to meet the Healthcare needs of target populations. There are a wide variety of Healthcare systems around the world. In some countries, the Healthcare system has evolved and has not been planned, whereas in others a concerted effort has been made by governments, trade unions, charities, religious, or other co-ordinated bodies to deliver planned Healthcare services targeted to the populations they serve. However, Healthcare planning has often been evolutionary rather than revolutionary. A Healthcare system is the organization of people, institutions and resources to deliver Healthcare services to meet the health needs of target populations.

There is a wide variety of Healthcare systems around the world, with as many histories and organizational structures as there are nations. In some countries, Healthcare system planning is distributed among market participants. In others, there is a concerted effort among governments, trade unions, charities, religious, or other co-ordinated bodies to deliver planned Healthcare services targeted to the populations they serve. However, Healthcare planning has been described as often evolutionary rather than revolutionary.

Goals

The goals for health systems, according to the World Health Report 2000 - Health systems: improving performance (WHO, 2000), are good health, responsiveness to the expectations of the population, and fair financial contribution. Duckett (2004) proposed a two dimensional approach to evaluation of Healthcare systems: quality, efficiency and acceptability on one dimension and equity on another. The goals for health systems, according to the World Health Organization, are good health, responsiveness to the expectations of the population, and fair financial contribution. Progress towards them depends on how systems carry out four vital functions: provision of Healthcare services, resource generation, financing and stewardship. Other dimensions for the evaluation of Healthcare systems include quality, efficiency, acceptability and equity. They have also been described in the United States as "the five C's": Cost, Coverage, Consistency, Complexity and Chronic Illness.

Providers

Healthcare providers are trained professional people working self-employed or as an employee in an organization, whether a **for-profit company, a not-for profit company,** a government entity, or a charity. Organisations employing people providing Healthcare are also known as Healthcare providers. Examples are doctors and nurses, dentists, medical laboratory staff, specialist therapists, psychologists, pharmacists, **chiropractors**, and optometrists. Healthcare providers institutions or individuals providing Healthcare services. Individuals including health professionals and allied health professions can be self-employed or working as an employee in a hospital, clinic or other Healthcare institution, whether government operated, private for-profit, or private not-for-profit (e.g. non-governmental organization). They may also work outside of direct patient care such as in a government health department or other agency, medical laboratory or health training institution. Examples of health workers are doctors, nurses, midwives, paramedics, dentists, medical laboratory technicians, therapists, psycholo-gists, pharmacists, chiropractors, optometrists, community health workers, traditional medicine practitioners and others.

Financial Resources

There are generally five primary methods of funding Healthcare systems:

- Direct or out-of-pocket payments,
- General taxation,
- Social health insurance,
- Voluntary or private health insurance, and
- Donations or community health insurance.

Most countries systems feature a mix of all five models. One study based on data from the **OECD concluded that all types of Healthcare finance** "are compatible with" an efficient Healthcare system. The study also found no relationship between financing and cost control.

The term health insurance is generally used to describe a form of insurance that pays for medical expenses. It is sometimes used more broadly to include insurance covering disability or long-term nursing or custodial care needs. It may be provided through a government-sponsored social insurance program, or from private insurance companies. It may be purchased on a group basis (e.g., by a firm to cover its employees) or purchased by individual consumers. In each case, the covered groups or individuals pay premiums or taxes to help protect themselves from high or unexpected Healthcare expenses. Similar benefits paying for medical expenses may also be provided through schemes organized by the government and funded through contributions from users.

By estimating the overall cost of Healthcare expenses, a routine finance structure (such as a monthly premium or annual tax) can be developed, ensuring that money is available to pay for the Healthcare benefits specified in the insurance agreement. The benefit is administered by a central organization, most often either a government agency or a private or **not-for-profit** entity operating a health plan.

Many forms of commercial health insurance control their costs by restricting the benefits that are paid by through deductibles co-payments coinsurance, policy exclusions and total coverage limits and will severely restrict or refuse coverage of pre-existing conditions. Many government schemes also have co-payment schemes but exclusions are rare because of political pressure. The larger insurance schemes may also negotiate fees with providers.

Many forms of government insurance schemes control their costs by using the bargaining power of government to control costs in the Healthcare delivery system. For example, by negotiating drug prices directly with pharmaceutical countries, or negotiating standard fees with the medical profession. Government schemes sometimes features contributions related to earnings as part of a scheme to deliver universal Healthcare, which may or may not also involved the use of commercial and non-commercial insurers. Essentially the more wealthy pay a little more into the scheme and to cover the needs of the relatively poor who therefore contribute a little less. There are usually caps on the contributions of the wealthy and minimum payments that must be made by the insured (often in the form of a minimum contribution, similar to a deductible in commercial insurance models).

Most countries' systems feature a mix of all five models. **Study based on data from the OECD concluded that all types of Healthcare finance** "are compatible with" an efficient Healthcare system. The study also found no relationship between financing and cost control.

The term health insurance is generally used to describe a form of insurance that pays for medical expenses. It is sometimes used more broadly to include insurance covering disability or long-term nursing or custodial care needs. It may be provided through a social insurance program, or from private insurance companies. It may be obtained on a group basis (e.g., by a firm to cover its employees) or purchased by individual consumers. In each case premiums or taxes protect the insured from high or unexpected Healthcare expenses.

By estimating the overall cost of Healthcare expenses, a routine finance structure (such as a monthly premium or annual tax) can be developed, ensuring that money is available to pay for the

Healthcare benefits specified in the insurance agreement. The benefit is typically administered by a government agency, a non-profit health fund or a corporation operating seeking to make a profit.

Many forms of commercial health insurance control their costs by restricting the benefits that are paid through deductibles, co-payments, coinsurance, policy exclusions and total coverage limits and will severely restrict or refuse coverage of pre-existing conditions. Many government schemes also have co-payment schemes but exclusions are rare because of political pressure. The larger insurance schemes may also negotiate fees with providers.

Many forms of social insurance schemes control their costs by using the bargaining power of their community they represent to control costs in the Healthcare delivery system. For example, by negotiating drug prices directly with pharmaceutical companies, or negotiating standard fees with the medical profession. Social schemes sometimes feature contributions related to earnings as part of a scheme to deliver universal Healthcare, which may or may not also involve the use of commercial and non-commercial insurers. Essentially the more wealthy pay proportionately more into the scheme to cover the needs of the relatively poor who therefore contribute proportionately less. There are usually caps on the contributions of the wealthy and minimum payments that must be made by the insured (often in the form of a minimum contribution, similar to a deductible in commercial insurance models).

Payment Models

In most countries, wage costs for Healthcare practitioners are estimated to represent between 65% and 80% of renewable health system expenditures. There are three ways to pay medical practitioners. There has been growing interest in blending elements of these systems.

- Fee-for-service
- Fee-for-service arrangements pay general practitioners (GPs) based on the service. They are even more widely used for specialists working in ambulatory care.

There are two ways to set fee levels:

- By individual practitioners.
- Central negotiations (as in Japan, Germany, Canada and in France) or hybrid model (such as in Australia, France's sector 2 and New Zealand) where GPs can charge extra fees on top of standardized patient reimbursement rates.

Other

- In capitation payment systems, GPs are paid for each patient on their "list", usually with adjustments for factors such as age and gender.[11] According to OECD, "these systems are used in Italy (with some fees), in all four countries of the United Kingdom (with some fees and allowances for specific services), Austria (with fees for specific services), Denmark (one third of income with remainder fee for service), Ireland (since

1989), the Netherlands (fee-for-service for privately insured patients and public employees) and Sweden (from 1994). Capitation payments have become more frequent in "managed care" environments in the United States.

According to OECD, "Capitation systems allow funders to control the overall level of primary health expenditures and the allocation of funding among GPs is determined by patient registrations. However, under this approach, GPs may register too many patients and under-serve them, select the better risks and refer on patients who could have been treated by the GP directly. Freedom of consumer choice over doctors, coupled with the principle of "money following the patient" may moderate some of these risks. Aside from selection, these problems are likely to be less marked than under salary-type arrangements."

In several OECD countries, general practitioners (GPs) are employed on salaries for the government. According to OECD, "Salary arrangements allow funders to control primary care costs directly; however, they may lead to under-provision of services (to ease workloads), excessive referrals to secondary providers and lack of attention to the preferences of patients." There has been movement away from this system.

Information Resources

There are different forms of Information Resources Likes

Healthcare delivery, Health information management, and Health informatics. Sound information plays an increasingly critical role in the delivery of modern Healthcare and efficiency of Healthcare systems. Health informatics is the intersection of information science, medicine and Healthcare and it deals with the resources, devices and methods required to optimize the acquisition and use of information in health and biomedicine. Necessary tools for proper **health information coding and management include** clinical guidelines, formal medical terminologies and computers and other information and communication technologies. The kinds of data processed may include patients' medical records, hospital administration and clinical functions and human resources information.

The use of health information lies at the root of evidence-based policy and evidence-based management in Healthcare.

Management

Health policy, Public health and Disease management (health)

The management of any Healthcare system is typically directed through a set of policies and plans adopted by government, private sector business and other groups in areas such as personal Healthcare delivery and financing, pharmaceuticals, health human resources and public health.

Public health is concerned with threats to the overall health of a community based on population health analysis. The population in question can be as small as a handful of people, or as large as all the inhabitants of several continents (for instance, in the case of a pandemic). Public health is typically divided into epidemiology, biostatistics and health services. Environmental, social, behavioural, and occupational health are also important subfields.

Today, most governments recognize the importance of public health programs in reducing the incidence of disease, disability, the effects of aging and health inequities, although public health generally receives significantly less government funding compared with medicine. For examply, most countries have a vaccination policy, supporting public health programs in providing vaccinations to promote health. Vaccinations are voluntary in some countries and mandatory in some countries. Some governments pay all or part of the costs for vaccines in a national vaccination schedule.

The rapid emergence of many chronic diseases, which require costly long-term care and treatment, is making many health managers and policy makers re-examine their Healthcare delivery practices. An important health issue facing the world currently is HIV/AIDS. Another major public health concern is diabetes. In 2006, according to the World Health Organization, at least 171 million people worldwide suffered from diabetes. Its incidence is increasing rapidly, and it is estimated that by the year 2030, this number will double. A controversial aspect of public health is the control of tobacco smoking, linked to cancer and other chronic illnesses.

Antibiotic resistance is another major concern, leading to the reemergence of diseases such as tuberculosis. The World Health Organization, for its World Health Day 2011 campaign, is calling for intensified global commitment to safeguard antibiotics and other antimicrobial medicines for future generations.

Special Healthcare Systems

Occupational safety and health

Occupational health and safety is a cross-disciplinary area concerned with protecting the safety, health and welfare of people engaged in work or employment. The goal of all occupational health and safety programs is to foster a safe work environment. As a secondary effect, it may also protect co-workers, family members, employers, customers, suppliers, nearby communities, and other members of the public who are impacted by the workplace environment. It may involve interactions among many subject areas, including occupational medicine, occupational (or industrial) hygiene, public health, safety engineering, chemistry, health physics.

Since 1950, the International Labour Organization (ILO) and the World Health Organization (WHO) have shared a common definition of occupational health. It was adopted by the Joint ILO/WHO Committee on Occupational Health at its first session in 1950 and revised at its twelfth session in 1995. The definition reads: "Occupational health should aim at: the promotion and maintenance of the highest degree of physical, mental and social well-being of workers in all occupations; the prevention amongst workers of departures from health caused by their working conditions; the protection of workers in their employment from risks resulting from factors adverse to health; the placing and maintenance of the worker in an occupational environment adapted to his physiological and psychological capabilities; and, to summarize, the adaptation of work to man and of each man to his job". This standard is based on the methodology known as Plan-Do-Check-Act (PDCA).

Relationship to Occupational Health Psychology

Occupational health psychology (OHP), a related discipline, is a relatively new field that combines elements of occupational health and safety, industrial/organizational psychology, and health psychology. The field is concerned with identifying work-related psychosocial factors that adversely affect the health of people who work. OHP is also concerned with developing ways to effect change in workplaces for the purpose of improving the health of people who work. For more detail on OHP, see the section on occupational health psychology....

Reasons for Occupational Health and Safety

The event of an incident at work (such as legal fees, fines, compensatory damages, investigation time, lost production, lost goodwill from the workforce, from customers and from the wider community).

Legal - Occupational requirements may be reinforced in civil law and/or criminal law; it is accepted that without the extra "encouragement" of potential regulatory action or litigation, many organizations would not act upon their implied moral obligations.

Occupational health and safety officers promote health and safety procedures in an organisation. They recognize hazards and measure health and safety risks, set suitable safety controls in place, and give recommendations on avoiding accidents to management and employees in an organisation. This paper looks at the main tasks undertaken by (Occupational Health & Safety) practitioners in Europe, Australia and the USA, and the main knowledge and skills that are required of them. "Like it or not, organisations have a duty to provide health and safety training. But it could involve much more than you think."

An effective training program can reduce the number of injuries and deaths, property damage, legal liability, illnesses, workers' compensation claims, and missed time from work. A safety training program can also help a trainer keep the required OSHA-mandated safety training courses organized and up-to-date.

Safety training classes help establish a safety culture in which employees themselves help promote proper safety procedures while on the job. It is important that new employees be properly trained and embrace the importance of workplace safety, as it is easy for seasoned workers to negatively influence the new hires. That negative influence however, can be purged with the establishment of new, hands-on, innovative effective safety training which will ultimately lead to an effective safety culture. A 1998 NIOSH study concluded that the role of training in developing and maintaining effective hazard control activities is a proven and successful method of intervention.

School Health Services

School health services are services from medical, teaching and other professionals applied in or out of school to improve the health and well-being of children and in some cases whole families. These services have been developed in different ways around the globe but the fundamentals are constant: the early detection, correction, prevention or amelioration of disease, disability and abuse from which school aged children can suffer. It was shown by statistics that many pupils were backward in their studies only because of lack of physical vitality. In 1920, it was shown that so many pupils in the schools of Brooklyn, New York, were compelled to pass through the same grades twice that, at the average cost of $40 a term for each pupil, the borough lost $2,000,000. On this basis various social organizations demanded an appropriation from the city of $100,000 for more effective medical aid to the school children, contending that more than half of the extra expense could thus be saved. Out of 252,000 school-children inspected in New York City in 1919, 74% were found defective physically, defective teeth and vision being the chief faults.

Military Medicine

The term military medicine has a number of potential connotations. It may mean:

A medical specialty, specifically a branch of occupational medicine attending to the medical risks and needs (both preventive and interventional) of soldiers, sailors and other service members. This disparate arena has historically involved the prevention and treatment of infectious diseases (especially tropical diseases), and, in the 20th Century, the ergonomics and health effects of operating military-specific machines and equipment such as submarines, tanks, helicopters and airplanes. Undersea and aviation medicine can be understood as subspecialties of military medicine, or in any case originated as such. (The American Board of Medical Specialties does not, however, certify or recognize a specialty or subspecialty of "military medicine").

The planning and practice of the surgical management of mass battlefield casualties and the logistical and administrative considerations of establishing and operating combat support hospitals. This involves military medical hierarchies, especially the organization of structured medical command and administrative systems that interact with and support deployed combat units. (See Battlefield medicine).

The administration and practice of Healthcare for military service members and their dependents in non-deployed (peacetime) settings. This may (as in the United States) consist of a medical system paralleling all the medical specialties and sub-specialties that exist in the civilian sector. (See also Veterans Health Administration which serves U.S. veterans.)

Medical research and development specifically bearing upon problems of military medical interest. Historically, this encompasses all of the medical advances emerging from medical research efforts directed at addressing the problems encountered by deployed military forces (e.g., vaccines or drugs for soldiers, medical evacuation systems, drinking water chlorination, etc) many of which ultimately prove important beyond the purely military considerations that inspired them.

The significance of military medicine for combat strength can be judged based on the fact that in every single major war fought until the late 19th century disease claimed more soldier casualties than did enemy action. During the American Civil War (1860-65), for example, about twice as many soldiers died of disease as were killed or mortally wounded in combat. The Franco-Prussian War (1870-71) is considered to have been the first conflict in which this ratio was reversed, at least in the German coalition army which lost 3.47% of its average headcount to combat and only 1.82% to disease. In new world countries, such as Australia, the United States and Canada, military physicians and surgeons contributed significantly to the development of civilian Healthcare.

Summary

Healthcare System are designed to meet the health need of target population. There are a wide variety of Healthcare Systems around the world. In some countries, Healthcare system planning is distributed among market participants. The Coal for health system are good health, responsiveness to the expectations of the population & fair financial contribution. Healthcare provides who are trained professional working self employed and are providing Healthcare. Examples are doctors, nurses etc. the financial resources should be provided so that organisation can run efficiently. By estimating the overall cost of Healthcare expenses, a routine financial structure should be developed. The Healthcare system can be effective by the different forms of information resources like Healthcare delivery, Health information management and Health Informatics. The management of Healthcare System is typically directed through a set of policies and plans adopted by government, private sector & other groups. It deals with occupational health & safety, the goal is to foster a safe working environment.

Question :

Q. 1. What is Healthcare system?

Q. 2. Explain the financial resources and types of Information resources of Healthcare system.

Short Notes:

Write short notes on

(*a*) Occupational health and safety

(*b*) Military medicine

(*c*) Healthcare System Management

8

HEALTH RESEARCH

Learning Objective

This chapter aims to provide the student with :

- An overview on Health Research
- Health System Research
- Role of Private Sector
- Role of Civil Society
- National Disease Surveillance Network.

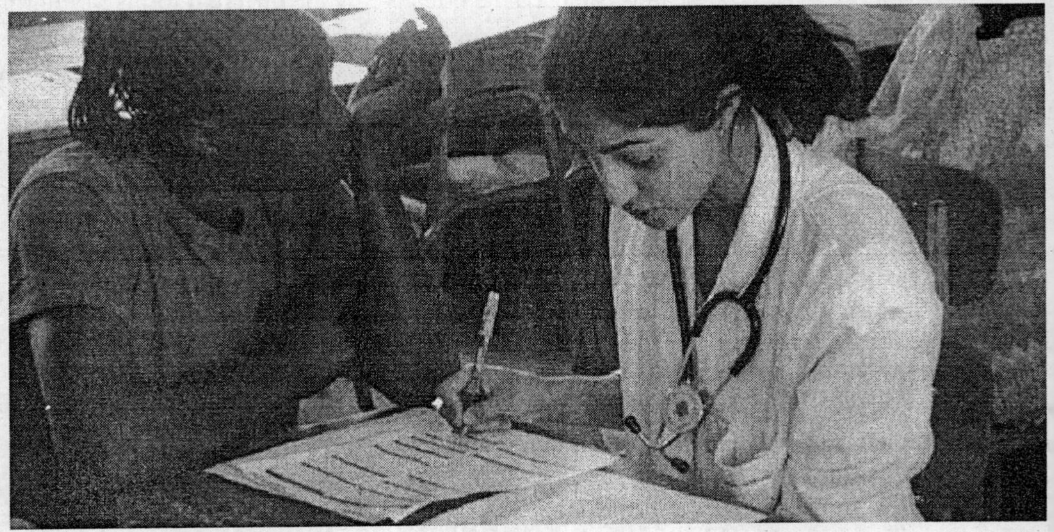

Over the years, health research activity in the country has been very limited. In the Government sector, such research has been confined to the research institutions under the Indian Counc of Medical Research, and other institutions funded by the States/Central Government. Research in the private sector has assumed some significance only in the last decade. In our country, where the aggregate annual health expenditure is of the order of Rs. 80,000 crores, the expenditure in 1998-99 on research, both public and private sectors, was only of the order of Rs. 1150 crores. It would be reasonable to infer that with such low research expenditure, it is virtually impossible to make any dramatic break-through within the country, by way of new molecules and vaccines; also, without a minimal back-up of applied and operational research, it would be difficult to assess whether the health expenditure in the country is being incurred through optimal applications and appropriate public health strategies. Medical Research in the country needs to be focused on therapeutic drugs/vaccines for tropical diseases, which are normally neglected by international pharmaceutical companies on account of their limited profitability potential. The thrust will need to be in the newly-emerging frontier areas of research based on genetics, genome-based drug and vaccine development, molecular biology, etc. NHP-2002 will address these inadequacies and spell out a minimal quantum of expenditure for the coming decade, looking to the national needs and the capacity of the research institutions to absorb the funds.

HEALTH RESEARCH

This Policy envisages an increase in Government-funded health research to a level of 1 per-cent of the total health spending by 2005; and thereafter, up to 2 percent by 2010. Domestic medical research would be focused on new therapeutic drugs and vaccines for tropical diseases, such as TB and Malaria, as also on the sub-types of HIV/AIDS prevalent in the country. Research programmes taken up by the Government in these priority areas would be conducted in a mission mode. Emphasis would also be laid on time-bound applied research for developing operational applications. This would ensure the cost-effective dissemination of existing / future therapeutic drugs/vaccines in the general population. Private entrepreneurship will be encouraged in the field of medical research for new molecules / vaccines, inter alia, through fiscal incentives.

The definition for the field of health services research to reflect its continuing evolution and sophistication. This new definition is intended to provide a cogent description of the field to interested parties from related fields such as health policy and clinical care. The definition, developed by the ad hoc committee, states the following: **"Health services research** is the multidisciplinary field of scientific investigation that studies how social factors, financing systems, organizational structures and processes, health technologies and personal behaviours affect access to Healthcare, the quality and cost of Healthcare, and ultimately our health and well-being. Its research domains are individuals, families, organizations, institutions, communities and populations."

In some respects, the definition of this field has not changed since the early days when health services research emerged in response to health policy concerns regarding access to care and the costs and quality of care. The name "health services research" was formally recognized in 1966 through the establishment of a federal government health services research study section to review grant proposals. The field gained broader recognition and increased funding with the establishment in 1969 of the National Center for Health Services Research and Development in the (then) Department of Health, Education and Welfare, under the leadership of Dr. Paul Sanazaro In the early 1970s, Dr. Sanazaro described health services research as a field that develops methods for improving access to care, moderating the rate of medical care prices and assuring the effectiveness of care. At approximately the same time, the Report of the Panel on Health Services Research and Development of the President's Science Advisory Committee (1972) stated, "Health services research seeks to improve the network for providing Healthcare so that the fruits of biomedical research are readily available to all citizens."

Health services research is inquiry to produce knowledge about the structure, processes, and effects of personal health services. In 1995, an IOM committee updated and expanded the definition to read, "Health services research is a multidisciplinary field of inquiry, both basic and applied that examines the use, costs, quality, accessibility, delivery, organization, financing and outcomes of Healthcare services to increase knowledge and understanding of the structure, processes and effects of health services for individuals and populations". The 1995 definition emphasized the multidisciplinary nature of the field, the range of basic to applied research, and the need to understand the effects of health services on both individuals and populations.

In the definition recently adopted by the AHSR Board and then by the Board of the Academy for Health Services Research and Health Policy, the scope of health services research interest broadened further to include personal behaviours and social factors. Personal behaviours (e.g smoking, use of seat belts, and diet) and social factors (e.g., income, educational attainment and occupation) are recognized as having important influences on the need for services and on the potential benefit or impact of health services on health status and well-being. The enumeration research domains further emphasizes the breadth of the field and the important influences of families, organizations, institutions and communities on the receipt of health services and health status outcomes.

The new definition will likely meet our needs for a few years. It is intended to indicate the range of factors that influences the need for health services, receipt of care, its quality and costs, and the health outcomes experienced by individuals and populations. Understandably, this definition is intended primarily for our research and policy colleagues and knowledgeable users of health services research. For the public, policy makers and others who may know relatively less about the field, we need to devise simpler and more effective ways of communicating the content and value of health services research, as indeed this issue has been true for the past three decades. The board and staff of the Academy are developing new communication tools that will permit all those in the field to have a hand in educating the broader community of people who benefit from the products of health services researchers. Without doubt, however, we can and should expect the field of health services research will continue to evolve and we will need to revisit in years to come the breadth and areas of contribution described above.

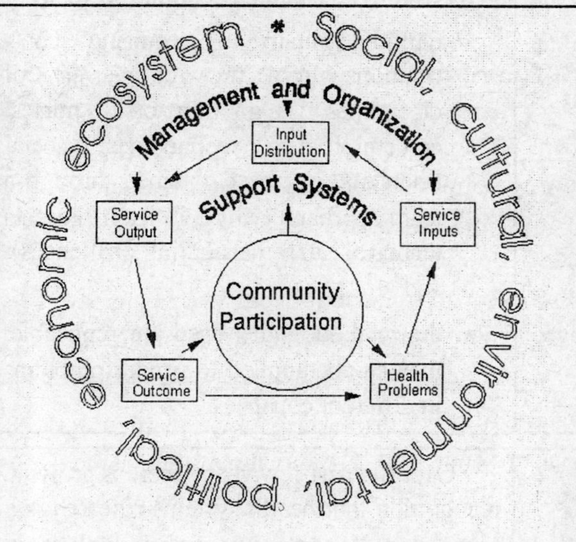

Health and health services have come to be seen in a much broader social, cultural and economic context, the interrelated parts of which are today considered as constituting the health system. It comprises three important elements:

(1) the community

(2) the health service delivery system and

(3) the environment in which both of them are located.

These three are highly interdependent. Health needs - objective and subjective - of the comunity are mostly determined by environmental ecology, i.e. its socio-cultural, demographic, ecoomical and political surroundings. Health problems and health needs, in turn, should determine the ientation of the Healthcare system. If the Healthcare system is to serve the community within a ven environment, there must be a close 'fit' between these three elements.

Health Systems Research is:

- problem and action oriented
- participatory
- multisectoral
- multidisciplinary
- methodically replicable

Health Systems Research is:

- problem and action oriented - it studies specific problems to find feasible, practical and affordable solutions;
- participatory - requiring active and continuous collaboration between those who identify the problems to be studied, those who are the main potential users of the research results (the health systems managers) and those who search for the facts and suggest alternative solutions (the researchers);
- multisectoral - deriving its inputs from various social and economic sectors;
- multidisciplinary - requiring contributions from a wide variety of disciplines, e.g. doctors, nurses, epidemiologists, economists, social scientists, etc. best obtained through a team approach (which in itself presents technical and managerial challenges); and
- the methodologies used are replicable, they can be applied to similar problems in different countries.

Health Systems Research aims to:

- improve decision making by providing relevant and timely information to health managers at all levels
- improve people's health through optimal use of research

Over the past few years, there is growing recognition that health systems research is a useful tool to empower policy makers in informed decision making. World-wide and especially in Africa, many initiatives were undertaken to strengthen HSR: the Commission of Health Research for Development (COHRED); the Commonwealth Regional Health Community Secretariat for East, Central and Southern Africa (CRHCS), the 'Joint Project on Health Systems Research' for the Eastern

	and Southern Africa Region - and the GTZ-supported Network for Health Systems Research for Reproductive Health and Healthcare Reforms in Eastern and Southern Africa.

The World Health Organisation (WHO) supported 'Joint Health Systems Research Programme' ınd the GTZ (German Development Co-operation) Programme for Health Systems Research HSR) have been supporting up to 17 countries of Eastern and Southern Africa in capacity building or HSR, giving financial and technical assistance to HSR studies, facilitating the implementation f research recommendations and trying to network the countries through newsletters, electronic ıedia, country visits, and inter-country workshops.

Role of the Private Sector : Considering the economic restructuring under way in the coun-y & over the globe in the last decade, the change role of private sector in providing Healthcare ill also have to be addressed in this policy. Currently, the contribution of private Healthcare is rincipally through independent practitioner. Also they contribute to secondary level care & some rtiary care. His widespread perception that private health services are very uneven in quality. rivate health services are perceived to be financially exploitative, and the observance of profes-onal ethics is noted only as an exception. With the increasing role of private Healthcare, the ıplementation of statutory regulation, and the monitoring of minimum standards of diagnostic enters / medical institutions becomes imperative. The Policy will address the issues regarding the tablishment of a comprehensive information system, and based on that the establishment of a gulatory mechanism to ensure the maintaining of adequate standards by diagnostic centers / edical institutions, as well as the proper conduct of clinical practice and delivery of medical rvices.

Currently, non-Governmental service providers are treating a large number of patients at the imary level for major diseases. However, the treatment regimens followed are diverse and not ientifically optimal, leading to an increase in the incidence of drug resistance. This policy will dress itself to recommending arrangements which will eliminate the risks arising from inappro-ate treatment.

The increasing spread of information technology raises the possibility of its adoption in the alth sector. NHP-2002 will examine this possibility.

e Role of Civil Society

Historically, it has been the practice to implement major national disease control programs ough the public health machinery of the State/Central Governments. It has become increasingly parent that certain components of such programs cannot be efficiently implemented merely through government functionaries. A considerable change in the mode of implementation has come about in the last two decades, with the increasing involvement of NGOs and other institutions of civil society. It is to be recognized that widespread debate on various public health issues has, in fact, been initiated and sustained by NGOs and other members of the civil society. Also, an increasing contribution is being made by such institutions in the delivery of different components of public health services. Certain disease control programs require close interaction with the beneficiaries for regular administration of drugs; periodic carrying out of pathological tests; dissemination of information regarding disease control and other general health information. NHP-2002 will address such issues and suggest policy instruments for the implementation of public health programs through individuals and institutions of civil society.

National Disease Surveillance Network

The technical network available in the country for disease surveillance is extremely rudimentary and to the extent that the system exists, it extends only up to the district level. Disease statistics are not flowing through an integrated network from the decentralized public health facilities to the State/Central Government health administration. Such an arrangement only provides belated information, which, at best, serves a limited statistical purpose. The absence of an efficient disease surveillance network is a major handicap in providing a prompt and cost-effective Healthcare system. The efficient disease surveillance network set up for Polio and HIV/AIDS has demonstrated the enormous value of such a public health instrument. Real-time information on focal outbreaks of common communicable diseases – Malaria, GE, Cholera and JE – and the seasonal trends of diseases, would enable timely intervention, resulting in the containment of the thrust of epidemics. In order to be able to use integrated disease surveillance network for operational purposes, real-time information is necessary at all levels of the health administration. The Policy would address itself to this major systemic shortcoming in the administration.

Health Statistics

The absence of a systematic and scientific health statistics database is a major deficiency in the current scenario. The health statistics collected are not the product of a rigorous methodology. Statistics available from different parts of the country, in respect of major diseases, are often not obtained in a manner which make aggregation possible or meaningful.

Further, the absence of proper and systematic documentation of the various financial resources used in the health sector is another lacuna in the existing health information scenario. This makes it difficult to understand trends and levels of health spending by private and public providers of Healthcare in the country, and, consequently, to address related policy issues and to formulate future investment policies.

NHP-2002 will address itself to the programme for putting in place a modern and scientific health statistics database as well as a system of national health accounts.

Women's Health

Social, cultural and economic factors continue to inhibit women from gaining adequate access even to the existing public health facilities. This handicap does not merely affect women as individuals; it also has an adverse impact on the health, general well-being and development of the entire family, particularly children. This policy recognizes the catalytic role of empowered women in improving the overall health standards of the community.

Health System Research

Over years, the health research activity in the country has been very limited. In the government sector, such research has been confined to the research institution under Indian Council of Medical Research. In our country, where the aggregate annual health expenditure is of the order of Rs. 80,000 crores, the expenditure on research (both public and private) was only of order of Rs. 1150 crores the define then for the field of health services research is inquiry to produce knowledge about the structure, processes and effects of personal health services. It comprises of three important elements that is community, the health service delivery system and the environment in which both of them are located. In Health Service Research the role of the private sector is providing private Healthcare through independent practitioner they also contribute to secondary & tertiary care. There are National Disease Surveillance Network whose efficient disease surveillance Network set up for polio and HIV/AIDs & developed enormous values.

Keywords: Health Statistics, Women's Health, Health System Research, National Disease Surveillance Network.

Question :

1. Explain the practical utility of Healthcare research.
2. What are the elements of health services?
3. Discuss in brief the role of private sector and civil society/
4. What is National Disease Surveillance Network?

Short Notes:

- Health Statistics
- National Disease Surveillance Network
- Health System Research

9

HEALTHCARE IN INDIA (TRENDS OF HEALTHCARE IN INDIAN SCENARIO)

Healthcare in India features a universal Healthcare system run by the constituent states and territories of India. The Constitution charges every state with "raising of the level of nutrition and the standard of living of its people and the improvement of public health as among its primary duties". The National Health Policy was endorsed by the Parliament of India in 1983 and updated in 2002. However, the government sector is understaffed and underfinanced; poor services at state-run hospitals force many people to visit private medical practitioners.

Government hospitals, some of which are among the best hospitals in India, provide treatment at taxpayer expense. Most essential drugs are offered free of charge in these hospitals. Government hospitals provide treatment either free or at minimal charges. For example, an outpatient card at AIIMS (one of the best hospitals in India) costs a onetime fee of rupees 10 (around 20 cents US) and thereafter outpatient medical advice is free. In-hospital treatment costs depend on financial condition of the patient and facilities utilized by him but are usually much less than the private sector. For instance, a patient is waived treatment costs if he is below poverty line. Another patient may seek for an air-conditioned room if he is willing to pay extra for it. The charges for basic in-hospital treatment and investigations are much less compared to the private sector. The cost for these subsidies comes from annual allocations from the central and state governments.

Primary Healthcare is provided by city and district hospitals and rural primary health centres (PHCs). These hospitals provide treatment free of cost. Primary care is focused on immunization, prevention of malnutrition, pregnancy, child birth, postnatal care, and treatment of common illnesses. Patients who receive specialized care or have complicated illnesses are referred to secondary (often located in district and taluk headquarters) and tertiary care hospitals (located in district and state headquarters or those that are teaching hospitals).

In recent times, India has eradicated mass famines, however the country still suffers from high levels of malnutrition and disease especially in rural areas. Water supply and sanitation in India is also a major issue in the country and many Indians in rural areas lack access to proper sanitation facilities and safe drinking water. However, at the same time, India's Healthcare system also includes entities that meet or exceed international quality standards. The medical tourism business in India has been growing in recent years and as such India is a popular destination for medical tourists who receive effective medical treatment at lower costs than in developed countries.

A Growing Healthcare Sector

Healthcare is one of India's largest sectors, in terms of revenue and employment, and the sector is expanding rapidly. During the 1990s, Indian healthcare grew at a compound annual rate of 16%. Today the total value of the sector is more than $34 billion. This translates to $34 per capita, or roughly 6% of GDP. By 2012, India's healthcare sector is projected to grow to nearly $40 billion. The private sector accounts for more than 80% of total healthcare spending in India. Unless there is a decline in the combined federal and state government deficit, which currently stands at roughly 9%, the opportunity for significantly higher public health spending will be limited. Growing population and economy One driver of growth in the healthcare sector is India's booming population, currently 1.1 billion and increasing at a 2% annual rate. By 2030, India is expected to surpass China as the world's most populous nation. By 2050, the population is projected to reach 1.6 billion. This population increase is due in part to a decline in Infant mortality, the result of better healthcare facilities and the government's emphasis on eradicating diseases such as hepatitis and polio among infants. In addition, life expectancy is rapidly approaching the levels of the western world. By 2025, an estimated 189 million Indians will be at least 60 years of age—triple the number in 2004, thanks to greater affluence and better hygiene. The growing elderly population will place an enormous burden on India's healthcare infrastructure.

Figure 1: India is forecast to grow by at least 5% a year for the next 45

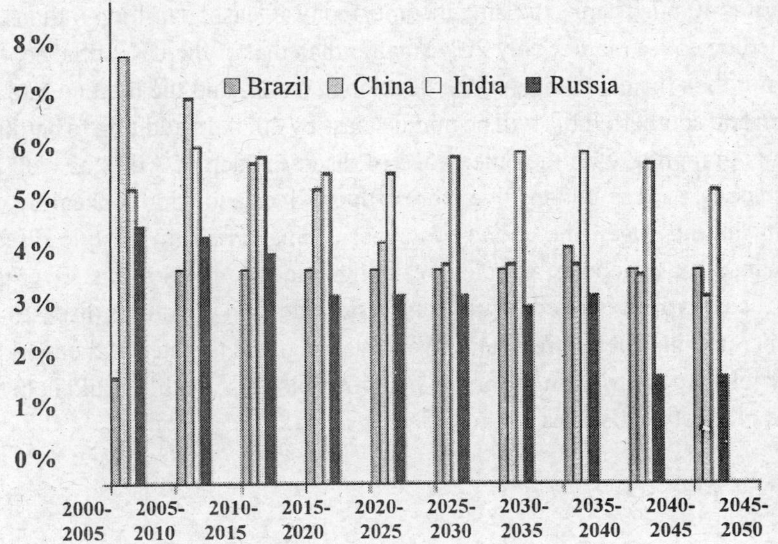

The Indian economy, estimated at roughly $1 trillion, is growing in tandem with the population. Goldman Sachs predicts that the Indian economy will expand by at least 5% annually for the next 45 years (see chart), and that it will be the only emerging economy to maintain such a robust pace of growth.

Expanding Middle Class

India traditionally has been a rural, agrarian economy. Nearly three- quarters of the population still lives in rural areas, and as of 2004, an estimated 27.5% of Indians were living below the national poverty line. Some 300 million people in India live on less than a dollar a day, and more than 50% of all children are malnourished.

Middle class % of entire population	
1998–99	44.92
2001–02	50.53
2009–10	(estimate) 62.95

However, India's thriving economy is driving urbanization and creating an expanding middle class, with more disposable income to spend on healthcare. While per capita income was $620 in 2005, over 150 million. Indians have annual incomes of more than $1,000, and many who work in the business services sector earn as much as $20,000 a year. While this is a fraction of the income that their US peers earn, it is the equivalent of more than $100,000 per year when adjusted for purchasing power parity. More women are entering the workforce as well, further boosting the purchasing power of Indian households. Between 1991 and 2001, the percentage of women increased from 22% to 26% of the workforce, according to the latest Indian government census. Many of these women are highly educated: the ratio of women to men who have a college degree or higher level of is 40:60. Thanks to rising income, today at least 50 million Indians can afford to buy Western medicines—a market only 20% smaller than that of the UK. If the economy continues to grow faster than the economies of the developed world, and the literacy rate keeps rising, much of western and southern India will be middle class by 2020. In addition to battling infectious diseases, India is grappling with the emergence of diseases such as AIDS as well as food- and water-borne illnesses. And as Indians live more affluent lives and adopt unhealthy western diets that are high in fat and sugar, the country is experiencing a rise in lifestyle diseases such as hypertension, cancer, and diabetes, which is reaching epidemic proportions. Over the next 5-10 years, lifestyle diseases are expected to grow at a faster rate than infectious diseases in India, and to result in an increase in cost per treatment. Wellness programs targeted at the workplace, where many sedentary jobs are contributing to an erosion of employees' health, could help to reduce the rising incidence of lifestyle diseases .

Pharmaceuticals

Paralleling the rise of disease is the emergence of a robust pharmaceutical industry in India. The Indian pharmaceutical market is one of the fastest growing markets in the world; sales increased by 17.5% to $7.3 billion in 2006, according to IMS Health. Many factors, including a strong economy and the country's growing healthcare needs have contributed to the accelerated growth, which is especially strong in the over-the-counter (OTC) market. Overall, the domestic pharmaceutical industry is highly fragmented; more than 10,000 firms collectively control about 70% of the market. Only three foreign multinationals rank in the top 10 companies, as measured by sales, and collectively they have only 11.9% of the market between them. But many of the local players are generics producers specializing in antiinfectives, and as the illnesses of affluence and age increase, the demand for innovative new pharmaceuticals will rise. The federal government uses price controls to ensure that vital drugs are affordable to the Indian population. Under the proposed pharmaceutical policy 2006, the government revealed its intention to raise the number of essential drugs under price controls from 79 to nearly 354, which would bring almost a third of the industry under price controls and adversely impact foreign pharmaceutical firms that want to business in India. It is an ongoing challenge to balance the commercial interests of pharmaceutical companies with the broader social objective of curing disease and preventing epidemics that could decimate the Indian population.

Deteriorating Infrastructure

India's healthcare infrastructure has not kept pace with the economy's growth. The physical infrastructure is woefully inadequate to meet today's healthcare demands, much less tomorrow's. While India has several centers of excellence in healthcare delivery, these facilities are limited in their ability to drive healthcare standards because of the poor condition of the infrastructure in the vast majority of the country. Of the 15,393 hospitals in India in 2002, roughly two-thirds were public. After years of under-funding, most public health facilities provide only basic care. With a few exceptions, such as the All India Institute of Medical Studies (AIIMS), public health facilities are inefficient, inadequately managed and staffed, and have poorly maintained medical equipment. The number of public health facilities also is inadequate. For instance, India needs 74,150 community health centers per million population but has less than half that number. In addition, at least 11 Indian states do not have laboratories for testing drugs, and more than half of existing laboratories are not properly equipped or staffed. The principal responsibility for public health funding lies with the state governments, which provide about 80% of public funding. The federal government contributes another 15%, mostly through national health programs. However, the total healthcare financing by the public sector is dwarfed by private sector spending. In 2003, fee-charging private companies accounted for 82% of India's $30.5 billion expenditure on healthcare. This is an extremely high proportion by international Standards. Private firms are now thought to provide about 60% of all outpatient care in India and as much as 40% of all in-patient care. It is estimated that nearly 70% of all hospitals and 40% of hospital beds in the country are in the private sector.

Per Lakh (100K) population			
Beds	Hospitals	Dispensaries	
Urban	178.78	3.6	3.6
Rural	9.85	0.36	1.49

The Healthcare Divide

When it comes to healthcare, there are two Indias: the country with that provides high-quality medical care to middle-class Indians and medical tourists, and the India in which the majority of the population lives—a country whose residents have limited or no access to quality care. Today only 25% of the Indian population has access to Western (allopathic) medicine, which is practiced mainly in urban areas, where two-thirds of India's hospitals and health centers are located. Many of the rural poor must rely on alternative forms of treatment, such as ayurvedic medicine, unani and acupuncture. The federal government has begun taking steps to improve rural healthcare. Among other things, the government launched the National Rural Health Mission 2005-2012 in April 2005. The aim of the Mission is to provide effective healthcare to India's rural population, with a focus on 18 states that have low public health indicators and/or inadequate infrastructure. These include Arunachal Pradesh, Assam, Bihar, Chhattisgarh, Himachal Pradesh, Jharkhand, Jammu & Kashmir, Manipur, Mizoram, Meghalaya, Madhya Pradesh, Nagaland, Orissa, Rajasthan, Sikkim, Tripura, Uttaranchal and Uttar Pradesh. Through the Mission, the government is working to increase the capabilities of primary medical facilities in rural areas, and ease the burden on to tertiary care centers in the cities, by providing Equipment and training primary care physicians in how to perform basic surgeries, such as cataract surgery. While the rural poor are underserved, at least they can access the limited number of government-support medical facilities that are available to them. The urban poor fare even worse, because they cannot afford to visit the private facilities that thrive in India's cities.

Lack of Insurance

A widespread lack of health insurance compounds the healthcare challenges that India faces. Although some form of health protection is provided by government and major private employers, the health insurance schemes available to the Indian public are generally basic and inaccessible to most people. Only 11% of the population has any form of health insurance coverage. For the small percentage of Indians who do have some insurance, the main provider is the government-run General Insurance Company (GIC), along with its four subsidiaries, The New India Assurance Company, Oriental Fire and Insurance Co., National Insurance Co., and The United India Insurance Co. GIC is able to obtain funds for underwriting from other countries, although foreigners are not allowed to own insurance companies. Only 1% of the population was covered by private health insurance in 2004-05. Group insurance accounted for 35% of the total health insurance business during that period. India's first medical insurance scheme for the poor was launched in the 1996-97 budget. The "**Janarogya Yojana**" scheme is marketed by the four subsidiaries of GIC, and covers people between the ages of 5 and 70 for pre– and post–hospitalization expenses, for up to 30 and 60 days, respectively. The insurance coverage costs around $122 per annum.

More than four million policyholders were expected to enroll during the first year of operation, although reports suggest this was not the case. One problem is that the insurance is provided on a reimbursement basis: patients are required to pay for treatment out of their own pockets and then claim reimbursement—a process that can take up to six months, according to local reports. While public sector health insurance has not fared well, the market for private health plans is expanding in India. In some cases, the government is partnering with the private sector to provide coverage at a low cost. For instance, the Yashaswini Insurance scheme, launched in 2002 in the state of Karnataka by a public–private partnership, provides coverage for major surgical operations, including those pertaining to pre-existing conditions, to Indian farmers who previously had no access to insurance. The premium is only Rs 60 annually (roughly $1.50), which virtually all workers can afford, and the government contributes an additional Rs. 30 annually for each policyholder. While the Yashaswini scheme has been successful, it only provides coverage for approximately 50,000 farmers. Because so little insurance is available to the population of India, out of-pocket payments for medical care amounted to 98.4% of total health expenditures by households, as of the most recent (2001–02) census. Without insurance, the poor must resort to taking on debt or selling assets to meet the costs of hospital care. It is estimated that 20 million people in India fall below the poverty line each year because of indebtedness due to healthcare needs. Clearly there is an urgent need to expand the health insurance net in India. Among other things, that will require more state governments to pursue micro insurance initiatives, such as the Yashaswini Insurance scheme in Karnataka, so that most or all of the population can afford to purchase at least a minimum level of coverage. The widespread availability of health insurance would help to drive demand for services and provide additional revenue to improve the quality of care.

Opportunities within India's Healthcare Sector

Given the current state of India's healthcare system, its challenges and its growth prospects, Price water house Coopers has identified a number of market opportunities for foreign companies that want to participate in the sector. **Medical tourism** on the rise Medical tourism is one of the major external drivers of growth of the Indian healthcare sector. A Google search of "India medical tourism" turns up more than two million results. The emergence of India as a destination for medical tourism leverages the country's well educated, English-speaking medical staff, state-of-the art private hospitals and diagnostic facilities, and relatively low cost to address the spiraling healthcare costs of the western world. India provides best-in-class treatment, in some cases at less than one-tenth the cost incurred in the US (see chart). India's private hospitals excel in fields such as cardiology, joint replacement, orthopedic surgery, gastroenterology, ophthalmology, transplants and urology.

Cost of Key Healthcare Procedures				
Currency: USD	**US**	**Thailand**	**India**	**India HC cost-x of US**
Cardiac surgery	50,000	14,250	4,000	12.5
Bone marrow transplant	62,500	62,500	30,000	13.33
Liver transplant	5,00,000	75,000	45,000	11.11
Orthopaedic surgery	16,000	6,900	4,500	3.56

According to a joint study by the Confederation of Indian Industry and McKinsey, Indian medical tourism was estimated at $350 million in 2006 and has the potential to grow into a $2 billion industry by 2012. An estimated 180,000 medical tourists were treated at Indian facilities in 2004 (up from 10,000 just five years earlier), and the number has been growing at 25-30% annually. India has the potential to attract one million medical tourists each year, which could contribute $5 billion to the economy, according to the Confederation of Indian Industries. In addition to receiving traditional medical treatments, a growing number of western tourists are traveling to India to pursue alternate medicines such as ayurveda, which has blossomed in the state of Kerala, in southwestern India. The number of medical tourists visiting Kerala was close to 15,000 in 2006 and is expected to reach 100,000 by 2010. To capitalize on medical tourism and build a sustained public-private partnership in the hospital industry, the Indian government is supporting an initiative by well known heart surgeon Dr. Naresh Trehan to build a "Medi City" in Gurgaon, on the outskirts of Delhi. The compound will include a 900-bed hospital that supports 17 super specialties, a medical college and paramedical college. The project, on 43 acres of land, will cost an estimated $493 million. The Medi City will integrate allopathic care with alternative treatments, including unani, ayurvedic and homeopathic medicine, and it will provide telemedicine services as well. To encourage the growth of medical tourism, the government also is providing a variety of incentives, including lower import duties and higher depreciation rates on medical equipment, as well as expedited visas for overseas patients seeking medical care in India.

Emerging Health Insurance Market

In recent years, there has been a liberalization of the Indian healthcare sector to allow for a much-needed private insurance market to emerge. Due to liberalization and a growing middle class with increased spending power, there has been an increase in the number of insurance policies issued in the country. In 2001-02, 7.5 million policies were sold. By 2003-04, the number of policies issued had increased by 37%, to 10.3 million. The Insurance Regulatory and Development

Authority (IRDA) eliminated tariffs on general insurance as of January 1, 2007, and this move is expected to drive additional growth of private insurance products. In the wake of liberalization, health insurance is projected to grow to $5.75 billion by 2010, according to a study by the New Delhi-based PHD Chamber of Commerce and Industry. The IRDA believes that eliminating tariffs will encourage scientific rating and adoption of better risk management practices, and lead to independent pricing for each line of business, so that premiums will be based on actual risks and costs. The implementation of the new policy also will encourage the development of innovative practices and customer-friendly options for policyholders, boosting penetration. Removal of tariffs also will result in wider acceptance of individual health coverage. Health insurance will make healthcare more affordable to larger segments of the populace, boosting healthcare expenditures per household and driving the demand for quality care. Finally, the elimination of insurance tariffs will serve as a litmus test for further legislation, such as co-payments and hospital accreditations, which the government plans to implement over the next two to three years. In the post liberalization era, some companies have been licensed to act as third party administrators of health services. The objective is to strengthen the health insurance industry and increase its penetration by bringing more professionalism to claims management, facilitating cashless services to policyholders, and reducing the claims ratio. Currently there are 25 licensed third party administrators in the Indian health insurance industry. In another effort to improve the insurance prospects for India, the IRDA is focused on standardizing medical definitions to ensure consistent pricing and products, and is providing incentives for stand-alone insurance companies. (Currently only Star Health exists as a stand-alone health insurance company.) In addition, government subsidies and tax incentives for health insurance are expected to attract key players to the industry.

In response to liberalization, a large number of international private insurance companies are moving into India and forming joint ventures. Two prominent examples are Max New York Life, a joint venture between Max India and New York Life, and ICICI Prudential Life Insurance, a joint venture between the ICICI Group and UK-based Prudential plc. Some companies are experimenting with more targeted forms of insurance coverage. For example, ICICI Prudential is offering plans designed specifically for diabetics. We can expect to see more innovations as the health insurance market evolves in the coming years. While the liberalization of the healthcare sector will increase the penetration of insurance policies, the widespread use of health insurance in India could take many years. One reason is that insurance companies lack the data they need to assess health risks accurately. In addition, today's insurance products work on an indemnity basis—that is, they reimburse patients only after they have paid their healthcare bills. Since many people cannot afford such large payments, even if they are subsequently reimbursed, they will not choose to purchase medical insurance.

Growth of Telemedicine

Only 25% of India's specialist physicians reside in semi-urban areas, and a mere 3% live in rural areas. As a result, rural areas, with a population approaching 700 million, Continue to be deprived of proper healthcare facilities. One solution is telemedicine—the remote diagnosis, monitoring and treatment of patients via videoconferencing or the Internet. Telemedicine is a fast-emerging trend in India, supported by exponential growth in the country's information and communications technology (ICT) sector, and plummeting telecom costs. Several major private hospitals have adopted telemedicine services, and a number of hospitals have developed public-private partnerships (PPPs), among them Apollo, AIIMS, Narayana Hridayalaya, Aravind Hospitals and Sankara Nethralaya. The early successes of telemedicine pioneers have led to increased acceptance and proliferation of telemedicine. Today there are approximately 120 telemedicine centers throughout India. The Asian Heart Institute (AHI) is planning to establish 60 more telemedicine satellite centers across the interiors of Maharashtra. The government has also made a major commitment to the growth of telemedicine. The Indian Space Research Organization (ISRO) plans to establish 100 **telemedicine** centers across the country. ISRO has already connected 25 major hospitals in the mainland and plans to link at least 650 district hospitals by 2008. The government also is reducing import tariffs on infrastructure equipment. And while India has yet to pass legislation on telemedicine related issues, the Ministry of Information Technology has developed "Recommended Guidelines & Standards for Practice of Telemedicine in India," with the goal of standardizing digital communication in telemedicine. The Medical Council of India has formed committees to explore this and other legal aspects of telehealth. There is a growing movement within India to establish a health grid that connects medical institutions and practitioners throughout the country. This would allow super specialists to exchange case studies, compare experiences, and hold virtual conferences to discuss critical disease patterns and provide treatment. Eventually, telemedicine likely will be practiced in the majority of Indian hospitals, initially in a separate department and eventually, integrated into medical specialties.

Healthcare Infrastructure Expansion

An enormous amount of private capital will be required in the coming years to enhance and expand India's healthcare infrastructure to meet the needs of a growing population and an influx of medical tourists. Currently India has approximately 860 beds per million population. This is only one-fifth of the world average, which is 3,960, according to the World Health Organization. It is estimated that 450,000 additional hospital beds will be required by 2010—an investment estimated at $25.7 billion. The government is expected to contribute only 15-20% of the total, providing an enormous opportunity for private players to fill the gap. Recently we have seen many new investments in healthcare infrastructure facilities in India. For instance, ICICI Venture, the country's largest private equity fund, has invested $8.6 million in a chain of diagnostics facilities, along with Metropolis Health Services Ltd. And in 2006, General Electric announced a $250 million investment in infrastructure and healthcare projects in India. With the advent of private insurance and the emergence of India as a medical tourism destination, there also has been a surge of growth in so-called "super specialty" hospitals, which have teams of specialists, sophisticated equipment, links to other medical centers, and the ability to treat a broad range of ailments. Some of these new facilities, such as the Rajiv Gandhi Super Specialty Hospital are public-private partnerships. Government fiscal constraints are driving the growth of PPPs to help meet India's growing demand for healthcare infrastructure. Such partnerships have gained legitimacy worldwide in recent years as a major strategy for health sector development. In addition to participating in infrastructure PPPs, opportunities are emerging for foreign companies to create super-specialty hospitals in collaboration with Indian corporations. For instance, Wockhardt Hospitals Group has partnered with Harvard Medical International to create a chain of super specialty hospitals in India. Two hospitals, in Mumbai and Bangalore, are attracting large volumes of medical tourists from the UK and US. There also is strong demand for tertiary care hospitals, which emphasize the treatment of lifestyle diseases, focusing on specialties such as neurology, cardiology, oncology and orthopedics. Tertiary hospitals are projected to grow faster than the overall healthcare sector, in response to the growing incidence of lifestyle disease and the accelerating growth of medical tourism.

In addition to a deteriorating physical infrastructure, India faces a huge shortage of trained

India Health Infrastructure

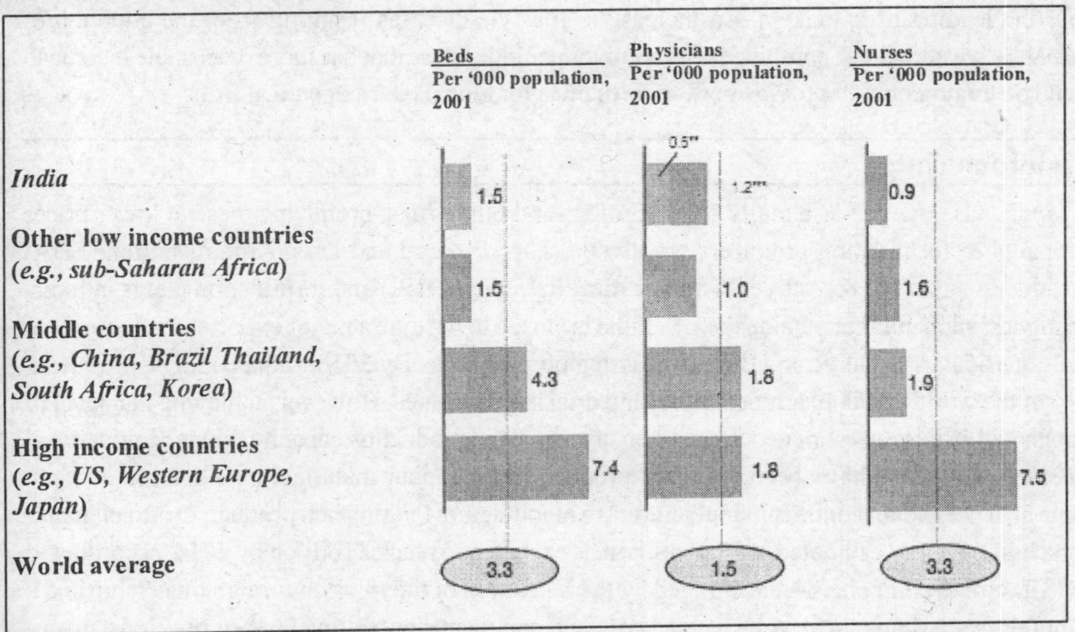

medical personnel, including doctors, nurses and especially paramedics, who may be more willing than doctors to live in rural areas where access to care is limited. There is an immediate need for medical education and training, which could provide additional opportunities for private sector providers or public-private partnerships. The communications technology that enables telemedicine could also be used to deliver training courses.

Medical Equipment Market

The rebuilding of India's healthcare infrastructure, combined with the emergence of medical tourism and telemedicine, will drive strong demand for medical equipment, such as x-ray machines, CT scanners and electrocardiograph (EKG) machines. Leading international companies market most high value medical equipment, while only consumables and disposable equipment are made locally. Many international companies have expanded their operations in the Indian market in recent years and established manufacturing facilities to assemble equipment for the domestic market and export sales. The competition is expected to intensify with the entry of more global firms into the medical equipment marketplace. The government is encouraging the growth of this market, through policies such as a reduction in import duties on medical equipment, higher depreciation on life-saving medical equipment (40%, up from 25%), and a number of other tax incentives.

Pharmaceutical Industry Opportunities

Despite widespread poverty and inadequate public healthcare provision, India has much to offer the leading drug makers. An increase in lifestyle diseases resulting from the adoption of unhealthy western diets, combined with a growing middle class that has more disposable income to spend on treatment, will provide new opportunities for global pharmaceutical firms.

Manufacturing

India has emerged as a major supplier of several bulk drugs, producing these at lower prices compared to formulation producers worldwide. The US Food and Drug Administration (FDA) already has approved 85 Active Pharmaceutical Ingredient (API) and formulation plants in India, the highest such number outside the US. India is poised to become a major exporter of pharmaceuticals, particularly generic and OTC drugs, to global markets. By 2010, India could be producing 15% of the world's bulk pharmaceuticals and drug intermediates. However, achieving that level of growth will require an estimated $1.2 billion investment in production capacity. Many multinational generics companies have been sourcing products from Indian manufacturers for some years. Some also use Indian contract manufacturers to manufacture the finished product. Contract manufacturing, currently estimated at $350 million, is expected to reach $1billion by 2010, according to CRISIL. Some companies—encouraged by the relaxation of the rules on foreign ownership and a favorable tax regime—have gone beyond contract manufacturing, setting up their own local manufacturing facilities. The financial incentive is compelling: Goldman Sachs estimates that the cost of setting up and running a new manufacturing facility in India is one-fifth of the cost of doing so in the West.

Pharmaceutical Research

Pharmaceutical research is one area that is expected to achieve tremendous growth in the coming decade, due to India's huge and growing population, low per capita drug usage and increasing incidence of disease. Global pharmaceutical alliances with Indian drug firms are finally beginning to look like a two-way street, with major R&D deals being struck. For instance, Glenmark Pharmaceutical has teamed with Dyax to identify biological entities for its three targets in cancer treatment and with Merck KGaA for its prospective diabetes molecule GRC 8200. GlaxoSmithKline is working with Ranbaxy Laboratories to identify new targets and has partnered with TCS for data management, through a global drug development support center in Mumbai.

Clinical Trials

India historically lacked the expertise to perform clinical trials, because most companies only tested different processes for producing copycat versions of Western products, and the rules were quite lenient. Several drug makers have also been caught behaving unethically or even illegally. However, in recent years, India has become a more attractive market for clinical testing. One reason is that in November 2004, the federal government amended Schedule Y of the Drugs and Cosmetics Act to make the rules on clinical trials more consistent with international practice. In addition, in January 2005 India became compliant with the Trade-Related Aspects of Intellectual Property Rights (TRIPS) Agreement and formally recognized product patents. This triggered growth in Indian clinical trial activity by contract research organizations, such as Quintiles, Omnicare, Pharma Net and Pharm-Olam, and by multinational corporations such as Novo Nordisk, Sanofi-Aventis, Novartis and GSK. Some multinationals, such as Pfizer and Eli Lilly, have been conducting tests locally for a while. Government taxation incentives are further boosting R&D in India.

As a market for clinical testing, India holds other attractions as well. According to a study by Rabo India Finance, a subsidiary of the Netherlands-based Rabo Bank, the huge patient population offers vast genetic diversity, making the country "an ideal site for clinical trials." It has the largest pool of diabetic patients, the population is relatively easy to access and many people are "treatment-naïve"; they have not been treated with medications being tested, which potentially could distort test results. As a result of these favorable factors, the Indian clinical trials market, currently estimated at $120 million, is expected to reach $1 billion by 2010, according to Infomedia. To achieve that level of growth, India will have to address a lack of skilled workers, high wage inflation, and inadequate infrastructure. For western companies that can navigate these obstacles, the rewards will be substantial: Clinical trials account for over 40% of the costs of developing a new drug, and Rabo India Finance estimates that a standard drug could be tested in India for as little as $90 million—60% of the cost of testing in the US.

Conclusion

The Indian healthcare sector can be viewed as a glass half empty or a glass half full. The challenges the sector faces are substantial, from the need to improve physical infrastructure to the necessity of providing health insurance and ensuring the availability of trained medical personnel. But the opportunities are equally compelling, from developing new infrastructure and providing medical equipment to delivering telemedicine solutions and conducting cost-effective clinical trials. For companies that view the Indian healthcare sector as a glass half full, the potential is enormous.

Summary

(Trends in Healthcare in Indian Scenario)

Healthcare in India is ruined by constituent states and territories. The constitution changes every state with raising of the level of nutrition and standard of living of its people. Government hospitals provide treatment at taxpayer expenses. Primary healthcare is provided by city and district hospitals. Its focussed on immunization, prevention of malnutrition, pregnancy, child birth, postnatal case and treatment of common illness. Healthcare is one of India's largest sector in terms of revenue and employment and the sector is expanding rapidly. India traditionally has been a rural, agrarian economy. Nearly three quarters of the population still lives in rural areas. However, India's thriving economy is driving urbanization and expanding middle class. The Indian pharmaceutical market is highly programented. The physical infrastructure is woefully inadequate to meet today's healthcare demands. A widespread level of health insurance compounds the Healthcare challenges that India faces. Although some form of health protection is provided by government and major private employer, the health insurance schemes available to the Indian Public are generally basis and inaccessible to most people. In the recent years, there has been a liberalization of the Indian healthcare sector. In response to liberalization, a large number of international private insurance companies are moving to India and forming joint ventures. Rural population is deprived of healthcare facilities & Solution is telemedicine in which the remote diagnosis monitoring and treatment of patients through internet and video conferencing is possible. Thus the development of technology is India has given a direction to Healthcare and the sector is booming.

Questions:

Q. 1. Discuss the contemporary trends of Healthcare in Indian context.

Q. 2. Explain the concept of insurance related to Healthcare.

Q. 3. Discuss the growth of telemedicine in India.

Short Notes:

- Clinical Trial
- Pharmaceutical Research
- Medical Equipment Market
- Healthcare Infrastructure Expansion

10

HEALTHCARE DECISION-MAKING

The tradition of medical decision making based on professional paternalism does not deal well with the complex trade-offs created by modern technology. Rates of elective surgery and other discretionary interventions are determined in large part by practice style and sometimes, by geographic variation in resources. These rates should be determined by the choices informed patients make. Patients should understand what is known, as well as what is not known, about the outcomes that matter to them. The outcomes commonly vary according to the treatment used. Patients should be able to make informed choices according to their own treatment preferences.

While there is a growing interest on the part of patients in challenging the paternalistic role of physicians as agents and sole decision makers, there are economic forces that have pulled in the opposite direction. Employers, as payers, have promoted the use of managed care, which challenges the autonomy of physicians but sometimes imposes its own rules on clinical medicine, and substitutes the managed care company for the physician as the decision maker. This transfer of agency power to third parties - payers, insurance companies, and health maintenance organizations - challenges the role of the patient in the choice of medical care.

A different model of the doctor-patient relationship is emerging in response to this rebellion against both paternalism and third party intrusion into medical decision making. Shared decision making recognizes that there are complex trade-offs in the choice of medical care. Shared decision making also addresses the ethical need to fully inform patients about the risks and benefits of treatments, as well as the need to ensure that patients' values and preferences play a prominent role. Most patients willingly participate in shared decision making, even when decisions are complicated and difficult.

Shared Decision Making Initiatives

Patients who are choosing among competing Healthcare interventions face an extraordinarily complex psychological challenge. So far, fundamental and applied investigators have successfully studied different aspects of this multi-faceted process. However, many research questions remain unanswered, and may best be solved by the collaborative efforts of multi-disciplinary scientific teams. The Institute's participants - advanced graduate students, research fellows, postdoctoral fellows, and junior professors - will debate how new insights in the fundamental decision sciences can guide future applied work in patients' decision support/decision aids, and how observations gained from applied work in patients' decision support/decision aids can point to new fundamental theories in human judgment & decision making.

Health Decision Research

The mission of Health Decision Research is to provide a scientifically rigorous and ethically sound basis for effective decision making in preventive, screening, diagnostic, treatment, clinical trials and palliative contexts.

Foundation for Informed Medical Decision Making

Research indicates that patient preferences are often less important in treatment decisions than factors having little to do with patients or their illnesses. The mission of the Foundation for Informed Medical Decision Making is to focus on the role patients play in selecting treatments for their medical conditions.

Questions :

Q. 1. What is the implication of Healthcare Decision-making in Healthcare Management?

Q. 2. What is meant by Health Decision Research?

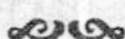

11

HEALTHCARE ISSUES FOR MEGA PROBLEMS

Health System is facing major problem related to different issues which are discussed as below :

1. Disease

India suffers from high levels of disease including Malaria and Tuberculosis where one third of the world's tuberculosis cases are in India. In addition, India along with Nigeria, Pakistan and Afghanistan is one of the four countries worldwide where polio has not as yet been eradicated.

Ongoing government of India education about HIV has led to decreases in the spread of HIV in recent years. The number of people living with AIDS in India is estimated to be between 2 and 3 million. However, in terms of the total population this is a small number. The country has had a sharp decrease in the estimated number of HIV infections; 2005 reports had claimed that there were 5.2 million to 5.7 million people afflicted with the virus. The new figures are supported by the World Health Organization and UNAIDS.

2. Pollution

According to the World Health Organization, 900,000 Indians die each year from drinking contaminated water and breathing in polluted air. As India grapples with these basic issues, new challenges are emerging for example there is a rise in chronic adult diseases such as cardiovascular illnesses and diabetes as a consequence of changing lifestyles.

3. Malnutrition

Half of children in India are underweight, one of the highest rates in the world and nearly same as Sub-Saharan Africa. India contributes to about 5.6 million child deaths every year, more than half the world's total.

4. Water and Sanitation

Water supply and sanitation in India is a matter of concern. As of 2003, it was estimated that only 30% of India's wastewater was being treated, with the remainder flowing into rivers or groundwater. The lack of toilet facilities in many areas also presents a major health risk; open defecation is widespread even in urban areas of India, and it was estimated in 2002 by the World Health Organisation that around 700,000 Indians die each year from diarrhoea. No city in India has full-day water supply. Most cities supply water only a few hours a day. In towns and rural areas the situation is even worse.

Medical Tourism

India is quickly becoming a hub for medical tourists seeking quality healthcare at an affordable cost. Nearly 450,000 foreigners sought medical treatment in India last year with Singapore not too far behind and Thailand in the lead with over a million medical tourists . As the Indian healthcare delivery system strives to match international standards the Indian healthcare industry will be able to tap into a substantial portion of the medical tourism market. Already 13 Indian hospitals have been accredited by the Joint Commission International (JCI). Accreditation and compliance with quality expectations are important since they provide tourists with confidence that the services are meeting international standards. Reduced costs, access to the latest medical technology, growing compliance to international quality standards and ease of communication all work towards India's advantage.

It is not uncommon to see citizens of other nations seek high quality medical care in the US over the past several decades; however in recent times the pattern seems to be reversing. As healthcare costs in the US are rising, price sensitivity is soaring and people are looking at medical value travel as a viable alternative option. In the past the growth potential of the medical travel industry in India has been hindered by capacity and infrastructure constraints but that situation is now changing with strong economic progress in India as well as in other developing nations. With more and more hospitals receiving JCI accreditations outside the US, concerns on safety and quality of care are becoming less of an issue for those choosing to travel for medical treatment at an affordable cost. The combined cost of travel and treatment in India is still a fraction of the amount spent on just medical treatment alone in western countries.

In order to attract foreign patients many Indian hospitals are promoting their international quality of healthcare delivery by turning to international accreditation agencies to standardize their protocols and obtain the required approvals on safety and quality of care .

Summary

Healthcare decision making deals with the electric surgery and other discretionary interventions. Patients should be able to make informed choices according to their own treatment preferences there should be shared decision making but research said that patient preferences are often less important in treatment rather than factors related to patient illness. There are maga problem related to Healthcare such as disease like Malaria, Tuberculosis, HIV/AIDsek. Other problems are pollution, malnutrition, water and sanitation. India is quickly becoming a hub for medical tourists seeking quality healthcare at an affordable cost. In order to attract foreign patients, many Indian hospitals are promoting their international quality of Healthcare delivery by touring to international a recitation agencies to standardize their protocols and obtain the required approvals on safety & quality of case.

Question :

Q. 1. Explain the concept of Healthcare decision making.

Q. 2. What are the maga problems related to healthcare?

Q. 3. Write short notes on medical tourism.

Q. 4. Explain the characteristics, goals and functions of Healthcare system in India.

Q. 5. Discuss in detail the Health System Research and its Application.

Q. 6. Explain the Healthcare issue & Major problems discussed.

Q. 7. Explain the concept of Healthcare decision making.

Q. 8. Discuss in detail the contemporary trends of Healthcare in Indian Context.

12

HEALTHCARE FINANCE

Learning Objectives

After studying this Chapter you should be able to understand:

- The reality of financial resources in public health.
- How the objective of reducing various types of in requires & imbalances is met?
- How does the delivery of National Public Health Programmes takes place?
- The State of Public Health Infrastructure.
- How to extend Public Health Services?
- The impact of Urban Health, Mental Health – Information, Education & Communication on Healthcare Financing?

Financial Resources

The paucity of **public health investment** is a stark reality. Given the extremely difficult fiscal position of the State Governments, the Central Government will have to play a key role in augmenting public health investments. Taking into account the gap in Healthcare facilities, it is planned, under the policy to increase health sector **expenditure** to 6 percent of GDP, with 2 percent of GDP being contributed as public health investment, by the year 2010. The State Governments would also need to increase the **commitment** to the health sector. In the first phase, by 2005, they would be expected to increase the commitment of their resources to 7 percent of the Budget; and in the second phase, by 2010, to increase it to 8 percent of the Budget. With the stepping up of the public health investment, the Central Government's contribution would rise to 25 percent from the existing 15 percent by 2010. The provisioning of higher public health investments will also be contingent upon the increase in the absorptive capacity of the **public health administration** so as to utilize the funds gainfully.

Equity

To meet the objective of reducing various types of inequities and imbalances – inter-regional; across the **rural – urban divide**; and between economic classes – the most cost-effective method would be to increase the **sectoral outlay** in the primary health sector. Such outlets afford access to a vast number of individuals, and also facilitate **preventive** and **early stage curative** initiative, which are cost effective. In recognition of this public health principle, NHP-2002 sets out an increased allocation of 55 percent of the total public health investment for the primary health sector; the **secondary and tertiary health sectors** being targeted for 35 percent and 10 percent respectively. The Policy projects that the increased aggregate outlays for the primary health sector will be utilized for strengthening existing facilities and opening additional public **health service outlets**, consistent with the norms for such facilities.

Delivery of National Public Health Programmes

This policy envisages a key role for the Central Government in designing national programs with the active participation of the State Governments. Also, the Policy ensures the provisioning of **financial resources**, in addition to technical support, monitoring and evaluation at the national level by the Centre. However, to optimize the **utilization** of the public health infrastructure at the primary level, NHP-2002 envisages the gradual convergence of all health programs under a single field administration. **Vertical programs** for control of major diseases like **TB, Malaria, HIV/AIDS**, as also the **RCH** and **Universal Immunization Programs**, would need to be continued till moderate levels of prevalence are reached. The integration of the programs will bring about a desirable optimization of outcomes through a convergence of all public health inputs. The Policy also envisages that programme implementation be effected through autonomous bodies at State and district levels. The interventions of State Health Departments may be limited to the overall monitoring of the achievement of programme targets and other technical aspects. The relative distancing of the programme implementation from the **State Health Departments** will give the project team greater operational flexibility. Also, the presence of State Government officials, social activists, private health professionals and MLAs/MPs on the management boards of the autonomous bodies will facilitate well-informed **decision-making.**

The Policy also highlights the need for developing the capacity within the State Public Health administration for scientific designing of public **health projects**, suited to the local situation.

The Policy envisages that apart from the exclusive staff in a **vertical structure** for the **disease control programs**, all rural health staff should be available for the entire gamut of public health activities at the **decentralized level**, irrespective of whether these activities relate to national programs or other public health initiatives. It would be for the Head of the District Health administration to allocate the time of the rural health staff between the various programs, depending on the local need. NHP-2002 recognizes that to implement such a change, not only would the public health administrators be required to change their mindset, but the rural health staff would need to be trained and reoriented.

The State of Public Health Infrastructure

As has been highlighted in the earlier part of the Policy, the decentralized Public health service outlets have become practically dysfunctional over large parts of the country. On account of resource constraints, the supply of drugs by the State Governments is grossly inadequate. The patients at the decentralized level have little use for diagnostic services, which in any case would still require them to purchase **therapeutic drugs** privately. In a situation in which the patient is not getting any therapeutic drugs, there is little incentive for the potential beneficiaries to seek the advice of the medical professionals in the public health system. This results in there being no demand for medical services, so medical professionals and paramedics often absent themselves from their place of duty. It is also observed that the functioning of the public health service outlets in some States like the four Southern States – Kerala, Andhra Pradesh, Tamil Nadu and Karnataka – is relatively better, because some quantum of drugs is distributed through the primary **health system network**, and the patients have a stake in approaching the Public Health facilities. In this backdrop, the Policy envisages kick-starting the revival of the Primary Health System by providing some essential drugs under Central Government funding through the decentralized health system. It is expected that the provisioning of essential drugs at the public health service centers will create a demand for other professional services from the local population, which, in turn, will boost the general revival of activities in these service centers. In sum, this initiative under NHP-2002 is launched in the belief that the creation of a beneficiary interest in the public health system will ensure a more effective supervision of the public health personnel through community monitoring, than has been achieved through the regular administrative line of control.

This Policy recognizes the need for more frequent **in-service training** of public health **medical personnel**, at the level of medical officers as well as paramedics. Such training would help to update the personnel on recent advancements in science, and would also equip them for their new assignments, when they are moved from one discipline of public health administration to another.

Global experience has shown that the quality of public health services, as reflected in the attainment of improved public health indices, is closely linked to the quantum and quality of investment through public funding in the primary health sector. Box-V gives statistics which clearly show that standards of health are more a function of the accurate targeting of expenditure on the decentralized primary sector (as observed in China and Sri Lanka), than a function of the aggregate **health expenditure.**

Box-V: Public Health Spending in select Countries

Indicator	% Population with income of <$1 day	Infant Mortality Rate/1000	% Health Expenditure to GDP	% Public Expenditure on Health to Total Health Expenditure
India	44.2	70	5.2	17.3
China	18.5	31	2.7	24.9
Sri Lanka	6.6	16	3	45.4
UK	-	6	5.8	96.9
USA	-	7	13.7	44.1

Therefore the Policy, while committing additional aggregate financial resources, places great reliance on the strengthening of the primary health structure for the attaining of improved public health outcomes on an equitable basis. Further, it also recognizes the practical need for levying reasonable user-charges for certain secondary and tertiary public Healthcare services, for those who can afford to pay.

Extending Public Health Services

This policy envisages that, in the context of the availability and spread of allopathic graduates in their jurisdiction, State Governments would consider the need for expanding the pool of medical practitioners to include a cadre of **licentiates** of medical practice, as also practitioners of Indian Systems of Medicine and Homoeopathy. Simple services/procedures can be provided by such practitioners even outside their disciplines, as part of the basic primary health services in under-served areas. Also, NHP-2002 envisages that the scope of the use of paramedical manpower of allopathic disciplines, in a prescribed functional area adjunct to their current functions, would also be examined for meeting simple public health requirements. This would be on the lines of the services rendered by nurse practitioners in several developed countries. These extended areas of functioning of different categories of medical manpower can be permitted, after adequate training and subject to the monitoring of their performance through **professional councils.**

NHP-2002 also recognizes the need for States to simplify the **recruitment procedures** and rules for **contract employment** in order to provide trained medical manpower in under-served areas. State Governments could also rigorously enforce a mandatory two-year rural posting before the awarding of the graduate degree. This would not only make trained medical manpower available in the underserved areas, but would offer valuable clinical experience to the graduating doctors.

Urban Health

NHP-2002 envisages the setting up of an organized urban primary Healthcare structure. Since the physical features of urban settings are different from those in rural areas, the policy envisages the adoption of appropriate **population norms** for the urban public **health infrastructure**. The structure conceived under NHP-2002 is a two-tiered one: the primary centre is seen as the first-tier, covering a population of one lakh, with a dispensary providing an OPD facility and essential drugs, to enable access to all the **national health programmes**; and a second-tier of the urban health organisation at the level of the Government general hospital, where reference is made from the primary centre. The Policy envisages that the funding for the urban primary health system will be jointly borne by the local self-government institutions and State and Central Governments.

The Policy also envisages the establishment of fully-equipped **'hub-spoke' trauma care networks** in large urban agglomerations to reduce accident mortality.

Mental Health

NHP – 2002 envisages a network of decentralised mental health services for ameliorating the more common categories of disorders. The programme outline for such a disease would involve the diagnosis of common disorders and the prescription of common therapeutic drugs, by general duty medical staff.

In regard to mental health institutions for in-door treatment of patients, the Policy envisages the upgrading of the physical infrastructure of such institutions at Central Government expense so as to secure the human rights of this vulnerable segment of society.

Information, Education and Communication

NHP-2002 envisages an **IEC policy**, which maximizes the dissemination of information to those population groups which cannot be effectively approached by using only the mass media. The focus would therefore be on the inter-personal communication of information and on folk and other traditional media to bring about behavioural change. The IEC programme would set specific targets for the association of PRIs/NGOs/Trusts in such activities. In several public health programmes, where behavioural change is an essential component, the success of the initiatives is crucially dependent on dispelling myths and misconceptions pertaining to religious and ethical issues. The community leaders, particularly religious leaders, are effective in imparting knowledge which facilitates such behavioural change. The programme will also have the component of an annual evaluation of the performance of the **non-Governmental agencies** to monitor the impact of the programs on the targeted groups. The Central/State Government initiative will also focus on the development of modules for information dissemination in such population groups, who do not normally benefit from the more common media forms.

NHP-2002 envisages giving priority to school health programmes which aim at **preventive-health education**, providing regular health check-ups, and promotion of health-seeking behaviour among children. The school health programmes can gainfully adopt specially designed modules in order to disseminate information relating to 'health' and 'family life'. This is expected to be the most cost-effective intervention as it improves the level of awareness, not only of the extended family, but the future generation as well.

Keywords : Public Health Investments; Equity; Universal Immunization Programme; Disease Control Programmes; Health System Network; In service training; Health Expenditure; IEC Policy; Health Education.

Summary : Investment in healthcare sector are merger. There is gap between healthcare delivery in various sectors. To cater this sectoral out lay in Primary Healthcare is required which requires not only the particular of centre but of State as well. The primary focus of the program should be increase capacity of staff. Global experience proves that investment in primary healthcare improves indices.

NHP-2002 envisages setting up a organised urban primary Healthcare structure, decentralised mental health services, a policy on Information, Education and Communication.

Question :

1. What are the key points of the policy of Government pertaining to financial enounces & equity?
2. How can the delivery of National Public Health Programmes be made effective?
3. What is the correct staff of Public Health Infrastructure? How can Public Health Services be extended to include Urban Health?

Short Notes:

- Mental Health Program
- Public Health Investments
- Disease Control
- In-service trainings
- Hus. Spoke Network.

13

HEALTHCARE ECONOMICS

Learning Objectives

After studying this Chapter you should be able to understand:

- The various problems of Healthcare relating to Healthcare Economics.
- How to approach the problems.
- The Healthcare dimension to the economies of scarcity. The study of wants and resources.
- Production Possibility Frontier in Healthcare.
- The study of opportunity cost.
- Understanding the various tradeoffs. viz. Allocation of Healthcare, Efficiency, Equity.
- The various approaches to rationing of health services.
- Understanding the Free Market Approach.
- Analyzing the buyings behaviour through demand curve.
- Analyzing the seller's behaviour through supply curve.
- Change in costs.
- The Economic Appraisal of Health Services Studying the Cost – Minimization Analysis and the key areas for critical appraisal.

Introduction

Discussion of Healthcare arouses great passion - who gets Healthcare and how much they get is both a moral and practical challenge to a civilized society and of personal interest to us all. We don't want to get ill and we want to be properly treated if we do.

Economics as a discipline can provide great insight into these issues. The fundamental problem of **scarcity** requires **choices**. Even if our **preference** is to spend more on Healthcare, there are limits as to how much of our national income we can spend on its provision. However, much we do decide to spend, we want to spend it efficiently so that we get more Healthcare for a given commitment of resources.

The Problem of Healthcare

Healthcare is something which touches all of our lives. Everybody visits the doctor and dentist and many of us have been treated in hospital. Yet Healthcare seems to be in almost permanent crisis – there are shortages of hospital beds and patients are left to lie in corridors while politicians argue endlessly over whether more or less is being spent on the NHS. Why it is that Healthcare is such a controversial area? Why is there never enough money to give us the level of Healthcare we want?

To answer these questions we need to introduce and apply a range of economic concepts. Each of the sections listed develops part of the answer:

(*i*) Approaching the Problems.

(*ii*) Scarcity-Health-care Dimension

(*iii*) Scarcity-A Theoretical Approach

(*iv*) **Trade-offs**

(*v*) Using the Theory

(*vi*) Approaches to **Rationing**

(A) Approaching the Problems

Asking people what they think. We should discover what 'ordinary people' thought should be the health service priorities by conducting a detailed survey and gathering responses from them.

Many economists would argue that the problem with these responses is that they mix up opinions and value judgments with facts. Economists believe that it is important to distinguish questions of fact from value judgments and opinions.

A statement such as "Specialist in heart-lung transplants resigns from the hospital in protest at lack of funding" is a positive statement: it can be shown to be true or false and is not dependent upon the value system of the observer. In contrast, "Healthcare is a basic right and should be provided free" is a **normative** statement. It cannot be proved true or false: our view of it depends on our value system.

One of the things which make the debate over the provision of Healthcare difficult to resolve is that positive and normative issues are very much intertwined. Sorting out fact from opinion is a first step but it does not explain why there are not enough beds in hospitals or why people might be refused treatment. To analyse this we need to explore the idea of scarcity

(B) Scarcity- The Healthcare Dimension

Scarcity has two sides: the infinite nature of **human wants** and the finite or limited nature of **resources** available to produce goods and services. What does this mean when related to Healthcare?

We'll examine the wants first.

The wants: Why do people **demand** Healthcare? The simple answer is that they want to be healthy. This desire to remain healthy has led to a continuous growth in the demand for Healthcare. However, there are also a number of specific reasons why the demand for Healthcare has expanded so dramatically in developed countries over the last 40 years:

- Changes in the age structure.
- Increasing real incomes.
- Improvements in medical technology

Let's look at these in more detail.

Changes in age structure: Changes in the age structure of the population have increased the demand for Healthcare. Countries like the UK and China have an ageing population. Elderly people require more Healthcare than other age groups. For instance, in 1998/99, 39% of hospital and community health services expenditure was used for treating people aged 65 and over, even though they are only 16% of the total population. Only 11% of the population was 65 or older in 1948.

Increasing real incomes: Increasing real incomes have led to an increase in people's expectations of Healthcare. Many of us are now not prepared to put up with the pain, discomfort and lack of mobility associated with afflictions like severe osteoarthritis of the hip - we demand a hip replacement operation. In the USA, people suffering from mild osteoarthritis of the knee often have an operation rather than give up playing golf.

Improvements in medical technology: Improvements in medical technology have continuously increased the range of treatments possible. A good example of this is the way in which the development of kidney dialysis machines has largely prevented kidney failure from killing people. As well as new and more effective medicines allowing us to treat conditions which were previously incurable, many new treatments now make chronic diseases like asthma manageable for patients, enabling them to have a good quality of life.

The resources : The other side of the scarcity equation relates to the finite nature of resources. The term 'resources' covers all **inputs** used to produce goods and services. Econo-mists also refer to these as the factors of production. They are divided into four categories:

1. **Land** - the physical resources of the planet including mineral deposits
2. **Labour** - human resources in the sense of people as workers
3. **Capital** - resources created by humans to aid production, such as tools, machinery and factories

4. **Enterprise** - the human resource of organising the other three factors to produce goods and services.

We can see all four factors at work in the **production** of healthcare. It is fairly obvious that the available quantity of these factors is limited; therefore there is some maximum quantity of Healthcare that can be produced at any one time. We can explore this idea theoretically by using what economists call a **Production Possibility Frontier (PPF).**

(C) Scarcity- A Theoretical Approach

Scarcity has two sides: the infinite nature of human wants and the finite or limited nature of resources available to produce goods and services. We can explore this idea theoretically by using what economists call a *Production Possibility Frontier (PPF).*

PPFs in Healthcare: Let us start by looking at the production of Healthcare within a single hospital and in particular at the ability of a specific hospital unit to carry out surgical procedures such as heart bypass operations. Suppose the heart bypass unit has 10 surgeons working in it, and assume that the only factor which affects the quantity of operations provided is the number of surgeons assigned to them.

If all the surgeons are assigned to heart bypass operations then the unit can carry out 50 heart operations per week. If, on the other hand, all the surgeons are assigned to other operations, then the unit can carry out 50 of these other operations per week.

Figure 1 shows the production possibility frontier for this unit. The graph charts all the possible maximum combinations of operations that the unit can achieve given the quantity and productivity of resources available.

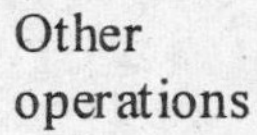

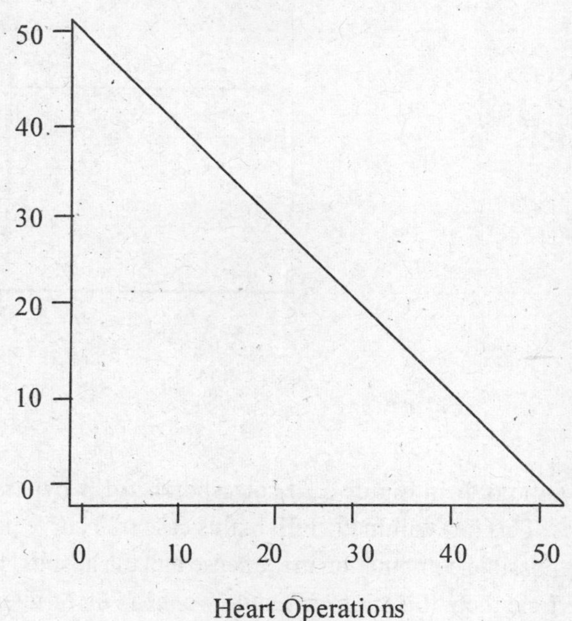

Figure 1

The shape of the graph: What determines the shape of the graph? Look at the graph (Figure 1). It is a **straight line**, with a **gradient** of -1. This reflects the fact that if we transfer one surgeon to heart bypass from other operations, we get five more heart bypasses but we lose five of the other operations, i.e. the **trade-off** between the two possibilities is one to one. This is what is called the **marginal rate of transformation**, MRT.

In fact it is highly unlikely that the marginal rate of transformation would be constant. The surgeons carrying out heart bypass operations would be working with a fixed quantity of operating theatres, heart monitors, and other inputs. So the more surgeons carrying out bypass operations, the less equipment each one would have. Therefore, the output per surgeon would fall.

So, the number of additional bypass operations carried out by an extra surgeon is different depending on how many surgeons are already doing bypasses. If there are already a lot of surgeons doing bypass operations, the extra one creates only a small increase in the number of bypass operations. This bends the line downwards, making it **concave**. This increase is smaller than, if there were only a few surgeons already doing bypass operations.

This phenomenon is called the **Law of Diminishing Returns** and makes the PPF concave to the origin (like Figure 2).

Efficiency :

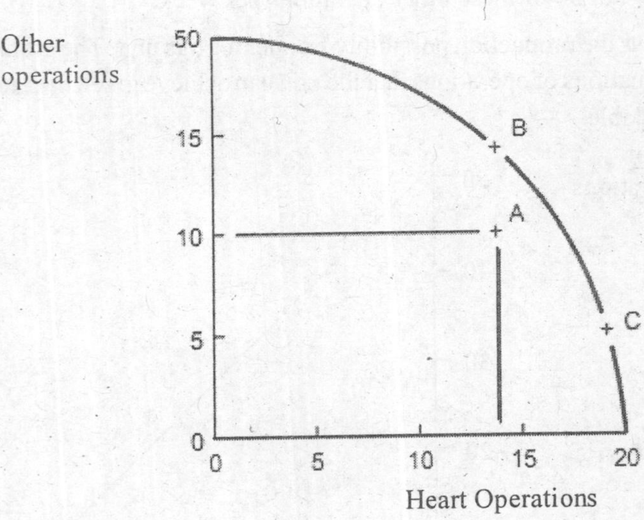

Figure 2

Now look at point A in Figure 2. It corresponds to 14 bypass operations combined with 1 other operations. This lies within the PPF in this case (the curve passing through points B and C Clearly this is a possible combination in the sense that the hospital has enough resources to achiev it, but is it an efficient combination? What do we mean by efficient?

The definition of **efficiency** used by economists is named after the Italian economist, Vilfredo **Pareto**, who formulated it. He said that an allocation of resources is efficient if it is impossible to change that allocation to make one person better off without making someone else worse off. Look at combination A again. Obviously it would be possible to re-organise the hospital's resources to increase the number of other operations without having to reduce the number of heart operations. This is shown by point B on the diagram. Moving from combination A to combination B is clearly in society's interests: we are getting an extra four other operations, i.e. more medical care from our scarce resources.

Opportunity cost: In fact at point B we are getting a maximum combination possible, given the resources we have. It is a Pareto efficient allocation. If we choose to move from combination B to combination C, then although we are getting five more bypass operations this has been at the expense of nine other operations. Thus moving from combination B to C involves a cost, which economists call an opportunity cost. Formally, this is defined as the benefit given up by not choosing the next best alternative. In this case the opportunity cost of moving from point B to C is nine other operations. All combinations which lie on a PPF are, by definition, pareto efficient.

Getting more treatment :

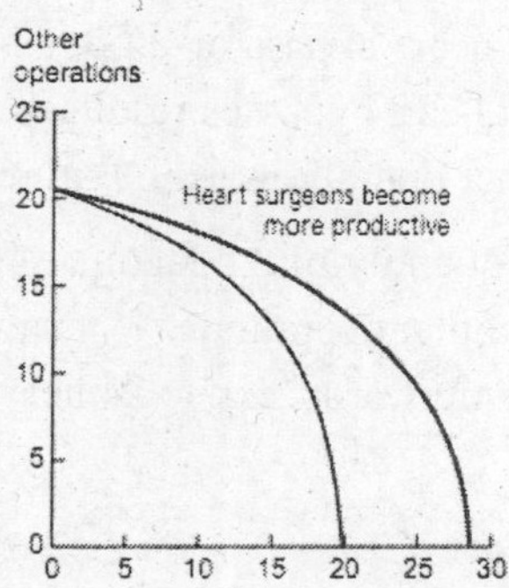

Figure 3

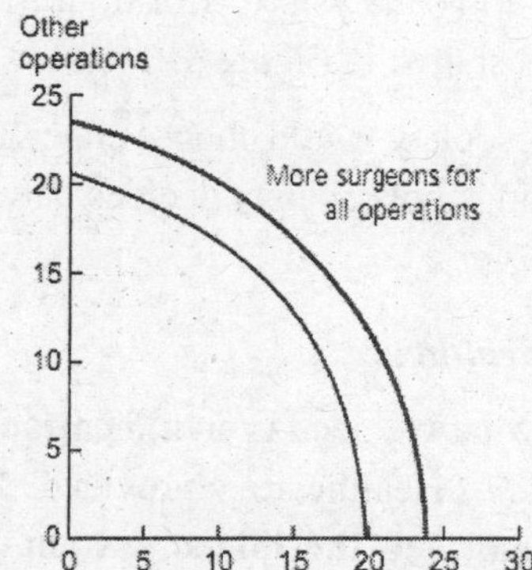

Figure 4

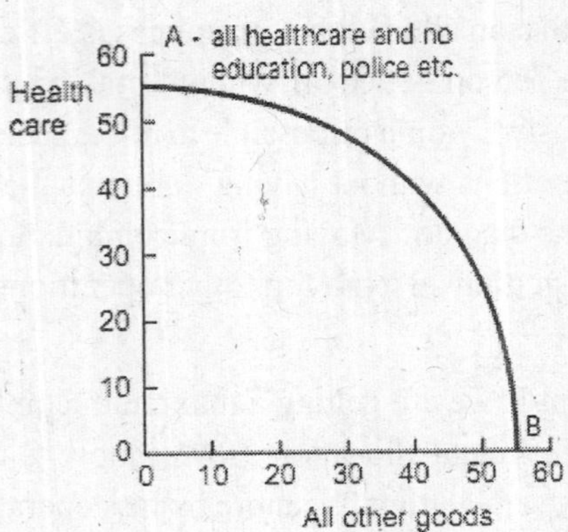

Figure 5

There are only two ways that society can get more treatment:

(*a*) By improving the productivity of the **factors of production**, so that the same quantity of factors produces more treatments. For example, Figure 2 showed surgeons being able to produce either 20 heart bypass or 20 other operations. Increased productivity of surgeons carrying out heart bypasses results in the PPF pivoting outwards, e.g. to 28 heart bypasses or 20 other operations as in Figure 3a.

(*b*) By increasing the quantity of the factors of production. The initial position is again 20 heart bypass or 20 other operations. When more surgeons are allocated to all operations then the PPF shifts outwards, e.g. to 24 heart bypass or 24 other operations as in Figure 3b.

The cost of more treatment

The PPFs we have been using relate to choices between different types of Healthcare. But we can equally use PPF analysis to illustrate the trade-off between Healthcare and all other goods. Such a PPF is shown in Figure 4.

It is unlikely that society would choose either point A or B, but they and all points between are feasible. The question is how society decides between them.

(D) Trade-Offs

Allocation of Healthcare

Given scarcity, what we need is an **allocation** or decision making system to determine how much of which kinds of Healthcare is provided. There are three possibilities: **the free market**; **the command system**; and **the mixed system.**

The free market would allocate Healthcare resources according to consumers' purchasing behaviour, while the command model would use planning to allocate Healthcare according to some predetermined criterion such as 'need.' The mixed system would combine parts of the free market with elements of the command model.

Efficiency

How can society decide which of these systems is most suitable in any given case? There are two criteria that economists use to assess the performance of an allocation system. The first is efficiency: does the system produce an allocation which is Pareto efficient (and thus on the economy's PPF). If the allocation is efficient then the economy is producing exactly the quantity and type of Healthcare that society wants (allocative efficiency) and it is producing that Healthcare for the lowest possible cost (productive efficiency).

Equity

The second criterion is equity: does the system produce an allocation which meets society's requirement for justice? Clearly, this is a normative issue: the decision made depends upon people's values. However, it is a very important consideration for many people when they consider the allocation of Healthcare.

Equity is a difficult concept to analyse but it helps if we differentiate between horizontal and vertical equity. **Horizontal equity** is concerned with the equal treatment of equal need. This means that to be horizontally equitable, the Healthcare allocation system must treat two individuals with the same complaint in an identical way. **Vertical equity**, on the other hand, is concerned with the extent to which individuals who are unequal should be treated differently. In Healthcare it can be reflected by the aim of unequal treatment for unequal need, i.e. more treatment for those with serious conditions than for those with trivial complaints, or by basing the financing of Healthcare on ability to pay, e.g. via progressive income tax.

(E) Using the Theory

What has the economic analysis in the previous pages added to our understanding of Healthcare problems? Look at this newspaper report. What can we say about this?

> "A unique hospital unit for children with severe learning disabilities and extreme behaviour problems faces closure so that much of its Rs. 350,000 annual budget can be diverted to run a scanner in another department."

Firstly, the statement is positive and so capable of being analysed objectively.

Secondly, the **conflict** has been partly brought about by the effects of developing medical technology - without the development of the scanner we would not have had the conflict.

Lastly, PPF analysis makes it clear that this situation reflects one of two possibilities. Either the hospital is operating on its frontier, or it is operating at some point inside its **frontier**. In the first case, either we have to find some way of deciding between the two efficient allocations (scanner versus children's unit) or we have to devote more resources to medical care in this hospital (shift the PPF outwards). In the second case, since the initial allocation was inefficient, there may be no need to choose between the two possibilities. If we just remove the **inefficiencies** we may then have enough resources to have both the scanner and the children's unit.

(F) Approaches to Rationing

It has been increasingly accepted at both local and national level that rationing is inevitable. This has led to initiatives to explore the best way of making such decisions. One approach has been to use surveys of **randomly sampled** adults. One such survey carried out in Great Britain in 1995/6 generated a 75% response rate and most of the people surveyed thought that surveys like this should be used in the planning of health services. The list below shows how this sample thought Healthcare services should be prioritized.

Priority Rating of Health Services

1. Treatments for children with life-threatening illnesses.
2. Special care and pain relief for people who are dying.
3. Preventive screening services and **immunizations.**
4. Surgery such as hip replacements to help people carry out everyday tasks.
5. District nursing and community services/care at home.
6. Psychiatric services for people with mental illnesses.
7. High technology surgery, organ transplants and procedures which treat life threa-tening conditions.
8. **Health promotion** / education services to help people lead healthy lives.
9. **Intensive care** for premature babies who weigh less than 680g with only a slight chance of survival.
10. Long stay hospital care for elderly people.
11. Treatment for infertility.
12. Treatment for people aged 75 and over with life threatening illness.

The Free Market Approach

One way in which the problem of scarcity can be overcome is to let people buy the Healthcare they want. This is what happens with most cosmetic surgery. "A man can have a facelift, a nose correction and his eyes tightened up. His whole face can be rebuilt for a third of the cost of the front end of an expensive car respray" - The Guardian 7.6.91.

All these treatments and more are available if you want to buy them and have the money to pay for them. This kind of Healthcare is sold just like any consumer good. People buy the treatment because they gain satisfaction from it, in just the same way that they would gain **satisfaction** from a car or a new dress. As consultant plastic surgeon David Sharpe puts it "There's nothing wrong with having plastic surgery, even if you don't need it. It's like buying a Porsche. You don't need one. It just makes you feel better".

The market for cosmetic surgery shows that it is possible to buy and sell Healthcare. To understand how such a market might work as a **resource allocation** system, we need to look at the different elements involved in any market. Look at 'What is a market' to see what these elements are. Even if a market can work for cosmetic surgery; what about the rest of Healthcare?

(A) What is a Market?

Overview

For many people the word market conjures up a picture of a town square with lots of small stall holders selling everything from fruit and vegetables to meat and fish. For economists, the term has a much wider meaning. It is used to describe any process of exchange between buyers and sellers. Formally, a market can be defined as any set of arrangements which allows buyers and sellers to communicate and thus arrange exchange of goods, services or resources. A free market is where such exchange occurs without interference from the government. **Information** is a vital ingredient for any market. Both buyers and sellers need to have access to sufficient information to allow them to make **rational decisions.**

Who are the Buyers and the Sellers?

So a market for Healthcare must involve two groups: the buyers and the sellers, who interact to trade Healthcare. Who would the buyers and sellers be in such a market? We all want good health and so most of us would be prepared, if necessary, to purchase medical treatment to cure an illness. This suggests that everybody is potentially a buyer (or **consumer**) of Healthcare. More precisely, at any moment, a buyer would be anybody who was ill or who wanted preventative medical treatment such as a vaccination or who wanted guidance about their health. The sellers would be those people who could provide medical and Healthcare services, such as doctors, nurses, physiotherapists, dentists and high street chemists.

Osteopathy provides an example of a Healthcare market which corresponds quite closely to the textbook model of a market.

Osteopaths manipulate and massage bones, muscles and ligaments which have been twisted or strained in some way. Increasingly, they specialise in dealing with the kind of sprains and strains that people get from sporting activities.

Earlier osteopaths either worked individually or in small practices and all of them sold a very similar service. In the next three sections, we use the example of osteopathy to look at demand and then supply and then put the buyers and sellers together to look at the market for osteopathy.

Demand-Analyzing the Buyer's Behaviour

What will influence how much osteopathy people are prepared to buy at any particular time?

Substitution and **Income Effects-**

Perhaps the most important factor will be the price of the treatment. The more expensive it is to buy osteopathy, all other factors remaining constant, the less we will buy. Why?

When osteopathy becomes more expensive two things happen:

1. Relative prices change; and
2. Our real income changes.

When we react to the price rise, we are taking both of these changes into account. The change in relative price means that osteopathy is now more expensive compared to other goods and services. How do we respond to this? Economists assume that people are **satisfaction maximisers**. This means that we all try to gain as much satisfaction as possible from our consumption of goods and services. So we react to the fact that osteopathy is now relatively more expensive by choosing to buy less of it and more of something else instead (substitution effect).

The increase in the price of osteopathy has also reduced our real income - we can now buy less than before with our money income. The way which we react to this change in real income depends on the kind of good or service. Osteopathy, like most goods, is a normal good - an increase in income leads to an increase in demand and vice versa. So a fall in real income will further reduce the amount of treatment bought (income effect).

The Demand Curve

This predictable relationship between **price** and **quantity** demanded allows us to define demand formally as the quantity of a good or service that buyers are willing and able to buy at every conceivable price. The demand curve (see Figure 6a) shows this relationship graphically.

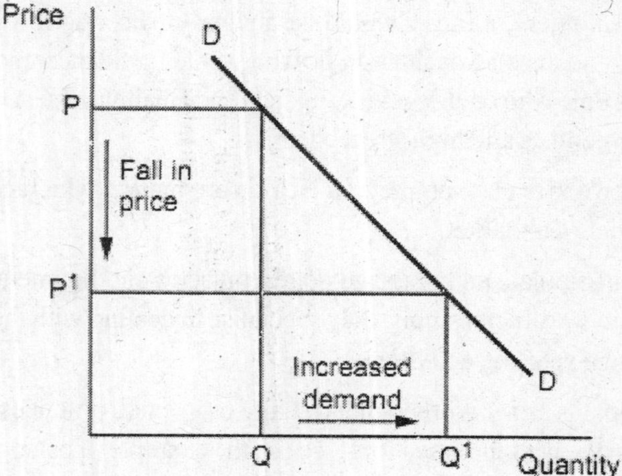

Figure 6

DD shows the quantity of osteopathy treatments that consumers are prepared to buy at every conceivable price. A change in price leads to a movement along the demand curve. When the price is P consumers will buy Q. If the price falls to P' then the quantity demanded will rise to Q'. A change in price has led to a movement along the demand curve.

What else will influence how much osteopathy we buy? The answer is our income, our **preferences** and the prices of other goods.

Osteopathy is a normal good so if our income rises we will buy more treatment at each price and if it falls we will buy less.

If our preferences change, we will buy more or less osteopathy at each price. If we decide we are keen on osteopathy, then we will buy more of it. If we go off the idea of osteopathy, then the amount we buy will drop.

Our demand for osteopathy will also be affected by the prices of related services. An obvious example is the price of physiotherapy, which is an alternative (or **substitute**) treatment for many of the conditions treated by osteopaths. If the price of physiotherapy falls then some people are likely to switch from osteopathy to physiotherapy, so the demand for osteopathy would fall.

Our demand for goods and services is also affected by changes in prices of complementary goods. These are goods and services which tend to be bought together. For instance, if the price of eye tests rose significantly, then many people would not bother to get their eyes checked regularly. This would lead to a fall in the demand for spectacles.

Whenever income, preferences or the price of a related good or service changes, the demand curve shifts. You can try out the effects of changes in the graph on the left.

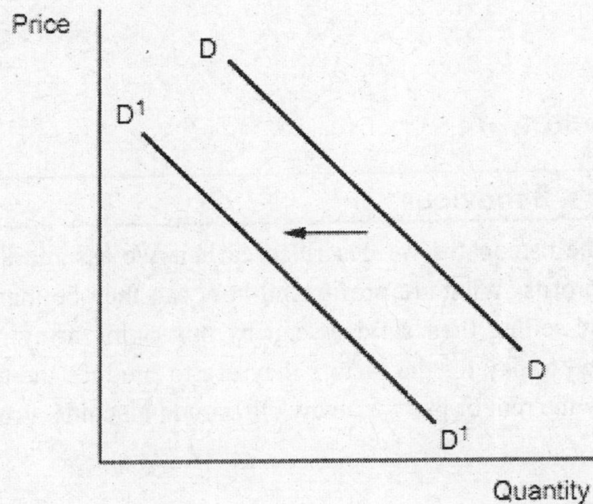

Figure 7

Demand curves shifts inwards from DD to D^1D^1 as a result of:

- a fall in income
- a fall in preferences
- a fall in price of substitute
- a rise in price of complement

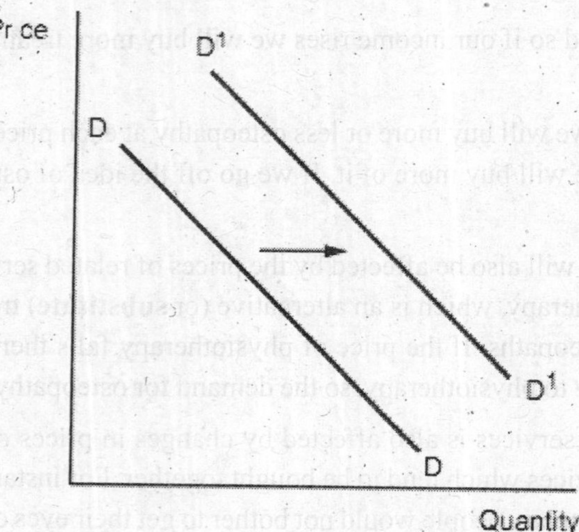

Figure 8

Demand curves shifts outwards from DD to D^1D^1 as a result of:

- a rise in income
- an increase in preferences
- a rise in price of substitute
- a fall in price of complement

Supply-Analyzing the Seller's Behaviour

The sellers in this market are the osteopaths we described earlier. We assume that these osteopaths want to maximize their profits. What are profits and how can they be maximized? Osteopaths earn money (revenue) by selling their services e.g. by massaging away muscular strains. Out of this revenue, they need to pay for the factors they use to produce the treatment (costs) e.g. pay their receptionist, pay the rent or pay for a new ultrasound machine. Profit is the excess of revenue over costs.

Maximizing Profits

Seeking to maximize profits leads each osteopath to want to sell more care at higher prices. There is a reliable and predictable positive relationship between price and quantity supplied. Formally, supply is defined as the quantity of a good or service that a population of sellers is willing and able to sell at every conceivable price. This positive relationship is shown graphically by the supply curve on the left - SS. If the price changes, there is a movement along the supply curve (see Figure 7). At price P the osteopath population is prepared to sell Q treatments. When the price rises to P' the osteopath population is prepared to sell Q' treatments - this might be because more people become osteopaths when it becomes a more lucrative job.

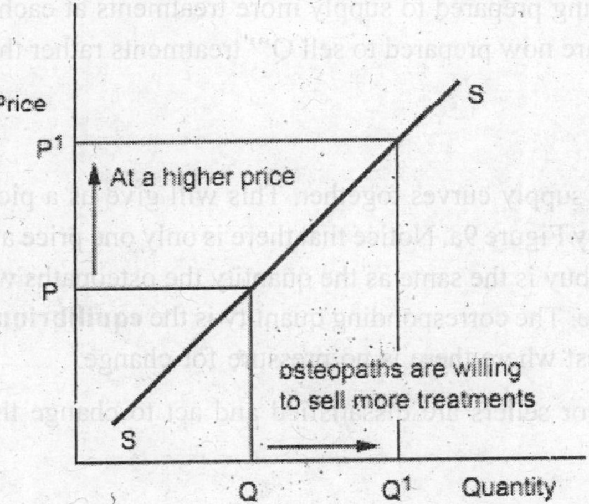

Figure 9: The supply curve for osteopathy treatments

Change in Costs

If the level of **factor costs** changes then the supply curve will shift. For example nurses' wages could go up or the rent could fall. Let's look at the effects of these.

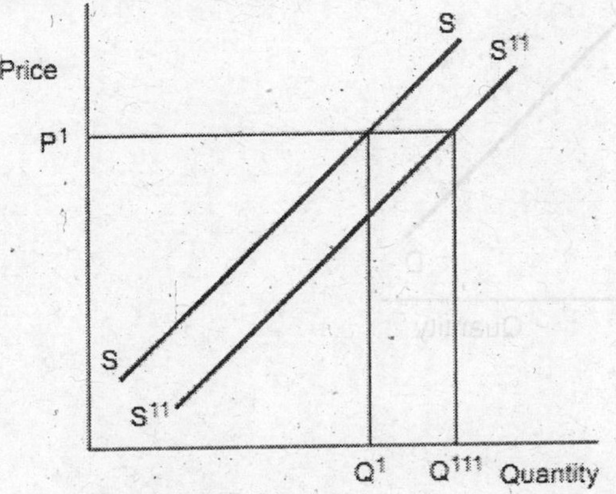

Figure 10: SS is the initial supply curve for treatments. Now rents fall and osteopaths react by being prepared to supply more treatments at each price. The supply curve shifts outwards to S" S". At a price such as P' osteopaths are now prepared to sell Q" treatments rather than Q'.

In Figure 8a, SS is the initial supply curve for treatments. Imagine that nurses' wages rise, pushing up osteopaths' costs. The osteopaths react by being prepared to supply fewer treatments at each price (this may be because there are fewer osteopaths). At a price such as P' osteopaths are now only prepared to sell Q" treatments rather than Q'. The supply curve shifts inwards to S'S'.

Now imagine that rents fall. The profit of osteopaths will increase for each treatment. The osteopath population will react by being prepared to supply more treatments at each price. See Figure 8b. At the price P' osteopaths are now prepared to sell Q"' treatments rather than Q'. The supply curve shifts outwards.

The Market

We can now put the demand and supply curves together. This will give us a picture of the market for osteopathy. This is shown by Figure 9a. Notice that there is only one price at which the quantity of treatments people want to buy is the same as the quantity the osteopaths want to sell. This is called the **equilibrium price** Pe. The corresponding quantity is the **equilibrium quantity** - Qe. The **equilibrium** is a state of rest where there is no pressure for change.

At any other price either buyers or sellers are dissatisfied and act to change the quantity demanded or supplied.

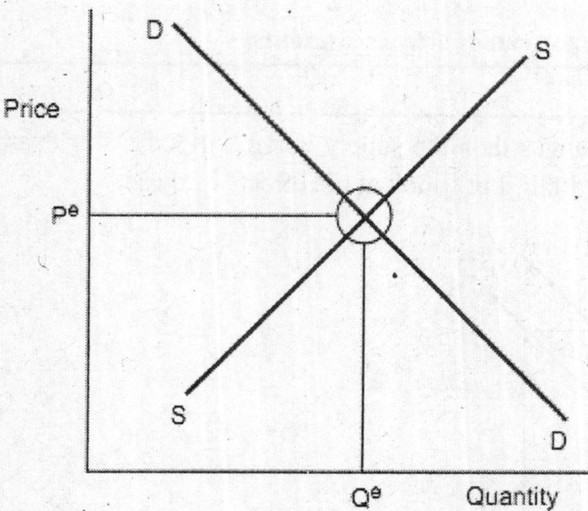

Figure 11

Excess Demand

If there is excess demand, consumers bid up the price. In Figure 9b, at price P' consumers demand Q'. The price is low so a lot of people are willing and able to buy treatments. However, the low price means that there aren't enough osteopaths prepared to provide this amount of treatment.

They are only prepared to provide Q”. The excess demand (Q’ – Q”) causes the consumers to bid the price up to the equilibrium price Pe.

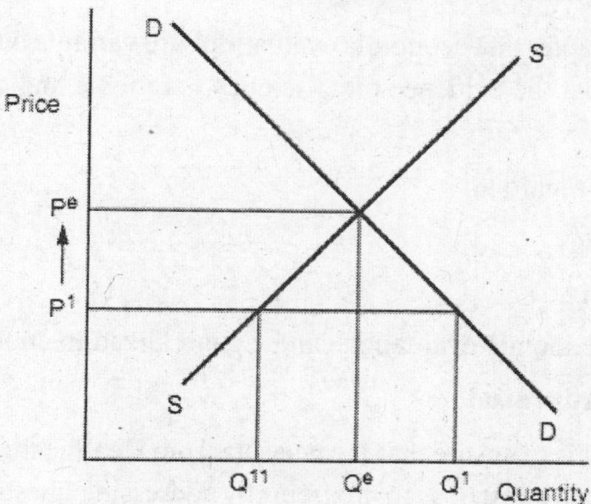

Figure 12

Excess Supply

In Figure 9c at P” the price is too high. Consumers only demand Q”’ treatments. However, ie osteopaths want to sell more treatment: Q””. So there is an excess of supply (Q”” – Q”’). his will lead to osteopaths having to cut their prices (to encourage more consumers to buy eatment). As sellers, they will have to reduce their prices until they reach the equilibrium price e. So the free interaction of buyers and sellers in the market automatically leads to a single price which the quantity traded ‘clears’ the market, i.e. the quantity supplied equals the quantity emanded.

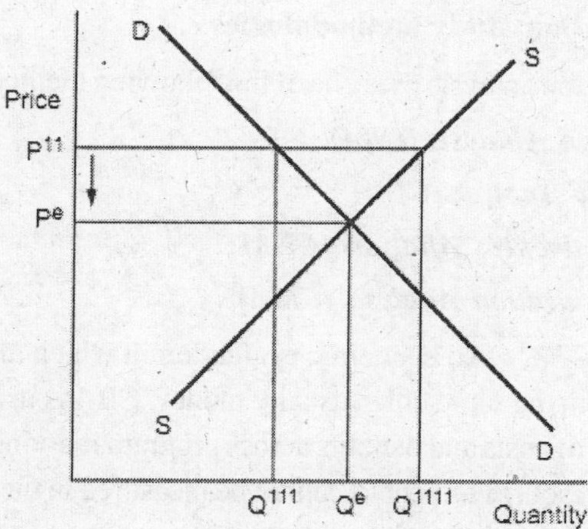

Figure 13

Economic Appraisal of Health Services

(A) Why Appraisal is Important?

We know from the previous chapter that economic evaluations are variable and that healthcare decision makers need to be sure that the evidence on efficiency is reliable and can be applied in situations.

Reliability must be checked in regard to:

- The quality of methodology
- The accuracy of reporting.
- Whether the results of economic evaluation can be generalized to another setting.

(B) The Aim of Economic Appraisal

The aim of economic appraisal is to ensure that the benefits from Healthcare programs implemented are greater than the opportunity cost of such programs by addressing questions of Allocative efficiency or Technical efficiency.

Allocative efficiency assesses competing programs and judges the extent to which they meet objectives.

Technical efficiency assesses the best way of achieving a given objective.

(C) Economic Appraisal defined

A full economic appraisal compares both the costs and consequences (effectiveness; benefits) of two or more interventions. A full economic appraisal requires the identification, measurement and valuation of both costs and consequences. A full economic evaluation is the only type of economic analysis that provides valid information on efficiency.

(D) Economic evaluation study methodologies

A full economic evaluation analysis uses one of the following methodologies:

- ***Cost-Benefit Analysis (CBA)***
- ***Cost-Utility Analysis(CUA)***
- ***Cost-Effectiveness Analysis (CEA)***
- ***Cost-Minimization Analysis (CMA)***

Cost-benefit Analysis (CBA) - An economic evaluation in which all costs and consequences of a program are expressed in the same units, usually money. CBA is used to determine allocative efficiency; i.e., comparison of costs and benefits across programs serving different patient groups. NB. Even if some items of resource or benefit cannot be measured in the common unit of account; i.e., money, they should not be excluded from the analysis.

Cost-utility Analysis (CUA) - A form of economic study design in which interventions which produce different consequences, in terms of both quantity and quality of life, are expressed as

'utilities'. These are measures which comprise both **length of life** and **subjective levels of well being**. The best known utility measure is the **'quality adjusted life year'** or QALY. In this case, competing interventions are compared in terms of cost per utility (cost per QALY).

(CUA) has its own strengths and limitations. CUA measures more aspects of health and well-being than a single natural unit. **QALYs** and **HYEs** assume that the only potential benefit from Healthcare is improvement in health-related quality of life. The different methods available to estimate QALYs may not provide identical results and CUA is more complex to undertake than CEA.

Cost-effectiveness Analysis (CEA) - An economic evaluation in which the costs and consequences of alternative interventions are expressed cost per unit of health outcome. CEA is used to determine technical efficiency; i.e., comparison of costs and consequences of competing interventions for a given patient group within a given budget.

CEA is relatively easy to undertake and the benefits are measured as a single one-dimensional outcome; however, other potentially important outcomes may be ignored. This unidimensionality may result in drawing erroneous conclusions from CEA.

Cost-minimization Analysis (CMA)

An economic evaluation in which consequences of competing interventions are the same and in which only inputs, that is, costs are taken into consideration. The aim is to decide the least costly way of achieving the same outcome.

These methodologies are distinct from each other and are used to address different efficiency questions. The distinction between the methodologies is found in the way in which the consequences are measured and valued.

(E) Key areas for critical appraisal

Two questions need to be addressed in relation to how the economic evaluation has assessed resource use and cost:

a. Are the main areas of resource use identified?

b. Are the appropriate costs measured?

It is important to remember that costs here do not equate with expenditure. Economic cost, that is, opportunity costs are the benefits of opportunities forgone; i.e., the best possible use of the same resources.

Are the main areas of resource use identified?

The main areas of resource use which may require specific identification and measurement of costs are:

- Healthcare resources
- Other related services

- Clients and their families
- Time lost from usual activity

This is not an exhaustive list but illustrates the main categories.

Examples of Healthcare resources include (but are not limited to) staffing, consumables such as supplies and equipment, overheads such as heating, lighting, cleaning, laundry services etc., and capital such as land, buildings and major items of equipment.

Other related services costs include resources associated with community, ambulance and voluntary services. As with Healthcare resources they may be categorized as staffing, consumables, overheads, and capital.

Resources used by clients and their families may take the form of inputs to treatment, e.g., informal care or expenses, such as transport costs.

Time lost from usual activity may take the form of time away from work, loss of leisure time, or unpaid work.

Are the appropriate costs measured?

The costs reported in an economic evaluation may suffer from a number of problems which require consideration at appraisal. These problems are:

- **effects of inflation**
- **double counting**
- **un-thinking acceptance of market values**

The key point to consider here is, has the economic evaluation attempted to correctly identify the opportunity cost of the resources used?

(F) Partial evaluation studies

Partial evaluations constitute a number of economic study types which consider costs and/or consequences, but which either do not involve a comparison between alternative interventions or do not relate costs to benefits.

Partial evaluations can be useful in that they can provide elements of information for a full evaluation and help answer questions not related to efficiency.

It is important to remember that partial evaluation do not provide information on efficiency.

Types of partial evaluation studies

Generally speaking, there are five types of partial evaluation studies. These are:

- **Cost Comparison / Cost Analysis**
- **Cost Outcome Description**
- **Cost Description**
- **Outcome Description**

- **Cost of Illness Study**

Keywords : Scarcity; Trade-offs; Rationing; Wants; Resources; Demand; Land; Labour, Capital. Enterprise; Production Possibility Frontier, Marginal rate of transformation; Law of Diminishing Returns, Efficiency, Pareto, Opportunity Cost; Factors of production; Equity; Free Market, Command System; Mixed System; Horizontal Equity; Vertical Equity; Substitution and Income Effects; Factor Costs; Equilibrium; Economic Appraisal; A vocative Efficiency; Technical Efficiency; Cost-Benefit Analysis; Cost utility Analysis; cost-Effectiveness Analysis; cost Minimization Analysis; Quality Adjusted Life year; Double Thinking; Partial Evaluation Studies.

Summary : It is crucial to know who gets the Healthcare and how much Economics comes in handy to know that. There are infinite human wants and finite nature of resources change in age structure. Increasing real income and improvement in medical technology has increased the demand of healthcare production possibility frontier shows maximum combinations which can be achieved given the quantity and productivity of resources available. Allocation of resources is efficient if it is impossible to change that allocation to make one person better off without making someone else worse.

Opportunity cost is the benefit giving up by not choosing the next best alternative. There are two ways by which a society can get more treatment :

(i) By improving the productivity of the factors of production.

(ii) By increasing the quantity of the factors of production.

Given scarcity, what we need is an allocation or decision making system to determine how much of which kinds of healthcare are provided. There are three possibilities: the Free Market: the command system and the mixed system. The free market would allocate Healthcare resources according to consumer's purchasing behaviour, which the command model would use planning to allocate healthcare according to some predetermined criterion such as 'need'. The mixed system would combine parts of the free market with elements of the command model. Healthcare decision-makers that evidence on efficiency is reliable and can be used is situations. Allocative efficiency assesses competing programs and judges the extent to which they meet objectives. Technical efficiency assesses the best way of achieving a given objective. A full economic evaluation uses one of the following methodologies :

(i) Cost – Benefit Analysis

(ii) Cost – Utility Analysis

(iii) Cost – Effectiveness Analysis

(iv) Cost – Minimization Analysis.

Questions:

1. Define the dimension of scarcity. What are the various factors affecting scarcity? How is the concept of production possibility frontier applicable?
2. Briefly describe the various trade – offs in Healthcare.
3. Describe the 'Free Market Approach'. Also give an overview of market, buyer and shelter, demand and supply.
4. Why is the Economic Appraisal of Health Services important? What is the aim of Economic Appraisal? Also describe the various methodologies by which Economic Appraisal is done.

Short Notes:

- Production Possibility Frontier
- Cost – Benefit Analysis
- Opportunity cost
- Profit Maximisation
- Efficiency
- Rationing

14

BUDGETING AND CONTROLLING OF HEALTH SERVICES

Learning Objectives

After studying this Chapter you should be able to understand:

- The Healthcare Controlling Process
- The various components of Budget
- Steps in Budget Preparation of Hospital
- Types of Budget
- What do you mean by Expenditure Survey understanding the various seasons behind growing hospital expenditure.

The budgeting and controlling process largely includes all the planning & organising activities f an organization. Most of the management control process involves informal communication and teraction. Informal communication occurs by means of **memoranda, meetings, conversa-ons** and even by facial expression but many organisation have formal **management control ystem**. A formal control system requires **programming, budgeting & controlling**. Program-ing is deciding on the programs that the company will undertake & appropriate amount of re-ources that should be allocated to each program.

Healthcare Controlling Process

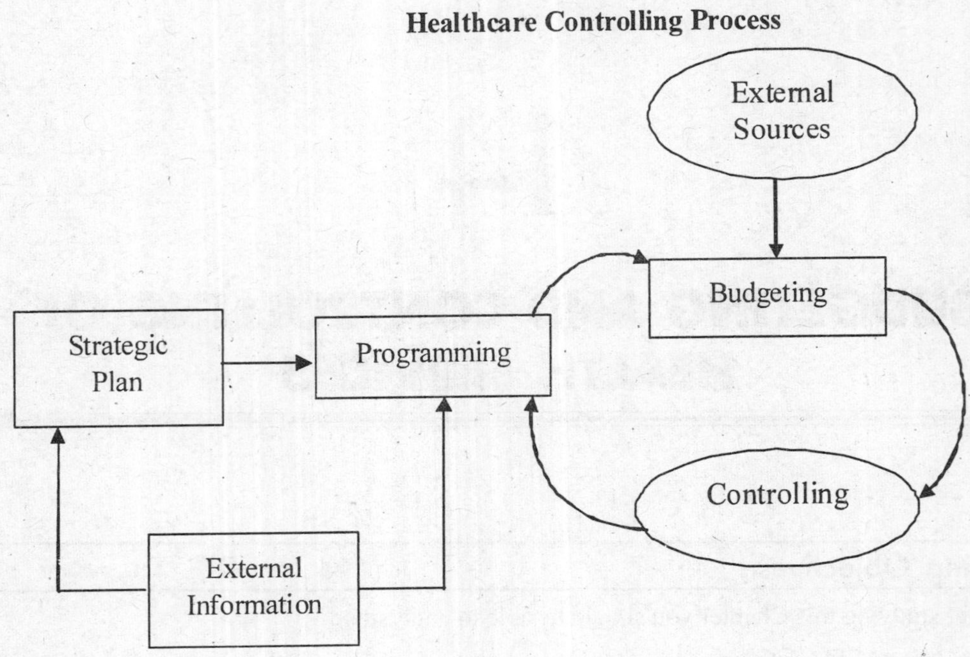

Adapted from R.N. Anthony and J.S. Reece [2, p. 670].

This aspect include formulation of **corporate strategies** and policies. During this stage Healthcare organizations would identify the type of medical services to be provided, the type of research activities, the populations to be served & general mode of operations in long & short run. The second stage is budgeting which expresses the programming decision in monetary terms and covers specific time period, generally one year. The budget represents the best plan for allocating resources to achieve the objectives & implement the programs approved. The agreed budget is considered a commitment in which responsibility center commit themselves to produce the planned output. The third stage is control process which represent a feedback mechanism in which plans & procedure can be modified based on experience from previous year. The process involves reporting & analysis of performance. Such reports and analysis provide the basis for control over expenditures and useful data for identifying the operating problems.

The programming decisions provide the **fiscal officer** and **budget committee** with a statement of **organisational objectives.** During the budget process, the approved programs are translated into a detailed statement of monetary requirements and financial consequence. The process of budgeting is useful because it formals communication between the hospitals governance, administration, department heads etc.

Components of Budget

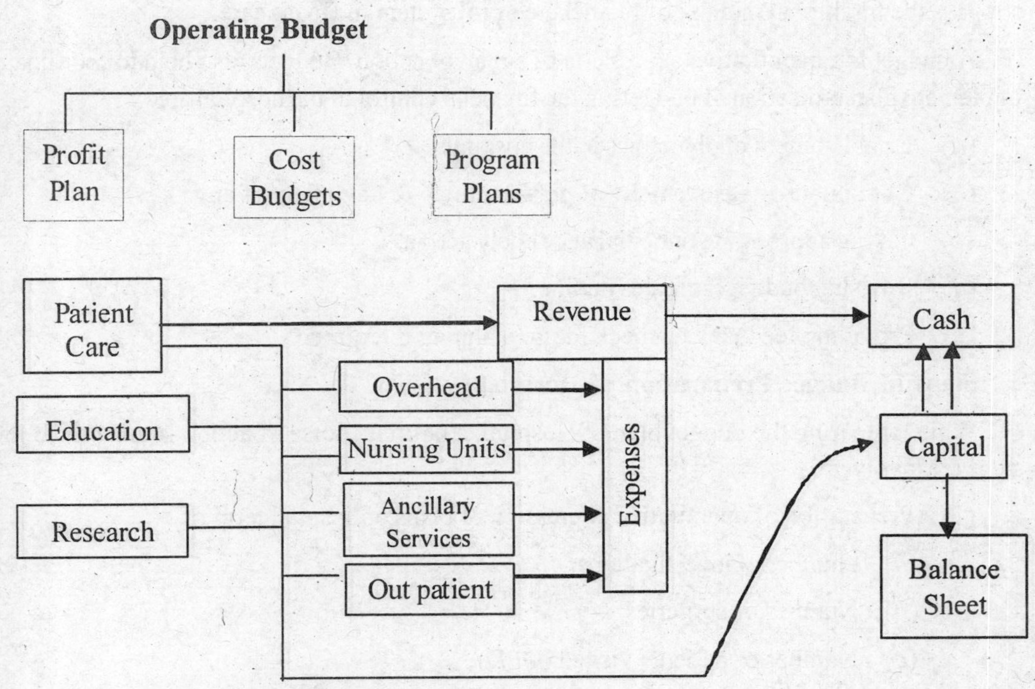

Adapted from Shilling-law, G. Managerial Cost Accounting, 4th ed., p. 137. Homewood, II; ichard D. Irwin, Inc., 1974

Management must develop the structure and processes of its control system. The major ele-ients of the controlling deal with establishment of standard & comparing the actual performance ith the standard. For the operation and financial aspect of the organisation, the operating and nancial budget generally provide the expected outcomes. They represent the best plans resulting om the analysis.

Operating Budget Includes Revenue, Expenses and other it includes process of examining the perations of different department & concerned with problem detection. Information about actual utcomes should be available from the organizations Management information system. The data hould be accurate, provided on a timely basis and must be compared with data from **budgeting ystem**. These generally means that **healthcare financial accounting system** must have the bility.

(1) Ability to accumulate expense by **responsibility center**

(2) Provide cost accounting system for calculating per-unit cost

(3) Collect operation of statistics as an integral part of Management Information System

H is the traditional method of financial control system in Healthcare.

A budget is a quantitative expression of a plan of action. Budgets also help to coordinate an implement plan utilisation of budgets in the financial control of the hospital are:

(*a*) Establishment of objectives in the hospitals.

(*b*) Continuous **measurement of performance** & deviations if any.

(*c*) Taking appropriate remedial and timely action.

(*d*) Revising budget estimates in time.

(*e*) Providing feedback to check future planning if required.

Steps in Budget Preparation of Hospital

While preparing the budget plan of Hospital, a normal course of action is taken & followi steps are involved:

(1) Preparation of quantitative expression of plans of hospital term of

 (*a*) Number of investigations

 (*b*) Number of surgeries

 (*c*) Number of patients visited (OPD)

 (*d*) Patient days of care

(2) Preparation of **economic forecast** in respect of new services, new person to be er ployed & new material to be procured etc.

(3) Establishment of quantifiable goals of budget in consultation with the finance depa ment.

(4) The chairman of the budget committee in the finance officer/ Accounts officer w prepare the budget and written communication will be given to the head of differe department through budget manual.

(5) The members of the budged committee had to analyze the statistical details available their departments & accordingly formulate their departments budget estimates.

(6) Presentation of the budget estimates to finance officer /chairman of the committ explaining the details to him for incorporating their **departmental budget** estimates the **hospital budget.**

(7) The chairman of the committee will prepare the **revenue budget** of the department a summarize **departmental expense budget.**

(8) The financer officer /chairman of the budget committee will prepare **preliminary op**

ating budget or the hospital.

(9) Summarize the total budget of hospital including **cash budget** and **capital budget**.

(10) The final budget is discussed in the budget committee for approval, obtaining signature of every member as a token.

(11) Presentation of budget before governing board.

(12) Communicating the final approved budget to all the heads of the department.

The budget making time in the hospital starts with the fiscal year. Hospital face a clear growth. Budgetary control is a way to check the enterprise to see on what its money is being spent. These are many types of budgets.

(1) Revenue and expense budget : This budget tells about plan related to revenue & operating expenses. It reflects anticipated income from Sales of products and services and by providing direct patient care. Patient care generates revenue. Revenue and expense budget are prepared by various professional departments (Medical, Surgical, Paediatries, Obstetrics and gynecology etc. and supportive services departments like - ray, laboratory & ancillary services etc.

(2) Programme Budgeting: It is a method of providing a systematic allocation of resources in a way that goal are achieved effectively. By concentrating on goals and programme in the light of available resources, it put stress on assessing costs against benefits in selecting the best course. It is a technique for achieving strategic decision and a balance between goals and allocation of resources.

(3) Zero Based Budgeting: Zero based budgeting involves an idea that for each programme budget should be calculated from base zero. It includes objective and goals of functional unit, the operational results required to achieve the goals, alternative approaches to these goal & the outcome & resource requirements for each approach. The heads successively consolidate responsibility and develop their own priorities.

Expenditure Survey

The general rise in market cost of almost all commodities had its effect on hospital expenditures current trends indicate that hospitals are increasing the capital intensity of their services because of expanding the scope of outpatient facilities, upgrading the quality of intensive care services, modernising the facilities and employing the latest technologies. Due to constant rise of medical care, funding and financing is getting difficult. It is apparent that the funding of hospital in future has to depend increasingly on non-governmental sources. The reason behind growing hospital expenditure are :

- **The changing character of services:** The Changing trend is shifted from few tests in diagnosis to more investigations. Hospitals not only add service, but they also deliver the existing ones more frequently. Physicians by their monopoly related to investigative procedures, have a significant role in cost aggravation.

- **Lack of commitment:** In government run hospitals, there is no commitment to lower the cost. Few doctors have sufficient information as to whether services delivered by a hospital are worthwhile. There are hardly any incentives for doctors to cut costs.
- **Technology Management:** The hospitals are adopting latest technology and because of which rising hospital cost. New technology often increases the utilisation and intensing of hospital care, two important factors in the growth of expenditure.
- **Changing: Lifestyle and Health Status**

  On one hand, control of communicable diseases has resulted in lower burden on hospital cost but on the other hand the changing lifestyle have given rise to cardiovascular & metabolic disorder and brought utilisation of medical care & increased expenditure.
- **Defensive Medicine:** It is primarily conducted not to ensure the health of patient, but as a safeguard against malpractise & fear of litigation because the introduction of consumer protection have involved these concept.
- **Lack of Awareness of Economy and Productivity:** Economy & Productivity has not a major concern & expenditure increases in that way.
- **Reimbursing practises:** The concept of Reimbursement say that employer has to pay for employee medical care. These concept has tempted hospital to over investigate patient and charge heavily.
- **More costly facilities:** The Hospital is providing more costly facilities to their patient and in the cost increase.

Due to constant rising cost of medical care, finding and financing is getting difficult. The budget needed to operate the hospital system alone may absorb upto 2 to 3 percent of GNP which is almost equal to the total budget of the entire health services.

Keywords : Programming; Budgeting; Controlling; External Sources; Strategic Plan; External Information; Operating Budget; Profit Plan; Cost Budgets; Program Plan; Revenue & expense budget; Programme Budgeting; Zero-Based Budgeting; Expenditure Survey.

Summary : All planning activities in an organisation is done through Budgeting and Controlling. It includes formulation of corporate strategies. The Budget Committee is provided with a statement of organisational objectives. Management must develop structure and processes of its control system. Operating Budget includes identifying the problem of various organisational departments. It also helps in coordinating and implementing plan. Various steps are involved while preparing a budget plan. The various types of budget are as follows: Revenue & Expense Budget; Programming Budget and Zero-Based Budgeting. An expenditure survey has suggested various reasons behind growing hospital expenditure.

Questions:

1. What do you understand by Budgeting and controlling of Health Services?
2. What are the various components of Budget? Remunerate the various steps in Budget Preparation of a Hospital.
3. List out the various types of budget.
4. What is an Expenditure Survey? What are the various reasons behind growing hospital expenditure?

Short Notes :

- Operating Budget
- Revenue & Expense Budget
- Zero-Based Budgeting
- Expenditure survey
- Profit Plan

15

PRICING AND EFFICIENCY

Learning Objectives

After studying this Chapter you should be able to understand:

- How is the efficiency measured and operationalized in Healthcare?
- What are the various factors on which efficiency should be based?
- What is pricing?

Efficiency Measurement and Operations in Healthcare

The usefulness of efficiency measurement act as a instrument of monitoring and resource allocation in health services. The methodological frame work of Healthcare have facilitated the efficiency in organization producing multiple output with the aids of multiple inputs where information about factor or product prices is lacking. The policy are formulated about the performance of Healthcare and monitoring may increase the efficiency of hospital. Measurement of efficiency may be done in terms of **allocation of resources** in health services. Using the **efficiency measurement** they can control the relative differences in the performance of health services for diagnostic purposes. The hospital may be grouped into high, medium or low performer. The hospitals are said to be technically efficient if it increase output.

Factors affecting the efficiency of the Healthcare:

(1) **The level of output:** The efficiency of Healthcare service will depend on number of output.

(2) **Technological change:** The efficiency of Healthcare increase when it is equipped with the latest technology.

(3) **Coordination and Cooperation:** There should be proper communication between the physician, patient and strategies related to Healthcare should be communicated at all levels.

(4) **Benchmarking:** It involves comparing one's business operations & performance to best industry where similar process exist and compare the results. The process allows organisation to develop plans to make improvement with the aim of increasing efficiency It is a continuous process to improve the performance and efficiency.

(5) **Integrated effort:** It is an integrated effort which deals with client, providers, organisation & collective orientation.

The assessment of performance should be as timely as data permits. Efficiency should be ased on the following:

(1) **Productivity monitoring:** In the assessment of input & output relationship of responsibility centres and individual providers are measured.

(2) **Variance Analysis:** It attempts to partition the total experience into parts which correspond to identify causes e.g. price, volume, supply, quantity.

(3) **Operational Audit:** Process of examining the operation of departments and organisational control system to assess their effectiveness.

(4) **Financial Statement Analysis:** The methodology for analyzing the organization's financial performance as a whole and assessing its position.

The reporting and analysis of performance serve several purpose. It tell management in-rmed about what is happening. Management can take appropriate action on the basis of report evaluate the performance of responsibility center heads. It helps in educating the head of de-rtment in their decision related to financial aspects. It makes proper staffing and **scheduling cisions** which are consistent with the overall goals of efficiency and effectiveness. It is con-cted for the purpose of improving the planning and budgeting processes gaining a better under-nding of production processes and improving management skills, performance evaluation can an essential link in a hospital's attempt to improve its cost effectiveness.

icing

In a changing health services Scenario, the existing operating and planning practices will need pe modified, where demands for new services, programmes, equipment or expansion of existing iveness should be based on expansion of existing activities should be based on **financial viabil-** . Generally, **hospital pricing practices** are based on a combination of input cost, including erheads plus profit or on rates which are prevalent in the neighbourhood hospital. The pricing icture of a hospital must be within areas unable range of charges with hospitals in the area with milar mix of service. A review of charges, including al the **direct** and **Indirect expenses** that y be related to a specific **cost centre**, may usually demonstrate little relationship to the actual t of providing and maintaining these services. Unlike all other countries, the Healthcare market erally lack transparent **market based pricing**. Patients cannot compare prices because the dical service providers do not typically disclose prices prior to service. Hospitals, doctors and other medical providers have traditionally disclosed their fee schedules only to insurance companies and other institutional payers but not to the individual patients. In critical care Government dew are enforced to treat any patient that has a life threatening condition, irrespective of patient's financial resources. Health services are raising to unprecedented heights and the estimates tc expenses are always higher than the income generated.

The pricing of health services should be **value based** & cost effective. It will help the organisation, provider & patient to be satisfied and there will be long term survival and goal will be achieved. There is no single price for a Healthcare service. The price will vary considerably depending upon who is paying for the service and where the service is obtained. Different insure may pay different amount to the same hospital and same physicians for the same procedur depending on their negotiated discounts. The governmental payer, uninsured also pay differe amounts for the same services. The amount paid for a Healthcare service will vary based on wh performs the service, where it is performed, and who pays the bill.

Keywords: Efficiency Measurement; Bench marking; Productivity Monitoring; Various Analysis Operational Audit; Financial Statement Analysis; cost centre; market based pricing

Summary : Efficiency Measurement facilitates resource allocation and monitoring in healt services. There are various factors affecting efficiency of the Healthcare viz., th level of output; Coordination and cooperation; benchmarking and Integrated effo Efficiency should be based on the following: Productivity monitoring; Varianc Analysis; Operational Audit and Financial Statement Analysis.

Questions :

1. How does Efficiency Measurement contribute to improving Healthcare Services? Wh are the factors affecting efficiency in Healthcare?
2. The assessment of performance should be timely. What are the factors on which eff ciency is based?
3. How is pricing done in Healthcare sector?

Short Notes :

- Market-based pricing
- Benchmarking
- Variance Analysis
- Efficiency Measurement
- Operational Audit

16

HOSPITAL : AN INTRODUCTION, CLASSIFICATION & ORGANISATION

Learning Objectives

This chapter deals with a picture regarding medical care services in developing countries including India. It provides awareness about diseases and managing & controlling of diseases. It evaluate health problems and advise patients to take physical, psychological factors and understand appropriate utilization of human resources, diagnostic Intervention, therapeutic modalities and healthcare facilities. It deals with basic diagnostic and technical procedures.

The hospital is an integral part of a social and medical organization, the function of which is to provide for the population complete healthcare, both curative and preventive and whose outpatient services reach out to the family and its home environment; the hospital is also a centre for the training of health workers and biosocial research (WHO).

The hospital is a very labor intensive organization in which the skills of varied group are being used efficiently and effectively. The hospital is a system comprising of sub system like clinical services, diagnostic services, therapeutic services, utility services.

History of Hospitals

The word hospital originates from Latin word 'hospice' which means a place where a guest is received or an institution for care of injured and sick.

Early History

In the earlier period of Greek and Roman civilization, the temples of the gods were used as hospitals. These hospitals were an integral part of temples. There was little distinction between the disease and the supernatural power that caused diseases. In those periods, superstition saddled medical practice where focus was more on social healing. The principle source of treating sick people was charity.

With the birth of Christianity, the concept of hospital gave rise to church and its monasteries. Gradually, Christian hospital replaced Greece and Rome. The earliest hospital was founded at Hotel Dieu, Paris in 542 AD. In 1123 AD St. Bartholomew's hospital in London was established. In 1524, Spanish were the first to build the hospital in Mexico. In 1751, the first general hospital operation in North America as Pennsylvania hospital.

Nineteenth Century

It evolved with the emergence of Florence Nightingale on the hospital scene. Florence Nightingale was born on 12th May, 1820, in 1832, Nightingale felt that God was calling her to do some work but wasn't sure about the work. She revolutionized nursing by supplementing good intentions and humane concern with the concept of training the nurses. Various developments in medical services gave impetus in the hospital field. Discovery of anaesthesia and steam sterilization in 1886, X-ray in 1895 and rubber gloves in 1890 revolutionized surgical treatment.

Condition of Hospital in India

The hospital could be traced at time of Buddha followed by King Ashoka. In ancient times, a well organized hospital were found. The writing of Sushruta and Charaka was considered as standard work by many countries. Medicine based on the Indian system was taught in Taxila University. The decline of Indian medicine gave rise to Hakims brought by Mohammedan. They followed the 'Yunani' system of medicine. The modern system was introduced in 17th century with the arrival of European Christian missionaries in South India. Organized medical training was started with first Medical College, opening in Calcutta in 1835, two in Delhi in 1835 and 1836, followed by Mumbai in 1845 and Chennai in 1850. In 1855 there were around 1250 hospital and dispensaries in British in India. But then also medical case reached only 10% of the total population.

Changing Concept of Hospitals

With the liberalization policy all over the world, the rapid advancement in the field of information technology have given the concept of Medical Tourism. The hospital concept have changed from service approach to profit making approach. Telemedicine is a new concept. There are a number of Community Health Centre (CHC), Primary Health Centre (PHC) and sub-centres in India. Most of the population in India lives in rural areas so the Healthcare is provided through PHCs, CHCs and sub-centres.

Factors Determining the Utilization of Hospital Services

There are many factors which influence hospital utilization directly or indirectly:

(1) **Demographic Factors:** Age, marriage rate, sex, distribution are the factors which influence hospital utilization.

(2) **Economic Factors:** Economic condition and income affects the utilization of hospital services.

(3) **Social Factors:** Social factors like values, culture, religion, customs, beliefs and ethics shape the attitude of people and determine the utility of hospital services.

(4) **Technological Changes:** The hospitals which are updated with the new and advanced technology have better utilization rates.

(5) **Transportation:** Transportation relates the connectivity with road, rail or air which can affect the positive utilization of hospital services.

(6) **Communication:** Effective communication is required for better utilization of hospital services on individual basis and organizational basis.

(7) **Adequate supply of manpower:** The adequate supply of manpower in form of doctors, nurses etc. on a regular basis is required for utilization of services in hospital.

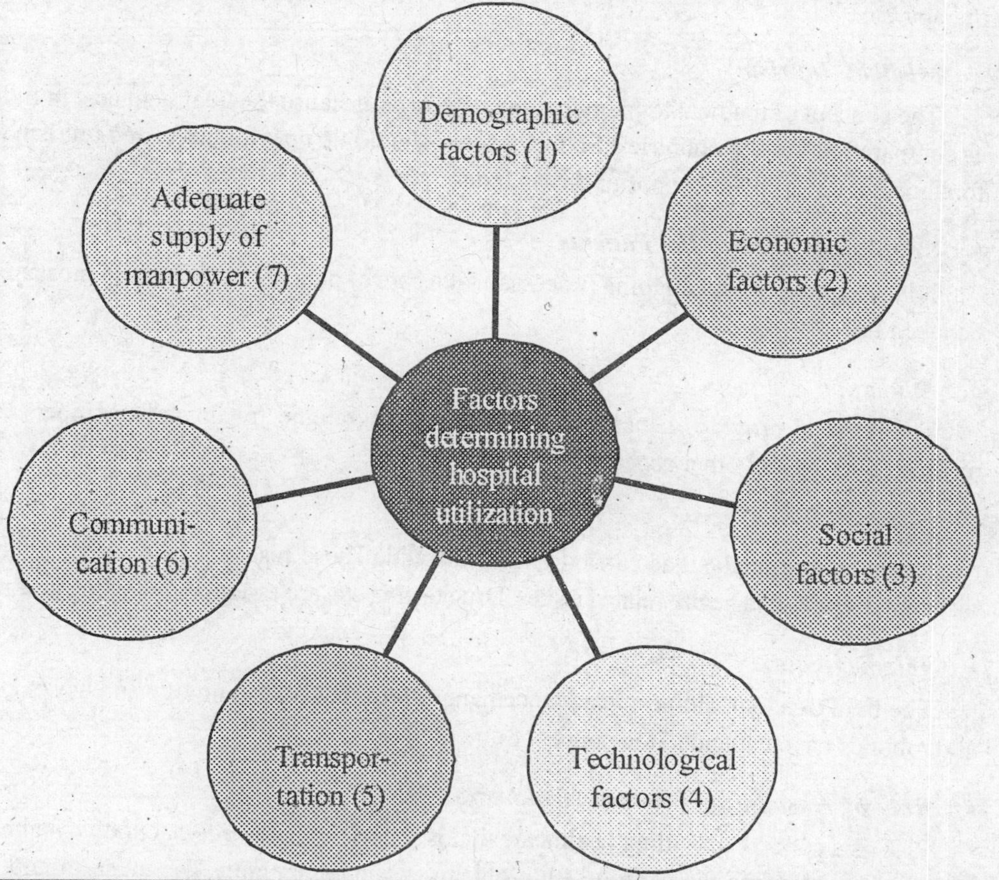

spital Function

The hospital is a peculiar organization because the output of hospital is not tangible product but ngible services. The service provided will be personalized, professional and directly related to doctor, nurses technical and non-technical personnel. The service provided in the hospital by varied skill that is form highly skilled to semi-skilled and unskilled also. The hospital role is to prepare for the demand of sick and injured patient. The hospital plays following different functions in the society:

- ***Care of Sick and Injured***

  The primary responsibility is to provide care to the sick and injured and to provide accommodation depending upon physical condition of the patient, financial status and availability. The hospital should be able to diagnose the disease and treatment should be given immediately.

- ***Rehabilitation***

  WHO defines rehabilitation and the combined and coordinated use of medical, social, educational and vocational measures for training or retraining the individual to the highest possible level of functional ability. Hospital provide rehabilitation through development of physiotherapy, speech therapy etc.

- ***Medical Tourism***

  The concept of medical tourism is a lucrative offer because the treatment cost in India is less as compared to foreign countries. So the hospital should tie up with travel and tourism to attract foreigners for availing the opportunities in India.

- ***Continuous Care of the Patients***

  It is a continuous and ongoing process to take care of patient and follow-up measures should be taken up.

- ***Education***

  The hospital provides education and training programme for its staff members related medical, nursing and other aspects.

- ***Research***

  Research and analysis is carried out in hospital. These research help to get remedy from different diseases and health related issues. Drug testing etc. are essential for testing new medicine

- ***Telemedicine***

  The field of telemedicine and advancement of information technology and use of computer and robotics have expanded the concept of medicine.

- ***Role of Hospital in Primary Healthcare (PHC)***

  PHC is a concept providing healthcare that is promotive, preventive, curative and rehabilitative services covering the main health problems in the community. The most important role related to adequate nutrition safe and adequate water supply, safe waste disposal prevention and control of locally endemic diseases diagnosis and treatment of common diseases and injury health education etc.

Function of a Hospital

The hospital can be divided into:

(1) Intramural

(2) Extramural

Intramural

Instrumental is related to:

(*a*) Restorative deals with

(*i*) ***Diagnostic*** – It include the in the patient services involving medical, surgical and other specialties.

(*ii*) ***Curative*** – Treatment of all ailment.

(*iii*) ***Rehabilitation*** – Physical, mental and social rehabilitation.

(*iv*) ***Care of Emergencies*** – Accidents as well as diseases.

(*b*) Preventive is related to:

(*i*) Supervision of normal pregnancy and childbirth.

(*ii*) Supervision of normal child growth.

(*iii*) Control of communicable diseases.

(*iv*) Prevention of prolong illness.

(*v*) Prevention of invalidism both mental and physical.

(*vi*) Health education.

(*vii*) Occupational health (Occupational safety and health hazards Act).

(*c*) Educational Function

(*i*) Medical undergraduates

(*ii*) Role of specialized and super specialized

(*iii*) Organizing conferences for doctors

(*iv*) General nurses and midwives

(*v*) Training of para-medicals

(*vi*) Community education

(*d*) Research – Medical and Nursing Research

Extramural

(*i*) Outpatient services

(*ii*) Psychiatric services

(*iii*) Day care hospitals

(*iv*) Mobile clinics

(*v*) Medical care camps

Role of Hospitals

Hospital is a place for the diagnosis and treatment of human ills and restoration of health. It plays different roles as discussed below:

(1) ***Role towards patients:***

- Treatment of patient
- Friendly care for patients
- Understanding the physical and emotional needs of patients
- Patient satisfaction
- Patient education

(2) ***Role towards organization:***

- Strategic planning and management of hospitals
- Determination of objective of hospitals
- Defining the present objective and strategies
- Environmental appraisal to determine the strength and weakness
- Finding out the opportunities and threats
- Modifying the present strategies according to situation
- Implementation of Strategies
- Monitoring and control of strategies

(3) ***Relating the Hospital to External Environment***

- Taking care of supply for example material, men, money machine etc.
- Political, legal, ethical aspects should be considered.
- Bringing charges in the technology according to the situation.

(4) ***Operational Management of Hospitals***

- Formulate policies, rules and procedure.
- Management of hospital staff
- Management of hospital materials (Inventory)
- Management of Finance
- Managing hospital information
- Maintaining good relations with medical staff
- Maintaining good relation with public

- Risk management
- Managing legal and ethical aspects
- Providing quality healthcare Service

(5) ***Role towards Community:***

- Education of Community
- Supporting and providing international services
- Providing extramural services

Hospital Organization

Organization is a combination of activities of a number of people for achievement of common purpose or goal. Hospital organization involves systematic approach of all technical, administrative and contingent activities to achieve customer satisfaction.

Organizing is the grouping of activities and responsibilities into workable unit. The structure is determined by the size of the hospital. The role of top management to supervise and coordinate the activities of heterogeneous group engaged in managing hospital services. The organizing of hospital involves following step:

- Identification of activities
- Grouping of the similar activities
- Assignment of authority and responsibility
- Proper communication and coordination

(1) ***Identification of Activities***

The activities performed in the hospital can be identified and recognized as follows:

- Registration of patient
- Consultation
- Examination of the case
- Investigation
- Minor surgical work
- Availability of drug and other services

(2) ***Grouping of Similar Activities***

In hospital, the activities which are similar are grouped in the departments for e.g. OPD, IPD, ICU, Operation Theatre etc.

(3) ***Assignment of Authority & Responsibility***

The hospital management is responsible for assigning authority to different department. The Head of the Department is responsible to plan and control the activities within the group.

(4) ***Proper communication & Coordination***

The hospital is a place where coordination and communication is essential for carrying out the function at different levels. To remove uncertainty from orgnaisation the role are very clear and hospital administrator acts as a coordinator in the organization.

Like other service organization, hospital is always connected with external environment that is patients, consumer, community and client.

The salient feature of hospital is the absence of single line of authority but the multiple pyramid of organization. The multiple pyramid deals with relationship of medical component to administrative components.

The Organizational Structure

Hospital Organization

(1) **Clinical & Nursing Services**

- **Inpatient services** – When people get admitted to hospital for treatment for e.g. cancer, heart and vascular services etc.
- **Outpatient services** – It is defined as part of the hospital with allotted physical facilities and medical with scheduled ......and to provide care for patients who are not registered as inpatients.
- **Emergency Services** – It is organization which ensures public safety and health by addressing different emergencies.
- **OT** – It is modern facility within a hospital where surgical operations are carried out in a sterile environment.

(2) **Supporting Services**

- Laboratory and Blood Bank
- Imaging services
- Drug supervisory
- Central Sterile Supply Services
- Medical Documentation
- Medical special work
- Physical, medicine & Rehabilitation

(3) **Central Advisory of the Administrative Services**

- Human Resource Department
- Finance Management
- Material Management

(4) **Deputy Services – Communication & Transportation**

- Fire safety and security services
- Laundry, housekeeping and emergency maintenance

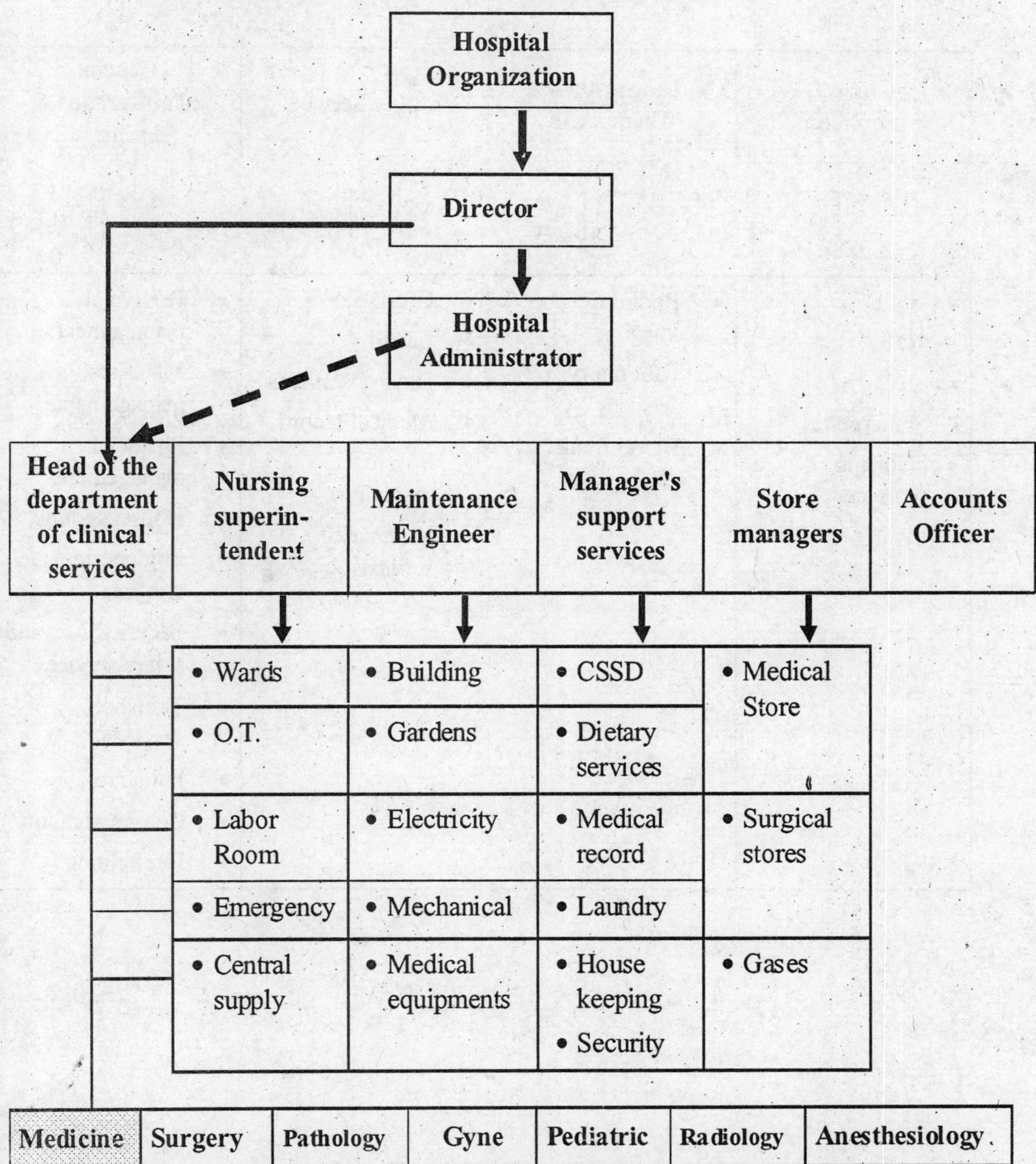

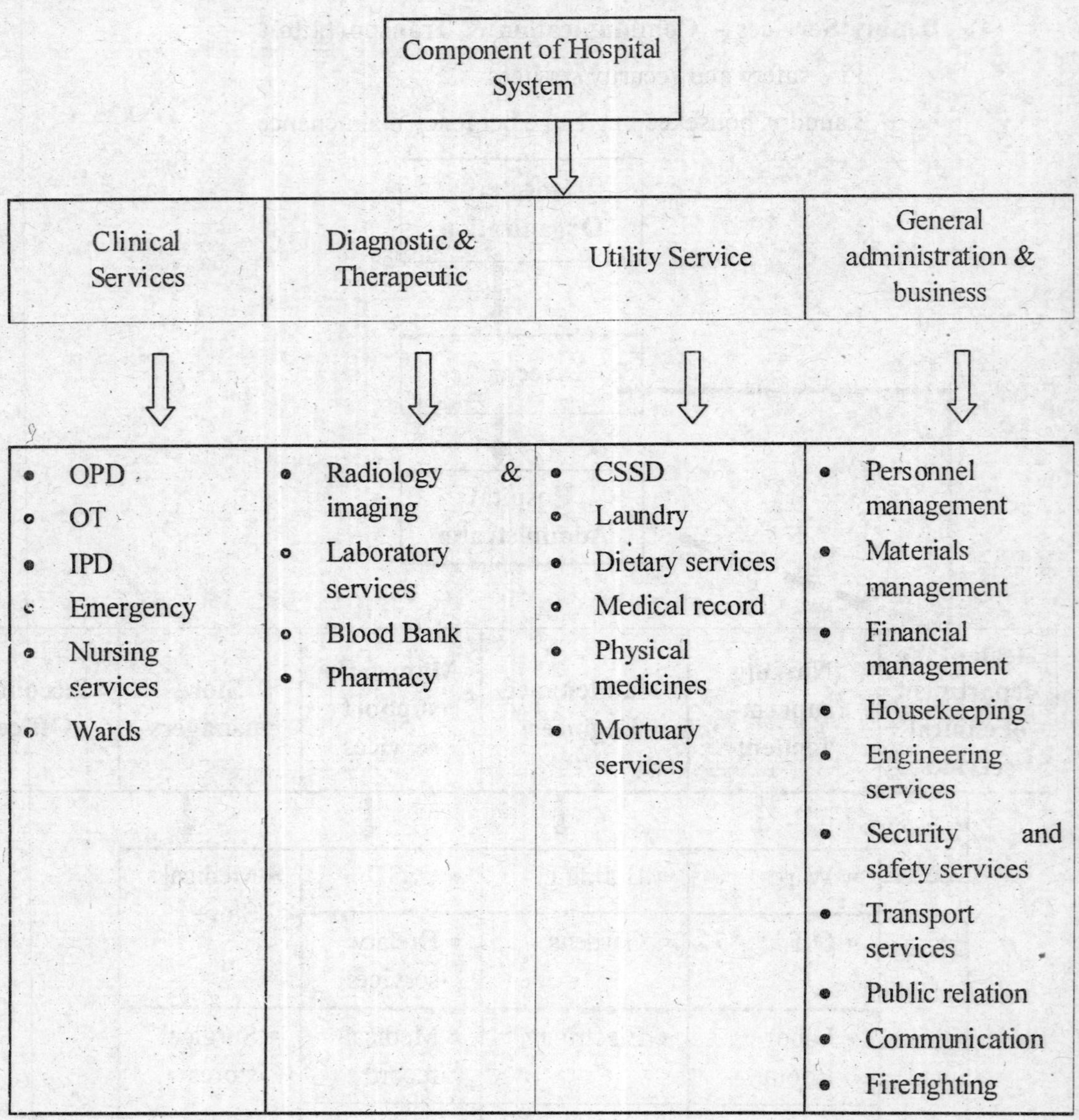
Component of Hospital System
Clinical Services
Diagnostic & Therapeutic
Utility Service
General administration & business
• OPD
• OT
• IPD
• Emergency
• Nursing services
• Wards
• Radiology & imaging
• Laboratory services
• Blood Bank
• Pharmacy
• CSSD
• Laundry
• Dietary services
• Medical record
• Physical medicines
• Mortuary services
• Personnel management
• Materials management
• Financial management
• Housekeeping
• Engineering services
• Security and safety services
• Transport services
• Public relation
• Communication
• Firefighting

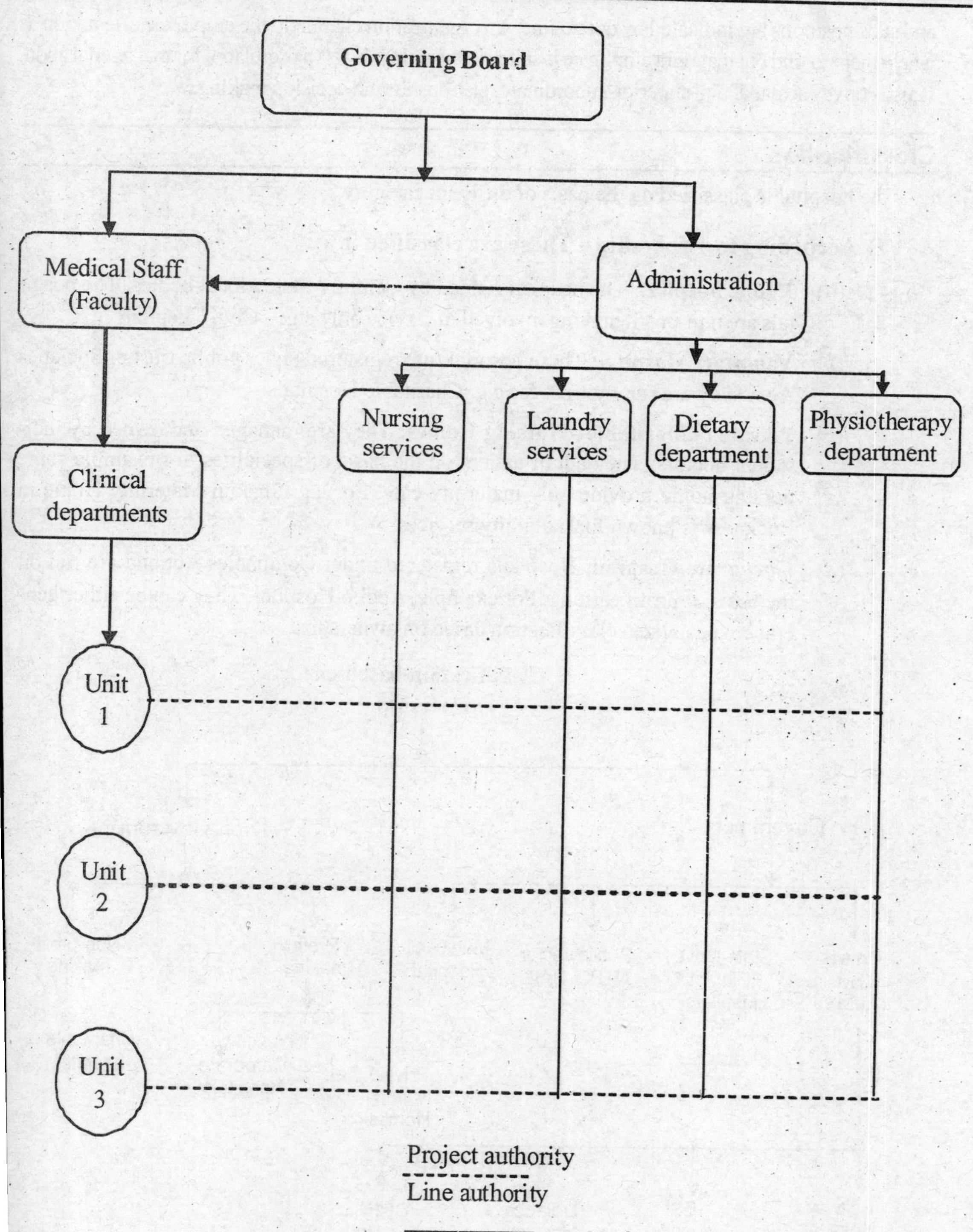

The organization structure of hospital is depicted in line or scales chain shading each layer in [se]quence. In drawing the organization, chart line authority and relationship are indicated by solid line and staff positions are indicated by dotted line. An organization chart help the employee orientation as it help them to find out that right employee is suited in the right job. It is a useful tool for managerial audit. It also convey scalar chain, superior-subordinate relationship and decision making.

Classification

The hospital is classified on the basis of different category.

(1) According to ownership – These are classified into:

(*a*) **Public hospital:** The hospital runned by Central / State / local bodies. The hospitals are non-profit making involved in service only e.g. – Civil Hospital.

(*b*) **Voluntary Hospital:** These hospitals are registered under public trust or Societies Act. They are run by trust for e.g. Charitable Hospitals.

(*c*) **Private / Charitable / Nursing Homes:** They are managed and owned by individual doctors. They admit patient on the basis of specialties, for example some nursing home provide only maternity care. For e.g. Shakun Maternity Home in Lucknow is known for maternity services.

(*d*) **Corporate Hospital:** Hospitals registered under Companies Act and are run on the basis of profit earning. For example, Apollo Hospital. They can be either general or specialized classification based on ownership.

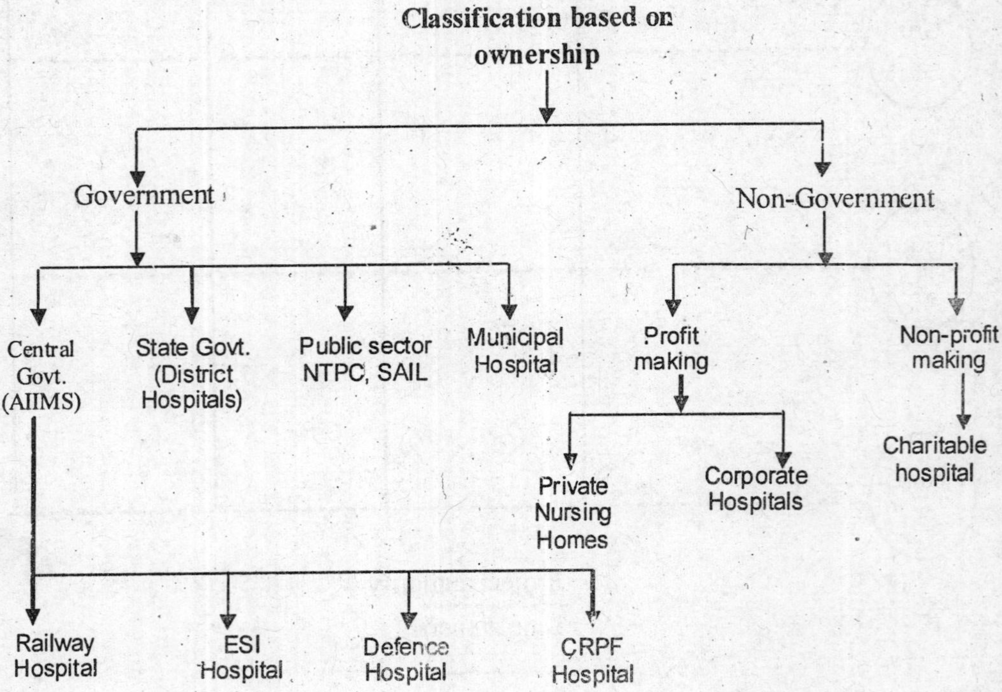

(2) Classification on the basis of length of stay of patient

It is classified into long term and short term. Long term when patient suffer from chronic care and short term or clinical basis for minor diseases.

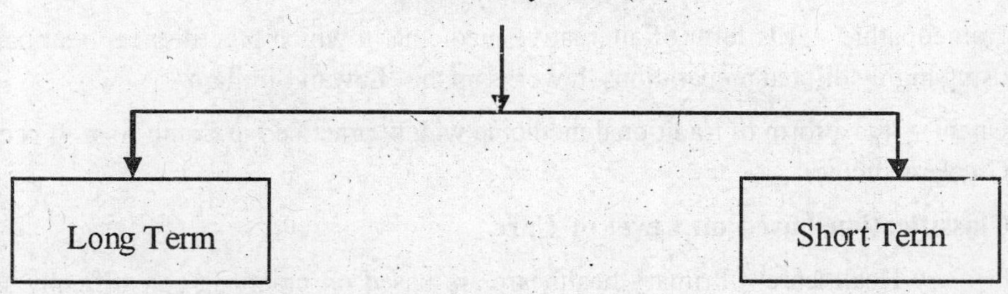

(3) Classification on the basis of Objective

(*a*) **Teaching & Research Hospital:** Hospitals are affiliated with universities for medical research and the training of medical personnel such as physicians and nurses are called teaching cum research hospital. These hospitals are attached to medical Colleges, Nursing Schools etc.

(*b*) **General Hospital:** The hospital which deals with many kinds of diseases and injuries.

(*c*) **Specialized Hospital:** Types of specialized hospitals include Trauma Centres, Children's hospital, Cardiac, Oncology and Orthopaedic.

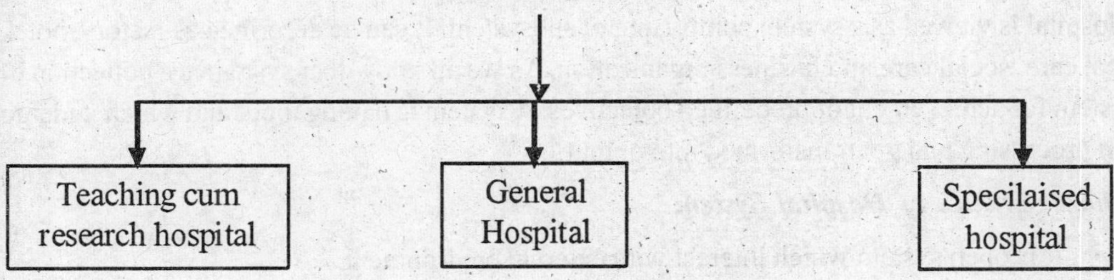

(4) Classification based on size

It can be classified small medium or large depending ob bed strength of hospitals:

- Teaching Hospital (500 Beds)
- District Hospitals (200 Beds)
- Taluka Hospital (50 Beds)
- Primary Health (6 Bedded)

(5) Classification based on System of medicine

- Allopathic – It refers to the practice of conventional medicine. It is broadly called as western, biomedicine, modern medicine.
- Ayurvedic – It is a system of traditional medicine native to India and practiced as an alternative medicine.
- Homeopathic – It is form of alternative medicine in which practitioners treat patients using highly diluted preparations. It works on the "Law of Similars".
- Unani – It is a form of traditional medicine widely practiced in South Asia. It is called Greek medicine.

(6) Classification based on Level of Care

- Primary Healthcare – Primary healthcare are based on practical, scientifically sound and socially acceptable methodology that are accessible to individual and families at a cost they can afford.
- Secondary Healthcare – It is the service provided by medical specialists who generally do not have first contact with patients for e.g. Cardiologist, Dermatologist.
- Tertiary Healthcare – It is specialized consultative care usually on referral from primary or secondary medical care, e.g. cancer care, neurosurgery.

(7) Classification based on Gender

- Male Hospital
- Female Hospital

Components of Hospital

Hospital is viewed as a system comprising of subsystem. It can be described as factory, hotel, medical care, social care and business organization. As we all know that system is a collection of subsystem for achievement of predefined objectives. A system is having input and which undergo certain processing and get transformed into output.

Characteristics of Hospital System

- It is open system which interact with external environment.
- A system is always limited by the boundaries.
- A system should always produce maximum output but it is not clear in hospitals.
- The system of hospital should be always dynamic.
- It is like other social system which tends to grow and elaborate in structure, functions etc.

The Dimensions of Hospital

The hospital was focused by Anand (1984) into four different areas which are as follows:

(1) ***Client Focused:*** These dimension deals with client autonomy, need, demand and requirement.

(2) ***Provider Focused***: It include the skilled and professional, staff working and include freedom of judgment, adequate compensation and maintenance of professional norms.

(3) ***Organization Focused:*** It includes cost control, quality control, ability to attract client, employee and staff.

(4) ***Collective Focused:*** It is the right allocation of resource according to need and coordination with other aggression.

Hospital is a Social System

A social system is used as a function of socio-demographic and economic variable which affect the manpower and overall system. Hospital is the most complex organization in modern society, characterized by extremely force division of labor and an exquisite talent of technical skill. The major role hospital play is multiple goal, patient care, reaching and research. It is at one time a hotel, a treatment centre, a laboratory or a university. Because the work is so specialized, staff of varied professional and technical these are problems related to authority, responsibility and coordinate. Staff relationships are distinguished by unclear patterns of authority and responsibility. The patient, both client and product of organization, enter a hospital then he encounters the situation of hospital with doctor, nurses etc. In the hospital, it is very essential to identify the patients' needs and satisfy them.

Hospital is an institution for healthcare providing patient treatment by specialized staff and equipment.

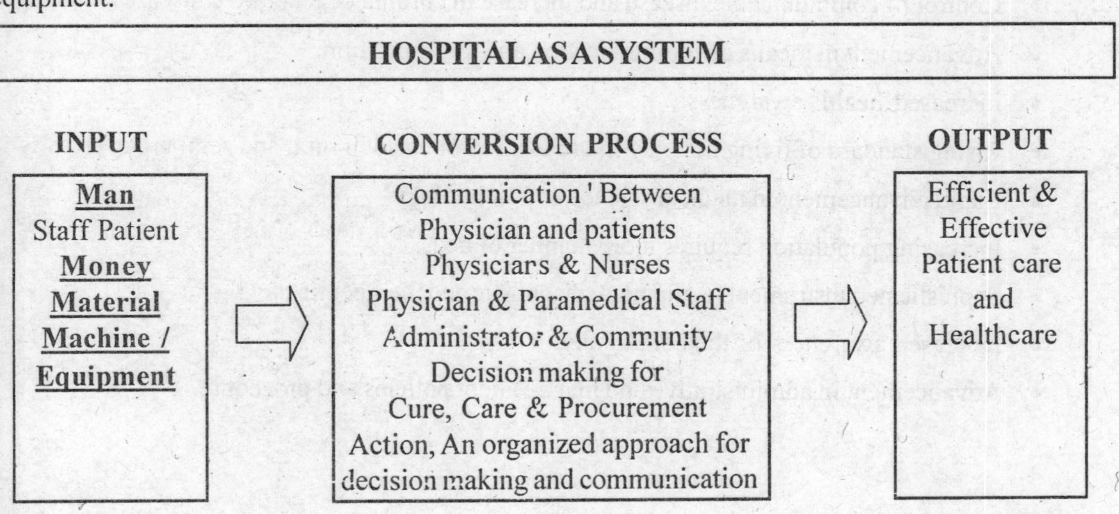

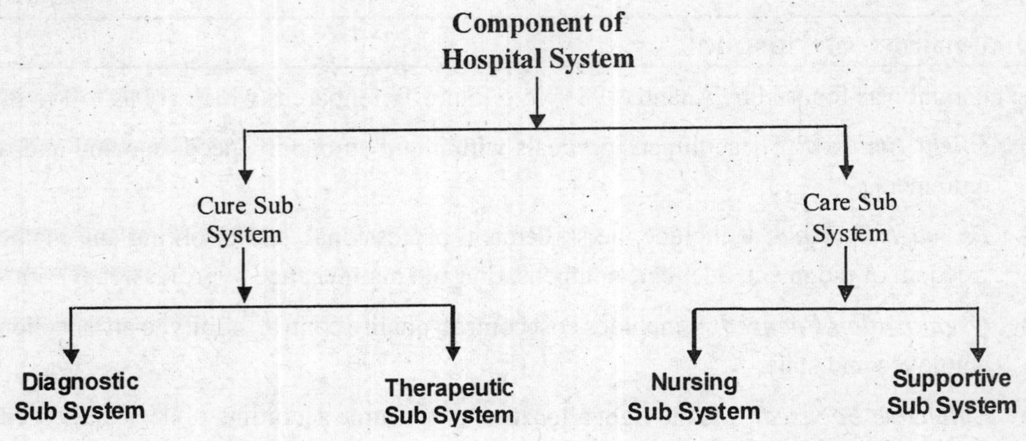

Changing Role of Hospital Administration

The hospital is an organization that mobilizes the skills of divergent group to provide a highly personalized services to individual patient. The hospital administration is concerned with general administration to meet the special need. The product is intangible and dependent on so many people individually and collectively. So it requires a high quality of management. The hospital administrator should undergo twin goal of efficiency and effectiveness. The changing role of hospital is shifted the acute illness to chronic illness. The hospitals not only deal with curative medicine but also preventive medicines. The role is focused from restorative to comprehensive medicine. It deals not only with inpatient case but also in outpatient and homecare. The changing role is related not only with individual but also with community. It deals not only with Primary Healthcare but secondary and tertiary healthcare also.

Changing role of hospital is due to factors like:

- Enhanced economic and social status of the community.
- Control of communicable disease and increase in chronic degenerative diseases.
- Advancement in means of communication and transportation.
- Increased health awareness.
- Rising standard of living not only in urban areas but also in rural and semi urban areas.
- Rapid advancement in medical science and technology.
- Increasing population requires more number of beds.
- Sophisticated instrument, equipment, diagnostic and therapeutic tools.
- Increased awareness of the community.
- Advancement in administrative and management policies and procedure.

- Health education to outpatient and inpatient.
- Establishment of counseling sessions in hospitals.
- Provide data to health planner.
- Organizing outreach programmes for the community.

The role of hospital is really challenging. It require trained and professional manpower not only nedicine but also in information technology. The hospital administrator will also develop new ls and techniques to manage their hospitals. It is not possible for hospital administrator to control coordinate until he is specialized in all the areas. Because the hospital administrator deals with nan resource planning, managing health insurance, material and equipment planning, medical ism, telemedicine, total quality management in hospital, quality circle and six sigma, legislation ealthcare mass media and management of Information Technology.

ource Utilisation and Control in Hospital

The hospital is an organization which provides medical care to the community, within the lable resources and with the satisfaction of professionals and patients and community at large. challenges faced by hospital administrator in utilization of resources are as follows:

(i) ***Division of Labour:*** The hospital is highly labour intensive organization. It comprises of many departments, staff, offices, coordination of task, duties and responsibilities. It cannot be achieved by a single person. It is the collective effort of all the member of departments whose work are interconnected and interdependent so it is complex job from the point of management.

ii) ***Highly inter-related and interconnected services:*** Each and every member working in hospital are dependent on each other for completion of task. The clinical department, diagnostic, therapeutic, support and utility department are interdependent and interconnected. The work of one department affects the working of other department.

ii) ***Hospital is a mix Autocratic and Democratic Style:*** The hospital is an organization where sometime a clear line of authority is seen and power flow in scale chain whereas at the same time participative management or working in team work is also essential for carrying out affective functions.

v) ***Highly Pubic Demand:*** Nowadays the demand of customer and patients are increasing and they expect best medical and nursing services. Because of costly equipment the price are higher and middle and low class people feel disappointed with the rise in cost of treatment.

v) ***Coordination:*** The control in hospital is exercised through coordination. The hospital comprises of subsystem. The work of each and every department is coordinated by hospital administrator. The responsibility of hospital administrator is very complex because he has to coordinate each and every part and function should be carried out efficiently and effectively.

Controlling in Hospitals

Controlling is one of the managerial functions which measure the performance of the hospital in order to ensure that objective are accomplished.

The basic purpose of control function is to ensure that the results, output is in accordance with the standard. If the deviation are more from standard then corrective action are taken:

The control process comprises of following steps:

(*i*) **Establishing Standard :** The first step in control process is to establish the standard that is criteria for performance. In hospitals, control standards are based on output and process control. In hospital length of stay, quality in patient care readmission of patient. Infection control are the dimensions on which quality can be checked and standards are compared.

(*ii*) **Measurement of Performance:** Appraisal in hospital is a very complex task because there are many activities and it is difficult to develop accurate measure. The job in hospital move away from routine pattern and standard varies from the nature of work so measurement and appraisal is difficult.

(*iii*) **Correction of Deviation:** The deviation in performance need to be corrected. A negative deviation gives wrong signal to the functioning of hospitals. They are corrected through appropriate measure:

- The entire staff and the member should be communicated about policies.
- Monitor current performance.
- Compare actual performance with the standard.
- Decide corrective action to control the plans of hospital.
- Take follow-up measure and adjust according to requirement.

Common Controlling Techniques used in the Hospitals

(*a*) **Break Even Analysis:** It is one tool useful in analyzing business decisions. In these methods, it forecast information about the volume of service and compare with break-even volume to predict profit or losses. The break even analysis requires the quantification of fixed and variable cost in order to identify the price of product and services and to determine the volume. The break even analysis provides data for:

- Profit Planning
- Policy-formulating
- Decision making

It tells the point where organization will not incur any loss nor make any profit. It analyses the relationship between revenue and expenses in such a way as to show at what volume of output, the institution would suffer a loss and at greater volume it would generate profit.

(*b*) **Internal Audit:** One most important tool used in management control is internal audit which is regular appraisal of accounting, functional and other operations of institution. Although internal auditing concentrates on accounts. The main source of income in hospitals is receipts from patients. The receipts of bills should be checked with cash book entries. The other receipt may be granted from different parties. They should be verified auditors should check payments, assets and liabilities on the balance sheet. It should be checked that they are shown at true value. Proper depreciation should be provided on the assets. Asset and liabilities should be actually physically verified by auditor on the balance sheet. It should be checked that the balance sheet and profit and loss account have been drawn according to the provision of the act.

Cost Accounting

Cost accounting system provides management with information crucial to operate more efficiently. In today's world, enhanced cost system are simple to implement. Healthcare organizations are beginning the arduous task of establishing cost accounting system that provide the information needed to make decision concerning operating performance, cost control, budgeting, prices and managed care contracting.

In a standard cost accounting system, the cost recorded are predetermined. The standard cost system requires a process of comparison between actual with standard.

In variable budgeting, the standard cost specification is a series of cost analysis for varying volume of output to develop reliable data. Once direct and indirect departmental cost are identified, statistic that describes production and correlates directly with departmental cost must be selected and used by revenue producing department.

Healthcare Communications

Healthcare communications are becoming extremely important in modern society. Since programmes in healthcare communication focus on training and communicating the importance of healthcare to the people. There are few types of communication in health and social care such as:

- Formal and informal
- Verbal and non-verbal
- One to one basis
- Group interaction
- Sign language
- Signs and symbols

Formal

Formal communication is a form in which sender and receiver communicate in a structured format.

Informal

It is the communication in family and social group.

Technological Aid

In these, laptops and phone are used to communicate with each other.

One to one basis → Just two people are involved in conversation related to healthcare issues.

Group → More than three people participating and communicating between each other.

Sign Language → It is a methodology used to deal with deaf and disabled people. In this, using of hands and gestures to communicate between each other.

Sign & Symbol

Street signs and symbols on the road help to get awareness about issue related to health.

AIDS

Acquired immune deficiency syndrome or acquired immunodeficiency syndrome is a disease of human immune system caused by the Human Immunodeficiency Virus (HIV).

The transmission can involve anal, vaginal, oral, blood transfusion, contaminated needles etc. Although treatment for AIDS and HIV can slow the course of disease but there is no vaccine or cure. Due to difficulty in treating HIV, the best means is preventing infection and promoting programme to slow down the spread of virus.

Healthcare Communications for Social Causes like AIDS Awareness, Antismoking, Anti-tobaccos

AIDS Awareness Programme

The HIV virus continues to spread, causing nearly 16,000 new infections a day in the world. During 1997 alone, that meant 5.8 million new HIV infections globally. Some 2.3 million people died of AIDS during the course of 1997. In India, the HIV/AIDS epidemic is now a decade old. Within this short period, it has emerged as one of the most serious public health problems in the country. HIV/AIDS, therefore, must be seen as a national calamity and can only be fought unitedly by forging co-ordination, and convergence in respect of HIV/AIDS prevention control strategies between civil society, voluntary and Government sectors.

The first AIDS case in India was detected in 1986. Since then HIV infection has been reported from almost all States and Union Territories of the country. But the emerging pattern of geographical distribution is not uniform. Though the dominant mode of transmission of HIV infection in the country still remains Heterosexual contact, the pattern of transmission in North Eastern States seems to be pre-dominantly through sharing of infected needles by injecting drug users.

The HIV sero surveillance report available to NACO tells, a cumulative total of 33.65 lakh persons have been screened for HIV, of which 79,574 have been found seropositive as on October 98. The HIV sero-positivity rate works out to be 23.65 (per thousand). A cumulative total of 6,609 AIDS cases have been reported in India during this period.

Realising the gravity of epidemiological situation of HIV infection prevailing in the country, the government of India launched a National AIDS Control Programme in 1987. A comprehensive Five Year Strategic Plan was launched during the 8th Plan period with the assistance from World Bank to the tune of US $84 million and another US $1.5 million in the form of technical assistance from World Health Organisation. Since AIDS has no cure, the main objective of this project is to slow down the spread ofHIV/AIDS infection through creation of awareness and aiming at behavioural change. The programme has the following components:

- Strengthening the Programme Management capacity at National and State levels;
- Surveillance & Clinical Management;
- Ensuring Blood Safety;
- Control of Sexually Transmitted Diseases;
- Public Awareness and Community support.

The Control of AIDs at three Levels

(*i*) **At the National level:** A National AIDS Committee, a National AIDS Control Board and a National AIDS Control Organisation have been created and are in operation.

(*ii*) **At the State and Union Territory level:** An AIDS Cell has been created in each State/UT. So far, 23 States have created registered societies exclusively for the implementation of this programme.

(*iii*) **Surveillance & Clinical Management:** There are 131 Blood Testing Centres and 9 Reference Centres. Surveillance system has been set up and is functioning in almost all the States.

Training of doctors is an ongoing process and Key Trainers are conducting training programme n Clinical Management including diagnosis of AIDS cases.

The overall goal of securing a safe blood supply is being tackled through 6 major strategies, amely,

(*i*) Mandatory Licensing of all Blood Banks;

(*ii*) Establishment of 154 Zonal Blood Testing Centres (ZBTCs) where HIV testing facilities are made available which could be availed of by all the blood banks linked to these ZBTCs;

(*iii*) Establishment of 40 component separation facilities for the purpose of reducing the wasteful use of blood in all 815 blood banks have been modernised in public and voluntary sectors;

(*iv*) Establishment of 40 blood component separation facilities;

(*v*) Training of the blood bank staff, and

(*vi*) Promotion of voluntary blood donation.

Public Awareness & Community Support

To reach the goal of public awareness of HIV/AIDS and to mobilise community support, efforts have been made in the areas of mass awareness, development of inter-personnel communication support material, NGO mobilisation, inter-sectoral collaboration and pilot interventions with vulnerable groups of population.

NACO has initiated a nationwide campaign using various media to spread awareness about the HIV/AIDS. This includes the use of television, radio, print media and folk theatre. An interpersonal communication programme is also being implemented through the Directorate of Field Publicity to spread awareness in the rural areas.

Funding support has been provided to the Non-Governmental Organisations to take up awareness and intervention programmes in vulnerable populations such as sex workers, truckers, intravenous drug users, street children and migrant labour.

A National Counselling Training Programme has been launched to train grassroots level counsellors. A National AIDS Helpline has been set up with a toll free number 1097 for telephonic counselling which maintains the confidentially and privacy of the caller. In School AIDS Education Programme has been started to provide life style education and information on HIV/AIDS to the student and youth.

A multi-sectoral approach has been devised by integrating an action plan of HIV/AIDS in the ongoing programmes of the social sector Ministries such as Education, Youth Affairs, Women and Child Development, Ministry of Empowerment and Social Justice, Labour, Railways and Defence.

Intensive awareness campaigns through electronic and print media and the field publicity units of the Ministry of Information & Broadcasting in both the urban and rural areas has resulted in generation of awareness about the disease both in the high risk groups and the general population. Awareness levels are of the order of 60-65 per cent on an average in urban areas land 35-40 per cent in rural areas. The highest awareness levels are in Tamil Nadu where it is 95% in urban areas and 75% in rural areas.

AIR is broadcasting a 10 minutes programme in Hindi and eleven regional languages on the Vividh Bharati channel for information and counselling on HIV/AIDS specially targetted towards rural audiences and migrant labour. The programme has an interactive component wherein the queries of listeners sent in through letters will be answered by experts.

The World AIDS Day was observed on 1st December 1998. In conjunction with the theme this year, "Youth-A Force for Change", a "Walk for Life", was held from Vijay Chowk to National Stadium. A music concert as organised at National Stadium. Senior Government Officials from the Central Ministries, leading celebrities, thousands of school children and street children from Delhi participated in both the events.

AIDS is not a health problem but a multi-faceted issue, NACO is tapping the networks available within the Government sector and private sector networks as well as resources available in associations, organisations and industrial sector.

NACO is providing direct funding and technical support to selected NGOs to establish "Best Practices" in the area of targeted interventions which would be trail blazers for the State AIDS Societies and help to expand NGO involvement in the National Programme. NACO has funded three NGOs in the last six months to set up "Best Practice" projects for street children, migrant labour and telephonic counselling for youth.

NACO has initiated an evaluation of NGOs which were provided financial assistance under the National AIDS Control Programme. The evaluation which would be carried out by independent agencies would help to measure the effectiveness and impact of the programme, provide an in-depth, integrated feedback about the programme, provide inputs for changes or modifications in the programme strategies, and possibly even in the overall approach.

NACO is targeting the youth through a combination of media campaign, education on AIDS for those attending school and those out of school and the provision of supportive services like counselling. NACO has also organised five regional workshops covering all states and Union territories for developing an action plan for the introduction of AIDS education in the school system. The workshops were held in collaboration with UNICEF, UNESCO, UNFPA under the umbrella of UN-AIDS and the Department of Education, Ministry of Human Resources Development.

Anti-Tobacco

The objective of the present study is to identify gaps in tobacco control and suggest ways of filling them. Tobacco use in terms of prevalence and product preferences are summarised. The costs and benefits of tobacco in the economy are symbolically weighed, using results of published studies.

India is home for 1/6th of global population and is second largest grower of tobacco leaf. About % of tobacco produce is consumed in the country. Tobacco is used in India in various forms. Bidis and Cigarettes, Hukka, Cheroots and other indigenous products are smoked where as tobacco leaf (with variable ingredients) and Gutka are chewed and some tobacco products are applied on teeth and gums as dentifrice. This chapter deals with tobacco controls efforts in India.

In India, policy-making and legislation are done at the levels of the States and the Union. Current tobacco control policy at Union level is in the form of Acts, Taxation, and Amend-ments tc Acts, Executive Orders, Codes of Conduct, Judicial Orders and Recommendations.

The Union Government took the first step in tobacco control legislation in 1975, after realisin to an extent the magnitude of tobacco related health problems in the country, with the promulgatio of the Cigarette Act, (Regulation of Production, Supply and Distribution), 1975. After that, tl Government of India and some State Governments, on the recommendations of the Parliamenta Committee or after some judgements of the Supreme Court/High Courts, passed some executi orders on tobacco control. Certain NGOs played a key role in following up the process of develo ment of these regulations.

Under the Cigarettes (Regulation of Production, Supply & Distribution) Act, 1975, all t manufacturers or traders in cigarettes have to display legible, prominent, colored and conspicuo "Cigarettes smoking is injurious to health," on all packets and cartons of cigarettes and cigare advertisements.

Under the Prevention of Food Adulteration Act (Amendment), 1990, chewing tobacco a pan masala need to bear the statutory warning, "Chewing of tobacco is injurious to health", a "Chewing of pan masala may be injurious to health", respectively.

The Drugs and Cosmetics Act 1940 (Amendment), 1992, bans tobacco in dental care prc ucts. The Cable Television Networks (Amendment) Act, 2000 prohibits tobacco adver-tising state-controlled electronic media and publications and on cable television.

In 1990, through an Executive Order, the Union Government prohibited smoking in all Healthc establishments, government offices, educational institutions, air-conditioned railway cars, ch cars, buses, suburban trains etc. Smoking is banned on all domestic flights in the country. In 19 use of tobacco and tobacco products within school premises by the students, teachers, parents a visitors was banned from 1995 for all CBSE schools.

In 1995, the Ministry of Health of India submitted the first draft of comprehensive tobac control legislation to the Parliament. The key issues were to:

(*i*) Prohibit advertising and promotion of all tobacco products;

(*ii*) Place restrictions on smoking in certain specified;

(*iii*) public places and

(*iv*) Make printing of nicotine and tar content on the packs a mandatory requirement.

After this, bill was withdrawn for various inadequacies, a new tobacco control bill was int duced in Parliament on 7th March, 2001 and was referred to the Standing Committee on the 1 March 2001. The Standing Committee gave its recommendations and the bill completed the p cess of going through Parliament in April, 2003. Rules and regulations are being formulated a notifications are on the way.

In 1999, the Railways Ministry banned the sale of tobacco products, smoking and gutka and pan masala advertisements on railway premises and trains. The apex courts like Supreme Court of India, Kerala High court a banned smoking in public places in 1999 and this was declared a punishable offence in November, 2001.

From the early 1990s, bidis began to be taxed, albeit at very low level. Gutka is also taxed and his tax has increased in subsequent years. Eighty-two percent of total tobacco excise revenue in ndia comes from cigarettes. The Union Government has continued to raise taxes on cigarettes in ubsequent years. The Union Government has taken some initiatives in public education. Among iem, the National Cancer Control Programme and Radio Dates, 1999, are important ones.

In India, a number of States have laws to control tobacco use and protect the rights of non-iokers. Current tobacco control policies at State level are in the form of Acts, Executive Orders d Judicial Orders.

The Goa (1999) and Delhi Prohibition of Smoking & Spitting Act, 1997, prohibits smoking or itting in places; prohibits tobacco advertising; the sale of tobacco products to minors; and prohib- the sale or distribution of tobacco products within 100 meters of educational institutions. In Goa, ditionally, this Act makes it mandatory for a "No Smoking/Spitting" board to be prominently played at all places of public work.

Smoking in public places is also banned by law in the States of Maharashtra, Andhra Pradesh, machal Pradesh, Tamil Nadu, Meghalaya, Jammu and Kashmir, Assam, Rajasthan and Sikkim.

In 2001, Tamil Nadu banned the sale, manufacture and storage of gutka, other forms of chew- ; tobacco and pan masala. Shortly thereafter, this had to be modified to permit the manufacture l storage of these products temporarily until certain issues were resolved.

Maharashtra, Kerala, Andhra Pradesh, Goa, UP, MP and Gujarat have also banned gutka. n-government organisations (NGO) and individuals have initiated some judicial interventions ough litigation. In addition, NGOs have taken interest in advocacy, initiatives for a smoke- free iety, and support for the Framework Convention on Tobacco Control (FCTC), research and motion of alternative crops, alternative uses of tobacco, community interventions and motiva- 1 for cessation. A cessation initiative by one of the private sector companies (Alkalis and Allied emicals Ltd.) is one of the most encouraging role models for cessation in India.

There have been several national and international consultations on tobacco control issues en by government and non-governmental institutions, mostly supported by the WHO. Existing 's and policies are not properly implemented. The main reasons behind this are corruption, lack political will and bureaucratic cooperation as well as high rates of tobacco use prevalence ong policy implementers and media personnel. Goa is implementing its policy better than any er States in India.

The results of the Global Youth Tobacco Survey in 15 States, till date, clearly indicate that 5% (median) (67.3% in the northeastern states) students of 13-15 years have purchased tobacco products without restrictions. About 80% of students were exposed to tobacco advertisements in various media.

Until the recent passing of the Act, 2003, there was no legal restriction on tobacco advertisements near educational institutions and sale of tobacco products to minors, except in Assam, Delhi, Goa, Sikkim and West Bengal. No data on enforcement of this legislation was available.

Some of the reasons identified by tobacco control activists for poor implementation of laws are as follows:

- People are poorly informed on tobacco issues,
- There is a lack of motivation to take up the issues,
- There is no clearly designated agency for policy implementation,
- Policies are weak,
- Selfish and shameless actions of the tobacco industries,
- There is a lack of opposition to the actions of the tobacco industry and
- A lack of follow-up action to policy implementation.

A multi-pronged approach and use of multiple sectors for true implementation is required Such an approach would include:

(*i*) Community mobilization,

(*ii*) Sustained motivation,

(*iii*) Powerful central and state-level mechanisms for implementation,

(*iv*) Comprehensive tobacco policies,

(*v*) Follow-up action and

(*vi*) Strong opposition to the actions of the tobacco industry.

The tobacco industry must be strongly opposed. Strong public opinion against evils of th tobacco industry needs to be created by informing the public of the true story of the multi-nationa and national tobacco industries killing millions of people globally and in India. The critical compo nents of opposition to tobacco industry include strong media advocacy on the Framework Conven tion on Tobacco Control, public interest litigations, moving into consumer courts for compensatio of victims and unyielding resistance to the targeting of youth by the tobacco industry.

There are many academic and Healthcare organizations involved in health research related t tobacco and other tobacco control activities but some potential institutions like Association c Health Professionals, the Association of School Personnel, the Association of Students, variou labour unions and the Association of Media Personnel need to be sensitized to be involved i tobacco control in India.

The WHO is sponsoring tobacco cessation programs in 12 centres in India, where pharma ceutical aids to tobacco cessation are being made available along with counseling and other thera pies. A special feature of this program is the inclusion of smokeless tobacco cessation (apart from smoking), which is a very new topic in tobacco control.

In the Union Government, The Ministry of Health, the Ministry of Information and Broadcasting, the Food and Drug Administration, the Ministry of the Environment, the Home Ministry, the Ministry of Labour, the Ministry of Industry and the Ministry of Excise are the concerned units of the Government of India involved in tobacco control. Under the Ministry of Health there is an active Anti-tobacco Cell. This cell has been putting lot of efforts for tobacco control. There is no such cell in any other ministry.

In state governments, there is no specific anti-tobacco cell. District Magistrates are expected to look into matters of implementation of tobacco control policies.

The strengths and weaknesses of non-government organizations (NGOs) involved in tobacco control were identified by self-reports, information from peers, documents of the World Health Organization, South-East Asian Regional Office (WHO, SEARO) on NGOs, and materials of meeting highlights. Analysis of the expertise of NGOs involved in tobacco control has been performed on the basis of their previous published and presented work.

The NGOs have expertise in advocacy, in judicial intervention, youth intervention, in community intervention, in tobacco related consumer movement, in material development for advocacy, in media advocacy, but only a few are involved at full priority to tobacco only.

The general weakness of almost all the organizations is with regard to action, whether it is legal action or mass-based action on the streets. There is poor networking amongst anti-tobacco groups and a lack of funds for anti-tobacco activities including counter-advertising.

Non-government institutions need to develop expertise in research, planning, designing and implementing of need-based interventions, fund raising and in working with all those sectors needing activation for effective tobacco control.

Mechanisms to strengthen the weaknesses of non-government institutions involved in tobacco control include increased use of collective and individual approaches by the NGOs themselves, capacity building by mutual training in their respective weak areas, outside support to NGOs by the WHO or other institutions and sensitizing of other institutions having the potential to work in tobacco control.

The strengths of government institutions in India involved in tobacco control include their power to enact laws, power of implementation, tremendous support from NGOs, the Judiciary, from the WHO and other international agencies, recommendations of expert committees and of the Parliamentary Standing Committee and their own research findings.

The weaknesses of government institutions involved in tobacco control have included a lack of political and bureaucratic will, large investments of public funds in the tobacco industry, corruption, opposition within the government, absence of a responsible nodal agency within the government, lack of coordination in actions, opposition from the tobacco industry in several agencies.

There are various gaps in current tobacco control efforts on the part of government institutions. Areas of inadequate legislation include faulty taxation policy that taxes cigarettes much more highly than other products and a lack of uniformity in rules and restrictions among the different States and Territories.

The approximately 200 million tobacco users in India consume eighty percent of Indian tobacco, spending Rs. 24,000 crore (Rs. 270,000 million) on tobacco annually. During 1950-1955, the annual per capita adult consumption of tobacco in India was around 900g, which declined to 700g by the late 1980s, small values compared to developed country standards. Per capita tobacco consumption has been increasing by about 3% per year according to industry sources. At least 30% in men and 12% of women use tobacco, according to the National Sample Survey of 1998-99 and the National Family Health Survey-2 of 1998-99. Information on prevalence of tobacco use available from house-to-house studies in six different parts of India ranged from 44% to 74% in the general population; specifically among men 60% to 80% and among women 15% to 67%. In India, tobacco is smoked, chewed and applied to gums and teeth. Less than one fifth (19%) of tobacco consumed in India is used in cigarettes, about half is smoked as bidis about a third is used in smokeless forms and the rest as other smoking products. In recent years, India has been witnessing a resurgence of smokeless tobacco consumption in industrially manufactured forms, especially amongst the young.

Tobacco is applied by millions for dental care. Although incorporation of tobacco in dental care products is prohibited, this continues. In the recent Global Youth Tobacco Surveys conducted on high school students aged 13-15 years in 12 north-eastern States, a range of 11.3% (in Sikkim) to 68% (in Bihar) regularly applied some form of tobacco, the most popular products being tobacco toothpaste and toothpowder, while several other products were also mentioned.

Data on yearly per capita consumption of bidis and cigarettes as reported in the WHO Country Profiles on Tobacco or Health, 2002 are shown in Table below:

Table 1. Annual Consumption Manufactured Cigarettes and Bidis in India, 1970-1999

Year	Cigarettes		Bidis	
	Year Annual Average Adult (15+ yrs) Per Capita Consumption	Total Consumption in Millions of Sticks	Year Annual Average Adult (15+ yrs) Per Capita Consumption	Total Consumption in Millions of Sticks
1970	190	62,908	840	284,971
1980	180	75,197	1,130	446,113
1990	101	54,867	1,220	601,911
1999	147	95,975	1,297	850,000

Tobacco and Health in India

Health researchers in India have been studying the association of tobacco with various diseases like cancers, heart disease and chronic obstructive respiratory diseases and they found that tobacco was responsible for nearly a third of cancers, over half of coronary artery disease cases and nearly a third or more of chronic obstructive lung disease cases.

Antismoking

The smoking ban are public polices, including criminal laws and health and safety regulation, which prohibit tobacco smoking in workplace and other public places.

The smoking has an effort on the people who don't smoke because of breaking they get second hand exposure which include increased risk of heart diseases, cancer, emphysema etc. The ban on indoor smoking has been introduced by many countries because of scientific evidences that tobacco smoking is injurious to smokes themselves and those inhaling second-hand smoke.

The World Health Organization considers smoke free laws to have an influence to reduce demand for tobacco by creating an environment where smoking becomes increase injury max difficult and to help shift social norms away frcm acceptance of smoking in everyday life.

Ban Based on Medical & Scientific Issue

Researcher has generated evidence that smoking causes problems including lung cancer, cardiovascular diseases, bronchitis and asthma. Scientific organizations conforming the effect of active and passive smokers. The effect of smoking is an Air quality one of the world's earliest smoking bans was a 1575 Mexican Council ban that forbade the use of tobacco in any Church in Mexico and Spanish colonies. These were many stands in tobacco control movement that is smoking is both offensive and harmful to non-smokers and that they have a risht not to be exposed to smokes waste gases and smoking is harmful to smoker's health and children and teenagers should be punished from smoking and smokes should be motivated to quit smoking. significant factors in the success of tobacco control movement is that smoking is both addictive and harmful to health which is used for creating awareness in the public mind and challenged the previous social consensus that smoking was a harmless and even beneficial habit. In particular, awareness of health risks of passive smoking shifted the debar from the right of smoker to the risks of non-smokers.

After centuries of smoking being seen as normal behaviour, and inspite of massive opposition from tobacco industry, the tobacco control movement have slowly achieved increasing success. On 1992, legislation was passed that increased the penalties of selling tobacco products to minors and the punishment was made more harsh for underage consumption of tobacco products.

The movement intended to enact a licensing bill that requires tobacco sellers obtain a license. Under the license, the tobacco business that violated the terms and conditions would be find and the money would be charged. Other states were beginning to enact limitations in smoking in public areas. This begin in late 1980s and continues today.

Advertising and the Impact of Smoking to Youth

Youth were a popular target because they were not only future consumer but also current consumer as well.

Effect on Health

Several studies revealed the effect of smoking on health and economic benefit. It was shown by lung infection, asthma, heart attack.

Effect on Tobacco Use

Smoking bans are generally acknowledged by reduce rate of smoking, work place ban reduces smoking rates and ban in public places. Restaurant smoking bans may help young people to stop becoming habitual smokers. In India, nation wise ban on smoking at the workplace and on restaurant, hotels, pubs, public transport (buses, trains and metros) airport and railway stations, educational. Institutions, cafes, theatres and other public places came into effect from 2nd October 2008. However, smoking in open area like roads, parks etc. and inside one's home and car is allowed. Smoking is also permitted in restaurants, bars and pubs having designated separate smoking areas. Anybody violating this law will be charged with a fine of Rs. 200. Advertising of tobacco products had already been prohibited nationwise by an earlier law.

In 2007, Chandigarh became the first city in India to become 'smoke-free' take cue from Chandigar's saucers, cities like Shimla also followed the smoke free Chandigarh model to became smoke free. The saucers of Chandigarh has been widely recognized and the architect of smoke free Chandigarh. Hemant Goswami was awarded global smoke free partnership award. The state of Kerala has implemented a more relaxed ban on public smoking thought it was never properly followed. However, the effect of nationwide ban is reflected in different part according to enforcement.

In order to create awareness among public, anti smoking slogan are an effective part of each and every advertising campaign. There are few slogans like Quit Smoking, it kills, stop smoking. Slogans make use of normal words and phrases that are interesting and understand to the general public.

Key Terms / Keywords

(1) Hospital Administrator : Hospital Administrator play a vital role in saving lives, without scalpel in hand. They manage hospital, outpatient clinics, drug-abuse treatment centre.

(2) **Medical Tourism:** Medical Tourism (Health Tourism) is a term covered travel agencies and the mass media to describe the rapidly growing practices of travelling across international borders to Healthcare.

(3) **Telemedicine:** Telemedicine is application of clinical medicine where medical information is transferred through interactive audiovisual media for the purpose of consulting and sometimes remote medical procedure.

(4) **Primary Healthcare:** It is essential healthcare based on practical, scientifically and acceptable method that are provided to individuals and families in the community through full participation and at a lower cost.

(5) **Organizing:** It is process of rational combination of activities of a number of people for achievement of common goals by division of labour and function and through a hierarchy of authority and responsibility.

(6) **Diagnosis:** It is the identification of the nature and cause of any disease related to healthcare.

(7) **Outpatient Services:** It is the first point of contact between the hospital and community and entry point into healthcare delivery system.

(8) **Rehabilitation:** It is the combined and coordinated use of medical, social, education and vocational measures for training the individual to the highest possible capacity.

(9) **Cost Accounting:** It is a technique used for controlling cost in hospitals.

(10) **Break-even Point:** It is interesting control device in which the relationship between revenue and expenses are calculated.

(11) **STD:** Sexually transmitted diseases like AIDS. It is a venereal disease, in an illness that has a significant probability of transmission between human by means of human sexual behaviour.

(12) **NACO (National Aids Control Organization):** It is a nation wise campaign using various media to spread awareness about HIV / AIDS.

Summary

In modern sense, the hospital is an institution for providing healthcare by specialized staff and equipment and often funded by public sector, by health organization, health insurance including direct charitable companies. There are about 17,000 hospitals in the world. The activities of hospitals are divided into two major types i.e. intramural and extramural. Intramural are confined with the walls of the hospital and extramural activities are the services provided outside the hospital. In the hospital, the effective management can be only done by an organized structure. The hospital is an organization that mobilizes the skill, efficiency and effectiveness of varied group to provide highly personalized services. The organizing of hospital involves identification of activities, grouping of similar activities, assignment of authority and responsibility to each department and lastly it deals with securing cooperation and coordination.

In hospital, control standard are essential to ensure the result and overall performance. In hospital a variety of control techniques and used like cost accounting, break-even analysis, internal audit etc. to maintain the standard of service. In healthcare communication, it deals with major diseases and the adverse effect of these diseases in health, society and community. The disease like HIV and AID affect economic growth by reducing human capital, social abuse etc. The effect of smoking and tobacco on health business, society and overall development and growth of a region.

17

THE CURRENT STATE OF PUBLIC HEALTH INFRA-STRUCTURE

The delineation of NHP-2002 would be required to be based on an objective assessment of the quality and efficiency of the existing public health machinery in the field. It would detract from the quaiity of the exercise if, while framing a new policy, it were not acknowledged that the existing public health infrastructure is far from satisfactory. For the outdoor medical facilities in existence, funding is generally insufficient; the presence of medical and para-medical personnel is often much less than that required by prescribed norms; the availability of consumables is frequently negligible; the equipment in many public hospitals is often obsolescent and unusable; and, the buildings are in a dilapidated state. In the indoor treatment facilities, again, the equipment is often obsolescent; the availability of essential drugs is minimal; the capacity of the facilities is grossly inadequate, which leads to over-crowding, and consequentially to a steep deterioration in the quality of the services. As a result of such inadequate public health facilities, it has been estimated that less than 20 percent of the population, which seek OPD services, and less than 45 percent of that which seek indoor treatment, avail of such services in public hospitals. This is despite the fact that most of these patients do not have the means to make out-of-pocket payments for private health services except at the cost of other essential expenditure for items such as basic nutrition.

Extending Public Health Services

While there is a general shortage of medical personnel in the country, this shortfall is disproportionately impacted on the less-developed and rural areas. No incentive system attempted so far, has induced private medical personnel to go to such areas; and, even in the public health sector, the effort to deploy medical personnel in such under-served areas, and has usually been a losing battle. In such a situation, the possibility needs to be examined of entrusting some limited public health functions to nurses, paramedics and other personnel from the extended health sector after imparting adequate training to them.

India has a vast reservoir of practitioners in the Indian Systems of Medicine and Homoeopathy, who have undergone formal training in their own disciplines. The possibility of using such practitioners in the implementation of State/Central Government public health programs, in order to increase the reach of basic Healthcare in the country, is addressed in the NHP-2002.

Role of Local Self-Government Institutions

Some States have adopted a policy of devolving programs and funds in the health sector through different levels of the Panchayati Raj Institutions. Generally, the experience has been an encouraging one. The adoption of such an organisational structure has enabled need-based allocation of resources and closer supervision through the elected representatives. The Policy examines the need for a wider adoption of this mode of delivery of health services, in rural as well as urban areas, in other parts of the country.

Norms for Healthcare Personnel

It is observed that the deployment of doctors and nurses, in both public and private institutions, is ad-hoc and significantly short of the requirement for minimal standards of patient care. This policy will make a specific recommendation in regard to this deficiency.

Education of Healthcare Professionals

Medical and Dental Colleges are not evenly spread across various parts of the country. Apart from the uneven geographical distribution of medical institutions, the quality of education is highly uneven and in several instances even sub-standard. It is a common perception that the syllabus is excessively theoretical, making it difficult for the fresh graduate to effectively meet even the primary Healthcare needs of the population. There is a general reluctance on the part of graduate doctors to serve in areas distant from their native place. NHP-2002 will suggest policy initiatives to rectify the resultant disparities.

Certain medical disciplines, such as molecular biology and gene-manipulation, have become relevant in the period after the formulation of the previous National Health Policy. The components of medical research in recent years have changed radically. In the foreseeable future such research will rely increasingly on the new disciplines. It is observed that the current under-graduate medical syllabus does not cover such emerging subjects. The Policy will make appropriate recommendations in respect of such deficiencies.

Also, certain specialty disciplines – Anesthesiology, Radiology and Forensic Medicine – are currently very scarce, resulting in critical deficiencies in the package of available public health ervices. This Policy will recommend some measures to alleviate such critical shortages.

Need for Specialists in 'Public Health' and 'Family Medicine'

In any developing country with inadequate availability of health services, the requirement of xpertise in the areas of 'public health' and 'family medicine' is markedly more than the expertise equired for other clinical specialties. In India, the situation is that public health expertise is nonxistent in the private health sector, and far short of requirement in the public health sector. Also, e current curriculum in the graduate / post-graduate courses is outdated and unrelated to conmporary community needs. In respect of 'family medicine', it needs to be noted that the more lented medical graduates generally seek specialization in clinical disciplines, while the remaining o into general practice. While the availability of postgraduate educational facilities is 50 percent f the total number of qualifying graduates each year, and can be considered adequate, the distriution of the disciplines in the postgraduate training facilities is overwhelmingly in favour of clinical ecializations. NHP-2002 examines the possible means for ensuring adequate availability of personnel with specialization in the 'public health' and 'family medicine' disciplines, to discharge the blic health responsibilities in the country.

ursing Personnel

The ratio of nursing personnel in the country vis-à-vis doctors/beds is very low according to ofessionally accepted norms. There is also an acute shortage of nurses trained in super-specialty sciplines for deployment in tertiary care facilities. NHP-2002 addresses these problems.

se of Generic Drugs and Vaccines

India enjoys a relatively low-cost Healthcare system because of the widespread availability of ligenously manufactured generic drugs and vaccines. There is an apprehension that globalization will lead to an increase in the costs of drugs, thereby leading to rising trends in overall health costs. This Policy recommends measures to ensure the future Health Security of the country.

Urban Health

In most urban areas, public health services are very meager. To the extent that such services exist, there is no uniform organizational structure. The urban population in the country is presently as high as 30 percent and is likely to go up to around 33 percent by 2010. The bulk of the increase is likely to take place through migration, resulting in slums without any infrastructure support. Even the meager public health services which are available do not percolate to such unplanned habitations, forcing people to avail of private Healthcare through out-of-pocket expenditure.

The rising vehicle density in large urban agglomerations has also led to an increased number of serious accidents requiring treatment in well-equipped trauma centers. NHP-2002 will address itself to the need for providing this unserved urban population a minimum standard of broad-based Healthcare facilities.

Mental Health

Mental health disorders are actually much more prevalent than is apparent on the surface. While such disorders do not contribute significantly to mortality, they have a serious bearing on the quality of life of the affected persons and their families. Sometimes, based on religious faith, mental disorders are treated as spiritual affliction. This has led to the establishment of unlicensed mental institutions as an adjunct to religious institutions where reliance is placed on faith cure. Serious conditions of mental disorder require hospitalization and treatment under trained supervision. Mental health institutions are woefully deficient in physical infrastructure and trained manpower. NHP-2002 will address itself to these deficiencies in the public health sector.

Information, Education and Communication

A substantial component of primary Healthcare consists of initiatives for disseminating to the citizenry, public health-related information. IEC initiatives are adopted not only for disseminating curative guidelines (for the TB, Malaria, Leprosy, Cataract Blindness Programs), but also as part of the effort to bring about a behavioural change to prevent HIV/AIDS and other life-style diseases. Public health programs, particularly, need high visibility at the decentralized level in order to have an impact. This task is difficult as 35 percent of our country's population is illiterate. The present IEC strategy is too fragmented, relies too heavily on the mass media and does not address the needs of this segment of the population. It is often felt that the effectiveness of IEC programs is difficult to judge; and consequently it is often asserted that accountability, in regard to the productive use of such funds, is doubtful. The Policy, while projecting an IEC strategy, will fully address the inherent problems encountered in any IEC programme designed for improving awareness and bringing about a behavioural change in the general population.

It is widely accepted that school and college students are the most impressionable targets for imparting information relating to the basic principles of preventive Healthcare. The policy will attempt to target this group to improve the general level of awareness in regard to 'health-promoting' behaviour.

Questions:

1. What is the current state of Public Health Infrastructure?
2. What is Role of Local Self-Government Initialises?
3. What is the need of specialist in 'Public Health' and 'Family Medicine'?

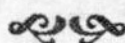

18

MEDICAL ETHICS

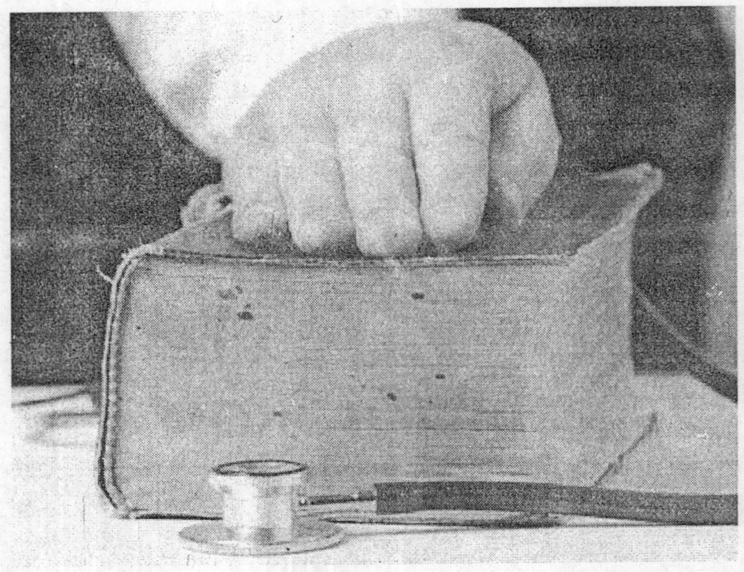

Professional medical ethics in the health sector is an area which has not received much att tion. Professional practices are perceived to be grossly commercial and the medical profession lost its elevated position as a provider of basic services to fellow human beings. In the p medical research has been conducted within the ethical guidelines notified by the Indian Counci Medical Research. The first document containing these guidelines was released in 1960 and comprehensively revised in 2001. With the rapid developments in the approach to medical search, a periodic revision will no doubt be more frequently required in future. Also, the frontier areas of research – involving gene manipulation, organ/human cloning and stem cell research _ impinge on visceral issues relating to the sanctity of human life and the moral dilemma of human intervention in the designing of life forms. Besides this, in the emerging areas of research, there is the uncharted risk of creating new life forms, which may irreversibly damage the environment as it exists today. NHP – 2002 recognizes that this moral and religious dilemma, which was not relevant even two years ago, now pervades mainstream health sector issues.

Enforcement of Quality Standards for Food and Drugs

There is an increasing expectation and need of the citizenry for efficient enforcement of reasonable quality standards for food and drugs. Recognizing this, the Policy will make an appropriate policy recommendation on this issue.

Regulation of Standards in Para Medical Disciplines

It has been observed that a large number of training institutions have mushroomed, particularly in the private sector, for Para medical personnel with various skills – Lab Technicians, Radio Diagnosis Technicians, Physiotherapists, etc. Currently, there is no regulation/monitoring, either of the curricula of these institutions, or of the performance of the practitioners in these disciplines. This Policy will make recommendations to ensure the standardization of such training and the monitoring of actual performance.

Environmental and Occupational Health

The ambient environmental conditions are a significant determinant of the health risks to which a community is exposed. Unsafe drinking water, unhygienic sanitation and air pollution significantly contribute to the burden of disease, particularly in urban settings. The initiatives in respect of these environmental factors are conventionally undertaken by the participants, whether private or public, in the other development sectors. In this backdrop, the Policy initiatives, and the efficient implementation of the linked programs in the health sector, would succeed only to the extent that they are complemented by appropriate policies and programs in the other environment-related sectors.

Work conditions in several sectors of employment in the country are sub-standard. As a result, workers engaged in such employment become particularly vulnerable to occupation-linked ailments. The long-term risk of chronic morbidity is particularly marked in the case of child labour. NHP-2002 will address the risk faced by this particularly vulnerable section of society.

Providing Medical Facilities to Users From Overseas

The secondary and tertiary facilities available in the country are of good quality and cost-effective compared to international medical facilities. This is true not only of facilities in the allopathic disciplines, but also of those belonging to the alternative systems of medicine, particularly

Ayurveda. The Policy will assess the possibilities of encouraging the development of paid treatment-packages for patients from overseas.

Questions:

What is the growing importance of Medical Ethics in healthcare industry?

Short Note:

Environmental & Occupational Health.

CASE STUDIES

ase 1: India's Demographics

India's favorable demographics are often touted as one of the major reasons behind the ›untry's growth. Millions of educated Indians under the age of 30 act as the pistons firing in a ulti-cylinder economic system, which continues to expand at enviable rates despite the global cession. There's no doubt that this confers upon India an enormous demographic advantage, an ›per-hand that will continue to fuel growth for decades to come.

What happens, however, to the Indian economy when the country's dependency ratio tilts gher as today's youth begin to retire? The Indian workforce is on pace to transform into an ıormous healthcare burden for the country as workers age, live longer and demand more medical rvices, as well as pensions and other correlated elements of social security. India will have no ıoice but to spend more of its GDP on healthcare. India's soaring birth rates will expound this lemma. By 2050, the United Nations expects India to boast the world's largest population. While dia cannot impose draconian rules such as its neighbor's "One Child" policy, the sheer scale of ese numbers places tremendous pressure on the country's ability to succeed in innovation in edical science and delivery models to help India avoid the burdens of healthcare costs that some untries, such as the United States, carry today.

The Planning Commission in India is well aware of this future problem. For years, innovators the life sciences have been racing to find novel ways to reduce costs and expand care in the pe of capitalizing on the economies of scale Indian consumers provide, such as the expansion of gital health records, the promotion of medical tourism, a focus on biostatistics for outcomes search, a drug patent system that protects generics for widespread distribution and inducing mpetition for cheaper medical devices. This rush of activity has produced so many new techques that India is beginning to export its expertise in these areas to other countries. Add to this ıt the Indian government will continue to liberalize the industry, doll out tax breaks, and encoure more private competition, and the recipe may be rotfust enough to put the country on a sustainle path to meet its future healthcare needs.

Question: Suggest some long term approaches to cater to the above problem.

ıse 2: Planning, Monitoring and Evaluation of Health Services

Over the years, planning monitoring and evaluation of health services and programmes have en hampered by dearth of reliable data. Availability of accurate, reliable, timely and relevant health information is the most fundamental step towards informed public health action. The essence of National Health Management Information System (NHMIS) is that it is designed to improve the health of the population. Much of the data will relate to medical and other biomedical, operation of health services for both private and public and also to other health related events and programmes. NHMIS should be able to provide reliable, relevant and timely information to health system's policy makers, managers, professionals, and to the other sectors for effective decision making, planning, monitoring and evaluation.

In 1988, the Federal Government adopted the first comprehensive National Health Policy which calls for among other things the establishment of a National Health Information System by all governments of the Federation to be used as a management tool for the health sector. Nigerian NHMIS support to PHC system is largely underdeveloped. There are serious limitations in the value of the health information that 'data led' national health information system could provide particularly regarding its availability and usefulness for the decision-making processes at local level. A lot of health events at the community level remain poorly recorded or collected as data Data from health facilities is often inadequate, incomplete, untimely and very little of the events are captured as generated data.

For effective NHMIS, the lower levels (Bottom) need to be well established and equipped to provide adequate health information on PHC components and services. Data and Information generated at the lower level if processed appropriately with completeness and timeliness will provide a basis for informed decisions at the top. There can't be any meaningful information at the top if data is not gathered properly from the bottom.

Question: How can you establish standards and procedures for analyzing and collectin health data?

Case 3: Healthcare Reforms

Healthcare reform was at the centre of the electoral debates in the United States. It is a liv issue in most developed countries. Europe is looking at new healthcare models.

Japan is opening up to generics. Yet India - where healthcare is still an out-of-pocket (OOI expense for the vast majority of citizens - is not part of the debate.

Should we be looking at free healthcare for all or affordable healthcare? Should we be contro ling the price of drugs or offering direct subsidy?

Is public-private partnership the way forward? The Indian healthcare system currently con bines the worst features of the public and private models - the public health system is in a po state and private care is unregulated and high cost.

1. No bureaucratic accountability leading to widespread corruption from top to bottom e
2. Lack of Political will

3. Lack of direction
4. Bewilderment at the grassroot level
5. Promotion and flourishing of Industrial houses sans ethics.

Thinking healthcare just from providing cure point of view can increase the expense on all accounts, instead to improve overall health of the country we need a comprehensive program which cover all aspect of health of a person. It involves:

- Clean drinking water
- Clean food
- Easy access to primary healthcare (Preferably free)
- Affordable access to high end medical treatments

Question: How will you achieve the above stated objectives? State some long term objectives.

Case 4:

While watching an intense debate on a TV channel today morning, over the repercussions of recent withdrawals of cash-less hospitalization benefits by most of the major Indian Insurance companies, a thought suddenly came to my mind: Do we need a OBAMA like leader, here, for streamlining "India's Healthcare System," which, no doubt, is, less fortunate than, even an orphan.

I'm sure, most of my Indian readers must have experienced, once at least, how painful it is, to get an appropriate cost-effective treatment in any private hospital these days.

Now read the verdict of Delhi High Court on one such incident,

The bills in respect of 22 employees (post at IGIA) and their family members listed in Annexure-2 have also been examined and it was found that bills are inflated and/or excess charged and the amount had been deducted from almost every bill. The details of which are given in Annexure-3.

It is seen from the name and designation of the patients that almost all of them are belonging to Class-IV (Group 'D') employees like Safaiwala, Belder etc., who are generally not much educated. The hospital took advantage of their lower educational level of the employees and had admitted them even for minor ailments and also raised the inflated bills which resulted in deduction as brought out in the foregoing paras.

It is also clear from Annexure-1 & 3 that approx.10-12% billing amounts are either inflated and/or charged in excess which clearly establishes that M/s. Sunil Nursing Home had been indulging in unfair practices.

Recently, my brother, suffering from high fever, went to a reputed hospital and in no time he was ill-advised for immediate admission terrifying him of the consequences if he decides against it.

He refused and consulted another doctor; this time not a consultant operating from private clinics but from residence. Trust me, it took him a few days to completely recover staying at home, and the treatment cost was less than a tenth of the estimated expenditure that the other doctor indicated.

For various reasons: High mortality rate, technological advancement etc, medical profession has recently undergone a major transformation in terms of corporatization; however, why in India, still, there's no effective regulatory system in place that can successfully eradicate so called healthcare malpractices.

DNA in April carried a story on how hospitals make money on syringes this way, drawing as much as Rs. 24,000 from 100 patients (assuming each used 24 syringes at an MRP of Rs. 12 each, which the hospital bought at Rs. 2 each). Now DNA has a copy of an agreement between a leading corporate chain running over 40 hospitals in the country and a manufacturer, proving the practice.

I think, we must learn a few lessons from the US in this respect and immediately treate a result-oriented infrastructure to regulate Indian healthcare system.

Question: Do you too thing in the similar way? IF so, what would you like to propose?

Case 5: Roadside Doctors are a thriving business in India

I had to read this one twice when I looked at the numbers quoted, there are twice as many "quack doctors" as qualified doctors in the country. It is against the law to practice medicine without a license but enforcement efforts or small or don't exist. They also pay "bribe" money to be left alone and if the heat rises, they move to another location.

The Street Doctors state they use traditional methods of healing and help the poor who cannot afford private healthcare. We have problems in the US but we don't see doctors on the street with a small outdoor office and practice. The doctors use many herbs to help consult and "cure" in their words problems as major as paralysis. Again, the numbers of Street Doctors when I read this article is mind boggling compared to licensed physicians

Sitting on an iron bench along a busy street, Chaman Lai sticks his fingers into a mug full of a greasy concoction and then applies the dark-red brew to areas where his patients complain of pain.

Lai - who does not have a license to practice medicine, but claims to be a successful bone doctor and traditional healer — says thir potion of 18 herbs is a cure-all. His large signboard, placed along the roadside, claims he can even treat paralysis.

Part of India's massive informal economy, these street-side medicine men and women are called quacks by the medical association here - but they say they are traditional healers. They cater to a huge market of poor people who cannot afford costly private Healthcare. The number of such practitioners is unknown.

"There's no firm estimate, but I can say that for every 100,000 qualified doctors in our country, there are 200,000 quacks," said Ashok Adhao, president of the Indian Medical Association. "The practice is condemnable."

"We do face problems when police and municipal officers come. But we manage it by paying bribes" said Shiv Kumar, a caretaker of a sexual disorder-treatment clinic.

Rajiv Singh, a clinic owner lying on a cot outside and under a bridge of New Delhi's prestigious Metro rail, said if his business starts to fall off, he will simply break camp and look for another location with potential new clients. Here, such a move is not a big deal.

He also said the work he and others like him are doing is effective.

Question: Comment on Health Education in India. What steps do you suggest?

Case 6: MassGen Hospital to enter India

This is a sign of the times ahead. As the purchasing power of the Indian middle class improves and insurance penetration increases, we will see more US based healthcare players look at India as a destination for expansion.

For these players the revenues from operations in India may not a huge impact on the top line in dollar terms. However, this could be seen as a medical tourism play and/or a pilot project to test out the Indian market. Though several US based payers have started to push medical tourism packages in India, the perception of quality has been an obstacle to adoption of India as a healthcare destination by employee unions, thus slowing the momentum. Mass Gen may be able to break those perception barriers and channel patients to its Indian venture. The other possibility is for MassGen to recruit high value patients for its centers in the US.

For the Indian healthcare industry, this could be turn to be an inflection point. Indian healthcare providers deliver some of the best quality care in the region. However, there is potential to adopt better management practices and technology in the hospitals.

The arrival of competition would definitely change the healthcare delivery model in India. Question: How do you think competition will change the face of India Healthcare Industry?

Case 7: An archaic Indian Healthcare System

Aruna Viswanatha describes India's Healthcare system as "an anarchic hodgepodge, with little insurance, little regulation and a range of services offered by hundreds of government-run, trust-run and corporate hospitals." It is by no means a purely free-market approach, but it's much more market-oriented than the American model.

Almost 25,000 doctors graduate from India's medical schools every year. Because there is so much competition, doctors and hospitals are forced to keep their prices low to get patients. Residents, who go to medical school straight from high school, only make the equivalent of a few hundred dollars a month. An average surgeon's salary would be around $8,000 per month. The take-home pay to fix a hip fracture, for example, might run between $100 to $300, out of the $1,000 fee to the patient, says orthopedic surgeon M.S. Phaneesha. At his hospital in Bangalore, he says, there are 20 orthopedic surgeons alone on staff. For 1,600 beds, the hospitals employs around 700 doctors full-time; 300 of them are surgeons. In the U.S., by comparison, a first-year resident might take home around $2,500 each month, and the average surgeon more than $20,000 per month. A hip fracture would cost a patient around $30,000, of which the surgeon's charge is $5,000. Even general practitioners in America earn on average more than $100,000 a year. Another factor in India's costs is the tiered system of beds that most hospitals employ. One night in a general ward at the private Artemis Health Institute in a New Delhi suburb, for example, costs around $20 per night. One night in a single room, or a deluxe, or a suite, though, will cost you between $100 to $200. Services are similarly tiered. A general ward patient at Artemis would only pay $2 for an X-ray, while single-room patients would pay more. There are so many hospitals, says Artemis' chief operating officer Jose Verghese, that rates at the lower end stay low. In addition, health insurance is uncommon in India, so patients typically pay out of their own pockets for routine care. That too plays a role in keeping costs low.

Instead, Viswanatha notes some similarities between the two nations' systems, then concludes that "it is remarkable that the healthcare system of the world's most powerful country has anything at all in common with the healthcare system of an emerging industrial nation, and so little in common with the systems of the other Western democracies." Apparently, in the mainstream Healthcare debate, the only models you're allowed to cite are countries that are relatively rich and white. Aside from some socialists smitten with Cuba, hardly anyone wants to look to the Third World. That's a mistake. The Indian system is far from perfect, and Viswanatha lists several problems with it. But from an American perspective, her two chief objections to the Indian approach shouldn't be deal killers.

At any rate, learning from a country doesn't mean copying it wholesale. It means adapting the things it's doing right to a different social context - by, say, reducing our reliance on insurance and eliminating our artificial restrictions on the supply of medical providers. There's an unstated assumption that the institutions that have grown up around the American and European medical systems are a *cause* of our higher standard of living. But what if they're a *product* of that wealth: vast bureaucracies that no nation needs but only the richest can afford? India is already a destination for medical tourists seeking more affordable care. If we could combine our wealth with Bangalore-style competition, they wouldn't need to travel: Prices would come down and doctors would be much more responsive to consumer demand, this time in a country where far more people can afford to participate in the medical marketplace.

Question: What is the difference between Indian model and American Model of Healthcare?

Case 8: India does not need Health Insurance

In the September 8th edition of the "mint", Mr. Gulzaar Natarajan made a case for starting a national healthcare scheme in India. While 85% of India's population is without any form of healthcare, and there is dire need for an affordable means to pay for healthcare, a national healthcare scheme is not the answer.

The Government already has several schemes to meet the healthcare needs of the poor, the most recent of which is RSBY (Rashtriya Swasthya Bima Yojana) which provides Rs 30,000 annually for hospitalization expenses for over 700 conditions. The cost to the beneficiary is a one-time fee of Rs 30. The Government must continue to provide this scheme for those living below the poverty line (BPL), and perhaps expand it to those 200% to 300% of the poverty line. But it does not need to provide this "free" health insurance for all Indians.

There is a large and expanding middle-class in India, which can well afford an annual premium for healthcare insurance. This segment of the population does not need the government's help to pay for their healthcare expenses. In fact, if the government were to pay for their healthcare, the middle-class will likely not have the incentive to remain healthy. If they are paying for their own care they are more likely to make lifestyle changes that keep them healthy and decrease the onset of sickness e.g. maintain their weight, watch their diet, exercise regularly, give up smoking.

There is a paucity of data for the purpose of building a risk profile, but one does not need a national health insurance scheme to build such a database. It can be done as more people buy health insurance, including private and RSBY, and as insurers start utilizing informatics to mine claims data.

Competition will reduce the cost of healthcare, not a national health insurance scheme.

Question: What is your point of view on requirement of Healthcare Insurance in India?

Case 9: Why is India not an International Healthcare Destination?

There are a lot of hospitals in India that provide better outcomes than what is provided in developed countries. But in general there is a lot that can be done to improve management practices in Indian healthcare sector.

There are a few projects underway, where healthcare groups from US and Europe are establishing presence in India. However, in general international providers are reluctant to set shop in India due to various reasons

US providers:

1. Many have a local and regional focus, not even expanding within US.
2. Profit in dollar terms would be miniscule, unless they build scale.

3. Healthcare projects have long gestation periods; medium term geopolitical risks could upset plans.
4. Availability of staff in the paramedical area.
5. Business models and marketing in India are vastly different from US.
6. Hyper competitive due to the presence of a lot of quality providers in India.
7. Many hospitals in US are barely getting by, profit margins are razor thin.
8. Potential for PE investments other co investment models leveraging existing infrastructure/business models.

Europe:

1. Since Europe in general has a public health system, the number of expert players in private sector is lesser compared to the US.

Many of the India centric issues listed above apply.

We may still see a couple make inroads in India, but would face intense competition from established Indian players.

If the financial system in Europe worsens, and senior patients struggle to find affordable public Healthcare, we may see investments in medical tourism projects in India coming from Europe. However, the first choice for such investments would be in Eastern Europe.

Middle East: Not many established healthcare brands in the Middle East.

However, we may see lot more co-investment in healthcare sector in India coming from the Middle East.

Question: What improvements do you suggest in the Indian Healthcare Model?

Case 10:

The healthcare industry in India has come a long way from the days when those who could afford it had to travel abroad to get highly specialized services such as cardiac surgery, while others had to do without it.

Today, patients from neighboring countries in Asia are coming to India to receive specialized medical treatment. Not only is India meeting international standards, but at prices that compare very favorably with developed countries.

The report takes a look at the healthcare industry in India; how it has evolved, the innovations that have taken place in the industry, the emerging trends and the opportunities for the future.

Through a few significant players in the industry, the report examines the competencies that India has developed in healthcare. It explores how these healthcare providers are endeavoring to provide services to India's vast and widely spread population, through innovative methods.

In 2003, a CM and Mckinsey study projected that India's healthcare market could touch Rs.3,200 million by 2012 from the existing Rs.1,030 million. It also predicted that India had a great future as a major destination for medical tourism.

India is already a preferred healthcare destination for neighboring countries due to the low cost and high quality treatment available here.

With the arrival of telemedicine in 1999, several large healthcare facilities in India have been linked up with healthcare facilities in the neighboring countries and the rest of Asia. Tele-medicine has enabled international patients to obtain specialized care in from India.

In the recent past, there have been several innovations in the healthcare services industry in India, giving patients a new experience of healthcare. The Amrita Institute of Medical Sciences' fully digital, computerized and networked facility enabled it to offer tele-medicine services such as tele-consultation, fetal tele-medicine and tele-surgery.

Aravind Eye hospitals' Internet kiosks in remote rural areas enabled poor villagers to consult top eye physicians online. Apollo Hospitals covered the entire gamut of healthcare services, from primary, secondary and tertiary care to diagnostic services and pharmacies.

The innovations in products and services have made its hospitals a one stop location for people's healthcare needs.

The hub and spoke model was another innovation in the diagnostic centers and pathology laboratories segment. All these innovations have given patients better service.

Some analysts feel that the hub and spoke model will be increasingly popular, not only for diagnostic tests, but for specialized tertiary healthcare too, in the near future. At present, small towns have limited health services. The presence of 'spokes' will improve accessibility to standard healthcare in small towns..

Questions:

- Understand the emerging trends in the healthcare industry.
- Understand the innovations that are happening in the industry.
- Understand the competencies developed by certain healthcare providers.
- Understand the growth opportunities the industry has created.

REFERENCES

1. Pandeya, Radhieka. "Outside the Sick Bay," Business Standard, June 28, 2007
2. CRIS INFAC
3. CRISIL
4. Finance Wire, July,2009 http://www.cdc.gov/ncidod/dvbid
5. http://www.pharmabiz.com/a rticle/detnews?articleid=46
6. http://www.ciionline.org/news_new/news01_ll_2006
7. http://www.bionet.com/2007/04/02/stories
8. Diderichsen, F., Evans, T. Whitehead, M. *The Social Basis of Disparities in Health.* From *Challenging inequities in health: From Ethics to action.* Edited by Evans, T., Whitehead, M., Diderichsen, F. Bhuiya, A., Wirth, M. Oxford University Press. New York, 2001.
9. Gartoula, R. P. (Ph.D). *Interview on social aspects of health and Healthcare in Nepal.* 6 January 2003, Kathmandu, Nepal Institute of Medicine, Department of Community Medicine and Family Health, Tribhuvan University, Kathmandu. 2003.
10. Ghimire, LP. (National Programme Manager). *Interview on gender, caste and health issues on 6 January 2003.* UNDP, Mainstreaming Gender Equity Programme, Kathmandu. Nepal 2003.
11. Gurung, Y. B. *Indigenous Peoples Plan for Rural Water Supply and Sanitation (RWSS-II).* Report submitted to The World Bank. SAMANATA, Institute for Social and Gender Equality. Kathmandu. 2002.
12. Limbu, B.M. (Secretary General - NEFEN). *Interview on gender, caste and health issues on 6 January 2003.* Nepal Federation of Nationalities (NEFEN). Kathmandu. Nepal 2003.
13. UNDP. *Nepal Human Development Report 2001 - Poverty Reduction and Governance.* Pulchowk, Kathmandu, Nepal. 2002
14. Brundtland, G. H. Director General (WHO). Speech to the International Consultation on the Health of Indigenous Peoples, 23rd November 1999. http://www.who.int/directorgeneral/speeches/1999/english/19991123_indegenous_people.html

15. World Fact Book (CIA), Nepal: http://www.cia.gov/cia/publications/factbook/geos/np.html • Nepal Federation of Nationalities (NEFEN): http://www.nefen.org The World Bank Group Recent Reports- Data and Publications (Nepal):

16. http://wblnl018.worldbank.org/sar/sa.nsf/d722d09e93ee6888852567d7005d7b35/848ab7bbb5699991 8525694600699ff9?OpenDocument

17. Akande T.M. Information Support for Primary Healthcare Issues in Health Planning & Management in Nigeria. 1996:1(1): 85-97.

18. Akande T.M., Monehin J. Health Management Information System in Private Clinics in Norm, Nigeria. Nigerian Medical Practitioner 2004; 46 (5): 103 - 107.

19. HERFON. Nigeria Health Review 2006. Health Reform Foundation of Nigeria

20. HERFON. Nigerian Health Review 2007. Primary Healthcare in Nigeria: 30 Years after Alma Ata.

21. FMOH (2004). National Health Management Information System Strategic Document.

22. FMOH (2004). Revised National Health Policy

23. FMOH. Health Information Management, Collaborating Centres Programme for Education and Training in Health Planning and Management. Student's Manual. FMOH Department of Planning, Research & Statistics.

24. FMOH (2006). National Policy on Integrated Disease Surveillance and Response (IDSR). Federal Ministry of Health, Abuja

25. NPHCDA. (2004) PHC Profile: Technical Report on PHCMIS Service Statistics. National Primary Healthcare Development Agency, Abuja, Nigeria.

26. NPHCDA (2006). Introduction to Ward Health System. Briefing Package for Sensitization on the Ward Health System.

27. Oyemakinde A. Update on NHMIS. Bulletin of Epidemiology 2007; 8(2): 7-10

28. WHO. Informatics and Telematics for Health. Present and Potential Uses. World Health Organization, Geneva.

29. WHO (2002). Report on Strengthening National Health Information Systems: Workshop on the use of Geographical Information System HealthMap *Harare, Zimbabwe, 1-4 July 2002*

30. *French foreign trade Secretary Meeting minutes' on GA TS meeting 17 November 2000 (translated)*

31. *Eg "How the World Trade Organization's new "services "negotiations threaten democracy" by Scon Sinclair*

32. *Canadian Centre for Policy Alternatives; 2000*

33. *Rewriting the regulations: how the World Trade Organisation could accelerate privatisation in health-care systems Allyson M Pollock, David Price Lancet 2000: 356: 1995-2000*

34. *"The WTO and the General Agreement on Trade in Services: What is at stake for public health" Public Services International and Education International (PSl & EI) July 2000*

35. *World Development Movement Report (WDM) "In whose service? The threat posed by the General Agreement on Trade in Services to economic development in the South "by Ellen Gould and Clare Joy December 2000 http://www. wdm. org, uki'cam briefs/WTO/1nwhoseservice. htm ' PSl & EI, p. 14 and annexe*

36. *Sinclair, section 2*

37. *Pollock and Price, Lancet 2000; 356: 1995*

38. *European Services Network "ESN POSITION PAPER ON GATS 2000 AND PUBLIC PROCUREMENT Final*

39. *Version - April 23, 1999*

40. *PSl & El, p. 15*

41. *ICFTU, Brussels, 8/6/00*

42. *OR BANKENSTEIN'S MONSTERS: THE WORLD BANK, THE IMF AND THE ALIENS WHO A IE ECUADOR by-Gregory Palast The Observer, London Sunday, 8 October 2000 [1] Source: Sarah Gnttsky, Globalization Challenge Initiative*

43. See PSIRU papers on "Independent Power Producers: A review of the issues" and "Privatisation of water and energy in Africa", both available at www.psiru.org/reports

44. *The source of the material in Annexe B is the World Bank's website www, worldbunk. org The various tables and reports are generated in response to queries submitted by scripts. ' World Bank Project ID PO58627 ' World Bank Project ID P049545' World Bank Project ID P055157*

45. *Document of The World Bank Report No. 20339 BUL PROJECT APPRAISAL DOCUMENT ON A PROPOSED LOAN IN THE AMOUNT OF US$63.3 MILLION TO THE REPUBLIC OF BULGARIA FOR A HEALTH SECTOR REFORM PROJECT May 30, 2000*

46. *Peter Woicke Annual Luncheon Speech 25 September 1999 "A New Direction"*

47. *http://www. ifc. org/ifc/pressroom/speeches/amlunch/amlunch. html*

48. *IFC INVESTS TO BOOST RUSSIAN HEALTHCARE SYSTEM" IFC Press Re/ease No. 01/36 Jan 2001*

49. *"IFC INVESTS IN HOSPITAL NETWORK IN THE DOMINICAN REPUBLIC" IFC Press Release 102, April 7, 2000*

50. *"IFC MAKES FIRST HEALTHCARE INVESTMENT IN BRAZIL "IFC Press release 99/124 March 19, 1999 ' IFC INVESTS IN HEALTHCARE AND MANUFACTURING IN NIGERIA" IFC Press release 00/25 Sept 9 1999*

'http://www.ifc. org/ifc/ABN/cic/nigeria/english'invest. htm#radmed

51. *"IFC TO INVEST USS8 MILLION IN MODERN MULTI-SPECIALITY PRIVATE HOSPITAL IN CALCUTTA INDIA "IFC Press Release No. 98/50 November 20, 1997 ' Hoovers profile ofDVI/nc. www, hoovers.com*

52. *"MIGA Insures Ground-breaking Healthcare Project in Brazil" MIGA Press release August (>. 1999 ' MIGA: "Latin Report: Public-Private Insurance" September 2000 ' www, who.org*

53. *See www, oecd. org- www, oecd. org/els/heallh*

54. *See www, encharter. org, www, encharter. org/English/Secretariat/index. html The website is recent. Learning form the lesson of the MAI, the Energy Charter Treaty was never available on the internet until it came into force in 1998.*

55. *Legal Opinion Appleton Associates 10/4/2000 "NAFTA Investment Chapter Implications of Alberta Bill-11*

56. *The existing procurement directives are currently being consolidated. The proposed new directive pnmsionsare published in "Proposal for a DIRECTIVE OF THE EL ROPE A N PA RI.1AML.NT AND OF THE COUNCIL on t in:coordination of procedures for the award of public supply contracts, public service contracts and public works contracts' Brussels, 30.8.2000 COMCOOO) 2"5final/2 2000/0115 (COD)*

57. *Restructuring and privatization of Healthcare services: Selected cases in the Americas by Sandra Polasyk. ILO*

58. *Action Programme on Privatization, Restructuring and Economic Democracy. November 1999*

59. *Restructuring and privatization of Healthcare services: Selected cases in western Europe by Stephen Bach. ILO*

60. *Action Programme on Privatization, Restructuring and Economic Democracy. November 1999*

61. *"Privatisation, the State and Healthcare Reforms: Global Influences & Local Contingencies in Malaysia" by*

62. *Chan Chee Khoon, Citizens' Health Initiative. Paper presented to 9th International Congress of the World*

63. *Federation of Public Health Associations Beijing, People's Republic of China September 2-6, 2000*

64. *http://prn. usm. mv/chi. html*

65. *flow the United States Exports Managed Care to Third-World Countries. By Howard Waitzkin and Celia Irian. Monthly Review May I, 2000*

66. *"AIHS Country workshop report" Modern Healthcare International J7/7/2000 ' "AIHS Country workshop report" Modern Healthcare International 17/7/2000*

67. *"AIMS Country workshop report" Modern Healthcare International 17/7/2000 www.modernhealthcare.com*

68. *See Buse &. Walt Bulletin of the World Health Organization, 2000, 78 (4)*

69. *See www, aihs. com/summit/sum mi tabout. html for information on speakers and agenda.*

70. *"A Spanish revolution; With surging economy, private sector plays vital role in healthcare system" FT 13/11/2000 ' ISS Half-yearly results August 2000*

71. *THE HINDU December 18, 2000: MCD move on hospitals to hit poor*

72. *Modern Healthcare International 13/11/2000 "Clash in Canada: Privatization legislation and NAFTA open healthcare market to protests"*

73. *For a review of the extent of these Global PPPs see "Global public-private partnerships: parts I and II- a new development in health?" K. Buse &G. Walt Bulletin of the World Health Organization, 2000, 78 (4)*

74. *Matthew Brault, "Americans with Disabilities: 2005,"* Current Population Reports* *(Washington, DC: U.S. Census*

75. *Bureau, 2008), p. 3.*

76. *Ibid, p. 5.*

77. *C. Boull, M. Allmann, D. Gilbertson, C. Yu, and R. L. Kane, "Decreasing Disability in the 21st (entury: The Future Effect of Controlling Six Fatal and Nonfatal Conditions, "*American Journal of Public Health *86, no. 10 (1996), pp. 1388-1393.*

78. *J. Waldrop and S. M. Stern,* Disability Status: 2000—Census 2000 Brief *(Washington DC: U.S. Bureau of the Census), p. 2.*

79. *Centers for Disease Control and Prevention, "Public Health and Aging: Projected Prevalence of Self-Reported Arthritis or Chronic Joint Symptoms Among Persons Aged > 65 Years—United States, 2005-2030,"* Morbidity and Mortality Weekly Report *52, no. 21 (2003), p. 489.*

80. *L.I. lezzoni and V. A. Freedman, "Turning the Disability Tide: the Importance*

Definitions," Journal of the American Medical Association 299(3), *(2008), pp. 332-334.*

81. *Kaiser Family Foundation, "Healthcare for Americans with Disabilities." <www.kff.org/medicaid/7202.cfm> (accessed April 19, 2008).*

82. *National Rehabilitation Hospital Center for Health and Disability, "Improved Healthcare Access May Help Prevent Secondary Conditions Among People with Disabilities,"* National Rehabilitation Hospital Research Update. *(2002), p. 3.*

83. *M.T. Neri and T. Kroll, "Understanding the Consequences of Access Barriers to Healthcare: Experiences of Adults with Disabilities,"* Disability and Rehabilitation, *25, no. 2 (2003), pp. 85-96.*

84. *Included are eight agencies within the Department of Health and Human Services (HHS), the lead Federal agency for Healthcare, health research, professional training, and health promotion and disease prevention. These are the Administration for Children and Families (ACF), the Administration on Aging (AoA), the Agency for Healthcare Research and Quality (AHRQ), the Centers for Disease Control and Prevention (CDC), the Centers for Medicare & Medicaid Services (CMS), the Health Resources and Services Administration (HRSA), the National Institutes of Health (NIH), and the Substance Abuse and Mental Health Services Administration (SAMHSA). NCD also reviewed the 33 institutes and centers that comprise NIH, and examined the activities of the Office of the Surgeon General and the Office on Disability, which reside within the Office of the Secretary of HHS. NCD reviewed the activities of the National Institute on Disability and Rehabilitation Research (NIDRR), an agency of the Department of Education, as well as the non-Federal Institute of Medicine of the National Academies of Science, whose mission is to serve as adviser to the nation to improve health.*

85. *Activities included (1) a review of the mission statement, strategic plan, annual and other significant reports, and major program goals and objectives for each agency to determine whether Healthcare disparities for people with disabilities had been identified as an area in which activities would be undertaken; (2) a keyword search of the agency Web sites to identify documents or other information that would reveal an agency's involvement in Healthcare disparity research or other health or Healthcare activities on behalf of people with disabilities that might not be readily apparent in the agency's priority program areas, goals, or objectives; and (3) key informant and informational interviews with certain agency representatives.*

86. *The datasets selected for examination were those listed as primary sources for the benchmarks in "Healthy People 2010 "and those that contained a large number of Healthcare questions. For these datasets, NCD examined the questionnaires, the*

documentation, and recent published works that used these datasets. NCD also reviewed reports by others who assessed the potential of Federal datasets, congressional testimony, Government Accountability Office reports, and some Webinar transcripts. Two key assessments are the NCD Indicators Report (2008/ and the University of California, San Francisco Disability Data Inventory (2005). Nine researchers were interviewed who had published papers on health disparities and people with disabilities or oilier aspects of Healthcare utilization, satisfaction with care, or the Healthcare experience of people with disabilities.

87. One or more key leaders in each program were interviewed to determine how the program came into being; what community need is being met; the extent to which the program is stable and fully integrated into a broader organization, if applicable; and how program beneficiaries rate the service they receive. Written evaluations and other related documentation were also obtained for each program that is reported as an effective practice, and in some cases NCD conducted client interviews to gain more insight into the program. Programs that do not meet all these criteria but appear to offer innovative or noteworthy services that meet specific Healthcare needs of people with disabilities or a subgroup of people with disabilities are reported as "practices with potential. 'World Health Organization, International Classification of Functioning, Disability and Health (1CF) (Geneva: World Health Organization, 2001).

88. Brault. "Americans with Disabilities: 2005," 2008, p. 14. [1] A. Stratton, M. Hynes, and A. Nepaul, "Issue Brief-Defining Health Disparities," Connecticut Health Disparities Project, Connecticut Department of Public Health, Summer 2007,

89. <www.ct.gov/dph/lib/dph/hisr/pdf7defining_health disparities.pdf> (accessed August 20, 2008); R.B. Warnecke el al., "Approaching Health Disparities from a Population Perspective: The National Institutes of Health Centers for Population Health and Health Disparities, "American Journal of Public Health, 98, no. 9 (2008), pp. 1608-1615; and O. Carter-Pokras and C. Baque, "What Is a 'Health Disparity'?" Public Health Reports, 117 (October 2002), pp. 30-90.

90. B AltmanandA. Bernstein, Disability and Health in the United States, 2001-2005, (Hyattsville, Ml): National Center for Health Statistics, 2008).

91. Please note that the study's methods for defining disability differ somewhat from the methods used by the 2000 U.S. Census. For more information about the disability questions from the 2000 Census, see <www.census.gov/prod/2003pubs/c2kbr-17.pdf>.

92. Altman and Bernstein, in Disability and Health in the United States, say, "Basic actions difficulty captures limitations or difficulties in movement and sensory, emo-tional, or

mental functioning that are associated with some health problem. NHIS data do not cover the full range of functional levels for all classes of basic actionsbut the available questions can identify [the following] range of difficulty levels in core areas of functioning: 1] movement (walking, standing, bending or kneeling, reaching overhead, and using the hands and fingers); [2] sensory functioning (the ability of a person to see and hear what is going on around him or her); [3j selected elements of emotional functioning—in particular, feelings that interfere with accomplishing daily activities; /4f Important elements in cognitive functioning, specifically difficulties with remembering or experiencing confusion, "p. 5. ' Altman and Bernstein, in Disability and Health in the United States, *say, "Complex activity limitation describes limitations or restrictions in a person's ability to participate fully in social role activities such as working or maintaining a household.*

93. *Complex activity consists of the tasks and organized activities that, when executed, make up numerous social roles. Complex activity performance requires the execution of a combination of more than one of the basic actions. NHIS obtains information on many (but not all) complex activities that comprise participation in social roles, including the following: flj difficulties experienced with social and leisure activities, represented in these data In questions about attending movies or sporting events, visiting with friends, pursuing hobbies, or engaging in relaxation activities; [2] perceived ability to work, which is a core aspect of social participation for the majority of the U.S. population and is represented by respondents' self-defined limitations in the kind or amount of work they can do or their inability to work at a job or business; [3] maintaining independence, including self-care and the ability to carry out activities associated with maintaining a household, such as shopping, cooking, and taking care of bills (measures are based on questions concerning ADL and IADL). These are the simplest of the complex activities, but limitations in doing them usually reflect the most severe difficulties in basic actions,".p. 8. ' Ibid, p. 27. ' Ibid, p. 34. ' Ibid p 37. ' Ibid. ' Ibid.*

94. *Ibid, p. 47. ' Ibid, p. 44. ' Ibid, p. 56. ' [bid.*

95. *Mari-Lynn Drainoni et al., "Cross-Disability Experiences of Barriers of Health-Care Access, "*Journal of Disability Policy Studies *17, no. 2 (2006), p. 102.*

96. *"Understanding the Healthcare Needs and Experiences of People with Disabilities: Findings from a 2003 Survey, "Henry J. Kaiser Family Foundation, <http://www.kff.org/medicare/iipload/Understanding-lhe-fleallh-Care-Needs-and-Experiences-of-People-with-Disabilities-Findings-from-a-2003-Survey.pdf> (accessed July 6. 2009)*

97. *"Medicaid: A Primer—Key Information on the Health Program for Low-Income Americans. "Henry J. Kaiser Family Foundation, Kaiser Commission on Medicaid*

and the Uninsured, March 2007, <www.kff.org/medicaid/upload7Medicaid-A-Primer-pdf.pdf> (accessedSeptember 3, 2008), p. 8. [1] *Ibid, p.6.*

98. *Jeffrey S. Crowley and Risa Ellas, "Medicaid's Role for People with Disabilities, "Henry J. Kaiser Foundation, Kaiser Commission on Medicaid and the Uninsured (August 2003), p. 12, <http://aging.senate.gov/minorih'/' files/hrl44jc.pdf>.*

99. *"Uninsured Americans with Chronic Health Conditions: Key Findings from the National Health Interview Survey, "Robert Wood Johnson Foundation, May 2005, p. 4., <www.urban.org/Uploaded!'DF/411161 uninsured americans.pdf>.*

100. *II. Stephen Kaye,* Disability Watch: The Status of People with Disabilities in the United States, *vol. 2 (San Francisco: Disability Rights Advocates, Inc., 2001) p. 9.*

101. *"The Uninsured and the Difference Health Insurance Makes, "Henry J. Kaiser Foundation, Kaiser Commission on Medicaid and the Uninsured, September 2008, <www.kff.org/uninsured/upload/1420-10. pdf> (accessed October 2, 2008).*

102. *("rowley and Elias, "Medicaid's Role for People with Disabilities," p. 11.*

103. *"California Health Insurance Plans-DME Coverage by 214 Health Plans As of February 2007, "Disability Rights Education and Defense Fund, <http://dredf.Org /healthcare/CADMFJ17 survey updatemlh.pdf> (accessed August 2003).*

104. *National Council on Disability,* Implementation of the Americans with Disabilities Act: Challenges, Best Practices, and New Opportunities for Success *(Washington, DC: NCD, July 26, 2007), p. 30*

105. *Marty Wyngaarden Krauss, Stephen Gulley, Mark Sciegaj, and Nora Wells, "Access to Specialty Medical Care for (liildren with Mental Retardation, Autism, and Other Special Healthcare Needs,"* Mental Retardation *41, no. 5 (2003).*

106. *Kaye,* Disability Watch, *pp. 7-9, 11-12. ' Ibid, p. 13.*

107. *Crowley and Elias, "Medicaid's Role for People with Disabilities," p. 11.*

108. *Carmen DeNavas-Walt, Bernadette D. Proctor, and Jessica C. Smith, "U.S. Census Bureau, Current Population Reports, P60-235,* "Income, Poverty, and Health Insurance Coverage in the United States: 2007 *(Washington, D(': U.S. Government Printing Office, 2008), p. 19. <www.census.gov/prod/2008pubs/p60-235.pdf> (accessed April 4. 2009).*

109. *"The Uninsured: A Primer: Key Facts About Americans Without Health Insurance, "Kaiser commission on Medicaid and the Uninsured, Henry J. Kaiser Family Foundation, October 2008. <www.kff.org/uninsured'uploud/'i'451'-04,pdf> (accessed April 4, 2009). ' Ibid.*

110. *Gloria L. Krahn and Charles E. Drumm, "Translating Policy Principles into Practice to Improve Healthcare Access for Adults with Intellectual Disabilities: A Re-*

search Review of the Past Decade," Mental Retardation and Developmental Disabilities Research Reviews *13 (2007), pp. 160-168.*

111. *J. M. Glionna, "Suit Faults Kaiser's Care for Disabled; Courts, Advocates Say Provider Fails to Give Equal and Adequate Treatment to the Handicapped. Chain Says It Complies with Disabilities Act,* "Los Angeles Times (record edition), *July 27 2000, p. 3.*

112. One Degree of Separation: Paralysis and Spinal Cord Injury in the United States *(Short Hills, N.l: ('hrisiopher and Dana Reeve Foundation, April 2008).*

113. *Centers for Disease Control and Prevention, "Women with Disabilities," <http://www.cdc.gov/ncbddd/women/default.htm> (accessed April 3, 2008); Office on Disability and Office on Women's Health,* Breaking Down Barriers to Healthcare for Women with Disabilities: A White Paper from a National Summit *(Washington, DC: Department of Health and Human Services, 2004).*

114. *"Healthcare for Minority Women, "Agency for Healthcare Research and Quality, Department of Health and Human Services, <www.ahrq.gov/research/minority.htm> (accessed September 17, 2008).* [1] *Brault," Americans with Disabilities: 2005, "2008, p. 5.*

115. *M. Lelhbridge-Cejku, J. S. Schiller, and L. Bernadel, "Summary Health Statistics for U.S. Adults: National Health*

116. *Interview Survey, 2002,* "National Center for Health Statistics. Vital Health Statistics *10, no. 222 (2004).*

117. *U.S. Census Bureau.* Characteristics of the Civilian Non-institutionalized Population by Age, Disability Status, and

118. Type of Disability 2000. *(Washington, DC: 2003).*

119. *Brault, "Americans with Disabilities: 2005," 2008, p. 5.*

120. *"Improving the Health and Wellness of Women with Disabilities: A Symposium to Establish a Research Agenda. "Executive Summary, Center for Research on Women with Disabilities (CROWD), Baylor College of Medicine, <www.ban.edu/crowd/?pmid=6107> (accessed March 22, 2008).*

121. *Susan L. Parish and M. Jennifer Ellison-Marti ı, "Health-Care Access of Women Medicaid Recipients: Evidence of Disability-based Disparities,* "Journal of Disability Policy Studies *18. no. 2 (2007). pp. 109-116.\ 'Margaret A. Nosek," Women, Disability, and Healthcare Reform, "presentation. National Women's Law Center. June 12, 2008.*

122. *Altman and Bernstein,* Disability and Health in the United States, *2008.*

123. *"Improving the Health and Wellness of Women with Disabilities," CROWD.*

124. *Frances Chevarley et al., "Health, Preventive Healthcare, and Healthcare Acce Among Women with Disabilities in the 1994-995 National Health Interview Survey, Supplement on Disability,"* Women's Health Issues *16 (2006), pp. 297-312.*

125. *Office on Disability and Office on Women's Health,* Breaking Down Barriers, *2004.*

126. *Altman and Bernstein,* Disability and Health in the United States, *2003. 'Kristina Hanson, Tricia Neuman, and Molly Voris, "Understanding the Health-C 'are Needs ami Experiences of People with Disabilities, Findings from a 2003 Survey, "Henry J. Kaiser Family foundation. <www.kff.org/medicare/6106.cfm> (accessed March 27, 2008). [1] Altman and Bernstein,* Disability and Health in the United States, *2008.*

127. *According to CROWD, nearly two-thirds of those with functional limitations who live in the community rely exclusively on family, friends, and volunteers for personal assistance services.*

128. *"Healthcare: Health Insurance," CROWD, Baylor College of Medicine. <wrn'. hem, edu/crowd'/PMID-1334> (accessed April 2, 2008).*

129. *Sandra A. Welner, "Gynecologic Care and Sexuality Issues for Women with Disa-bilities."* Sexuality and Disability *15, no. 1 (1997).*

130. *H. Becker, A. Stuifbergen, and M. Tinkle, "Reproductive Healthcare Experiences of Women with Physical Disabilities: A Qualitative Study, "*Archives of Physical and Medical Rehabilitation *12, no. 5 (1997): S26-S30. [1] J. Panko Reis, M. L. Breslin, L. I. lezzoni, and K. Kirscher,* It Takes More Than Ramps to Solve the Healthcare Crisis for People with Disabilities *(Chicago: Rehabilitation Institute of Chicago, 2004).*

131. *AG. Steinberg et al., "Deaf Women: Experiences and Perceptions of Healthcare System Access, "*Journal of Women's Health *//, no. 8 (2002), p. 733.*

132. *N. I. Gavin, M. B. Benedict, and E. K. Adams, "Health Service Use and Outcomes Among Disabled Medicaid Pregnant Women,"* Women's Health Issues *16, no. 6 (2006), pp. 313-322.*

133. *Susan L. Parish and Jungwon Huh, "Healthcare for Women with Disabilities: Population-Based Evidence of Disparities,"* Health and Social Work *32, no. 1 (2006), pp. 7-15.*

134. *Rosemary B. Hughes, "Achieving Effective Health Promotion for Women with Disabilities"* Family Community Health / *(2006), 44S-51S.*

135. *W. Wei, P.A. Findley, and U. Sambamoorthi, "Disability and Receipt of Clinical Preven-tive Services among Women,"* Women's Health Issues *46, no. 6 (2006), pp. 286-296.*

136. *N. Mele, J. Archer, and B. D. Pusch, "Access to Breast Cancer Screening Services for Women with Disabilities,"* Journal of Obstetrics and Gynecology—Neonatal Nurs-

ıng *34, no. 4 (2005), pp. 453-464.* [1] *Drainoni et al., "Cross-Disability Experiences of Barriers, "pp. 101-115.*

137. *Ellen P. McCarthy, Long H. Ngo, Richard G. Roetzheim, Thomas N. Chirikos, Donglin Li, Reed E. Drews, and Lisa I. lezzoni, "Disparities in Breast Cancer Treatment and Survival for Women with Disabilities,"* Annals of Internal Medicine *145, no. 9 (2006): 637-645, <www.annals.org/cgi/content/abstract/145/9/637> (accessedMarch 9, 2009).*

138. *Kristi L. Kirschner, Mary Lou Breslin, and Lisa I. lezzoni, "Structural Impairments That Limit Access to Healthcare for Patients with Disabilities,"* Journal of the American Medical Association *297 (2007), pp. 1121- 1125. ' R. G. Roetzheim, T. N. Chirikos, K. J. Wells, E. P. McCarth, L. H. Ngo, D. Li, R. E. Drews, and L. I. lezzoni, "Managed Care and Cancer Outcomes for Medicare Beneficiaries with Disabilities,"* American Journal of Managed Care, *14, no. 5 (May 2008), pp. 287-296.*

139. *Office on Disability and Office on Women's Health,* Breaking Down Barriers, *p. 4.*

140. *G. Steinberg et al., "Deaf Women: Experiences and Perceptions of Healthcare System Access."* Journal of Women's Health *11, no. 8 (2002), pp. 729-741.*

141. *Lisa 1. lezzoni et al., "Mobility Impairments and Use of Screening and Preventive Services,"* American Journal of Public 1 lealth *90, no. 6 (2000), p. 140; Lisa I. lezzoni et al., "Use of Screening and Preventive Services Among"*

142. *Women with Disabilities,* "American Journal of Medical Quality *16, no. 4 (2001), pp. 135- 144."*

143. *Leighton Chan et al., "Do Medicare Patients with Disabilities Receive Preventive Services/ A Population-based"*

144. *Study,* "Archives of Physical Medical Rehabilitation *80, no. 6 (1999")", pp. 642-646.*

145. *Altman and Bernstein,* Disability and Health in the United States.

146. *Drainoni et al., "Cross-Disability Experiences of Barriers," pp. 101-115.*

147. *Kirschner et al., "Structural Impairments," 2007. Legal actions that have targeted Healthcare professionals and organizations include about 157 cases settled by the Department of Justice between 1994 and 2006* [1] *Theresa Capriotti, "Inadequate Cardiovascular Disease Prevention in Women with Physical Disabilities,* "Rehabilitation Nursing *31, no. 3 (2006)," pp. 95-101.*

148. *Office on Disability and the Office on Women's Health,* Breaking Down Barriers.

149. *Lisa M. Harmer, "Healthcare Delivery and Deaf People: Practice, Problems, and Recommendations for Change,"* Journal of Deaf Studies and Deaf Education *4, no. 2 (1999), pp. 74-110.*

150. *A. Schoenborn and K. Heyman, "Health Disparities Among Adults with He Loss in the United States. 2000-2006, "National Center for Health Statistic. <www.cdc.gov/nchs/products/pubs/pubd/hestats/hearingOO-06/hearing00-06.html> (accessed June 27, 2008). Hearing status is based on the question "Which statement best describes your hearing without a hearing aid: good, a little trouble, a lot of trouble, deaf?"*[1] *S. Barnett and P. Franks, "Healthcare Utilization and Adults Who Are Deaf: Relationship with Age at Onset of Deafness,* "Health Services Research *37, no. 1 (2002), pp. 105-120.*

151. *University of Rochester Medical Center, <www.unnc.edu/pr/News/stoiy.cfm? id"623> (accessed April 14. 2008);*

152. *Harmer, "Healthcare Delivery"; and P. W. Reis, "Prevalence and Characteristics of Persons with Hearing"*

153. *Trouble: United States, 1990-1991,* "Vital Health Statistics *10, no. 188 (1994)."*

154. *Schoenborn and Heyman, "Health Disparities Among Adults with Hearing Loss."*

155. *University of Rochester Medical Center.*

156. *Barnett and Franks, "Healthcare Utilization."*

157. *Lisa lezzoni et al., "Communicating About Healthcare: Observations from Persons Who are Deaf or Hard of Hearing,* "Annals of Internal Medicine *140, no. 5 (2004), pp. 356-362.*

158. *A.G. Steinberg et al, "Healthcare System Accessibility: Experiences and Perceptions oj Deaf People,"* Journal of General Internal Medicine *3 (2006), pp. 260-266.* [1] *Schoenborn and Heyman, "Health Disparities."*

159. *Guthmann and K. Sandberg, "Assessing Substance Abuse Problems in Deaf and Hard-of- Hearing Individuals,"*

160. American Annals of the Deaf *143, no. 1 (1998), pp. 14-21.*

161. *Schoenborn and Heyman, "Health Disparities."*

162. *Harmer, "Healthcare Delivery."*

163. *Barnett and Franks, "Healthcare Utilization."*

164. *Ibid.*

165. *lezzoni et al., "Communicating About Healthcare." University of Rochester Medical Center.*

166. *Paul C. Ajumian, "Don 7 turn a deaf ear; patients with vision loss are also more likely to have hearing loss. As a primary-care doctor, here's how you can help them. "(Comanagement Q+A),* Review of Optometry *145, no. 7 (July*

, *2008), p. 81.*

"Guidelines for Services to Deaf and HOH Adults, "Delmarva Foundation for Medical Care, Inc., Gallaudet University, and the Healthcare Financing Administration. www, hearing! ossweb. com/lssues/A ccess/Medical/dele. htm> (accessed March 2, 2009).

169. *Arthur Wingfield, Patricia A. Tun, and Sandra L. McCoy, "Hearing Loss in Older Adulthood.* "Current Directions in Psychological Science *14, no. 3 (2005), pp. 144-148.*[1] *Steinberg et al., "Healthcare System." Teri Hedding, deaf access program manager, Mt. Sinai Hospital, Chicago, Illinois, email correspondence (August 16, 2008).*

170. *lezzoni et al., "Communicating About Healthcare"; Steinberg et al., "Healthcare System." Steinberg et al., "Healthcare System."*

171. *Steinberg et al, "Healthcare System" ; lezzoni et al., "Communicating About Healthcare."*

172. *Ibid.*

173. *Drainoni et al., "Cross-Disability Experiences of Barriers," pp. 101—115. ' Ibid.*

174. *Steinberg et al., "Healthcare System."*

175. *D.A. Ebert and P.S. Heckerling, "Communication with Deaf Patients: Knowledge, Beliefs, and Practices of Physicians,"* Journal of American Medical Association *273, no. 3 (1995), pp. 227-229.*

176. *J.M. Orsi et al., "Cancer Screening Knowledge, Attitudes, and Behaviors Among Culturally Deaf Adults"*

177. *Implications for Informed Decision Making,* "Cancer Detection Prevention *31, no. 6 (2007), pp. 474 479.*

178. *Sternberg, V. Sullivan, and R. Loew, "Cultural and Linguistic Harriers to Mental Health Services" The Deal*

179. *Consumer's Perspective,* "American Journal of Psychiatry *157, no. 7 (1998)," pp. 982-984.*

180. *Teri Hedding, email correspondence (August 16, 2008).*

181. *D.M. Feldman and A. Gum, "Multigenerational Perceptions of Mental Health Services Among Deaf Adults in Florida,"* American Annals of the Deaf *152, no. 4 (2007), pp. 391-397.*

182. http://www.bbc.co.uk/history/historic figures /nightingale_florence. shtml

183. Management, Principles and Functions – John M. Ivancerich, et al 1996

184. Harold Koontz, et al. Essentials of Management (5th Edn.), McGraw_Hill International

Edition, 1999

185. Dalton E Mc Farland, Management Principles and Practice, McMillan, New Work

186. Primary Healthcare: World Health Organization, Geneva, 1978.

187. Anand RC: Modern Approach for Management of Hospital as a System, Seminar on Hospital Administration: AIIMS, New Delhi, 1984

188. Sakharkar B.M., Principles of Hospital Administration & Planning (2nd Edn.), Jayree Brothers Medical Publishers (P) Ltd.

189. Joshi D.C., Joshi Mamta, Hospital Administration, Jaypee Brother Medical Publisher (P) Ltd.

190. Koontz H., O'Donell C, Weihrich H: Management, McGraw Hill Book Co., New Delhi 1993

191. Rakich JS, Darr K, Hospital Organization and Management Spectrum Publication, Jamaica, 1983.

192. Landmark J, The effect on Hospitals of Expanding PHC in Sweden. World Hospital XXII (3): 1986

193. Hhtp://en,wikipedia,org/wiki/hospital

194. http://www.ncki.nim.nih.gov/pmc/articles/pmc 182

195. http://www.tob_cntrl_edited8.doc

196. https://mail,google.com/mail/?ui=2@ik=c14f4553bi

197. http://www.google.co.in/image?hi=en&q=anti+smokin

198. http://en,wikipedia.org/wiki/smoking_ban

199. http://www.who.int/en

QUESTION PAPERS

B. B. A. (Vth Semester) Examination, 2008
Healthcare Management
(BBA- 503)

Time Allowed: Three Hours **Maximum Marks: 70**

Note: Attempt *Five* questions in all, including Question No. 1, which is compulsory.

1. Read the case and solve the questions given bellow : 3

It is increasingly being recognized that good health is an important contributor to productivity and economic growth, but it is first and foremost, an end in itself. In a poor country like India, where the only asset most people have in their bodies, health assumes even greater significance.

The Indian state has articulated the responsibility often enough. Since indepen-dence, the government ostensibly driven by socialistic goals has expressed its intentions to discharge this responsibility in one five year plan after the other.

Ambitious systems, programmes, schemes have been drawn up to alleviate poverty while promoting the goal of universal Healthcare, although the close linkages between the two have not been fully appreciated. There have been large gains in health status since independence. Life expectancy has gone up, infant mortality rate gone down, reduced crude birth rate and crude death rate. There has been 3-tier system of rural health infrastructure with subcentres. The National Health Policy has set some targets. The states role in health has fallen well short of its declared intentions. The private sector is almost entirely, unregulated and not guided by national health goals. National family health survey shows only slight improvement. Non-communicable diseases will gradually become the dominant contributors to the burden of disease their share increasing from estimated 33 percent in 1998 ti 57 percent by 2020. The recurring refrain in any discussion of Indian health system is fincers, a refrain that grows more shrill and urgent because of policy failures and state neglect. 115

(*i*) Define Healthcare management.

(*ii*) Discuss the present challenges in current health scenario.

(*iii*) Reasons for health scenario being so bleak.

(*iv*) Major communicable and non-communicable diseases prevailing in India.

(*v*) Explain the flow of fund from Centre to states for financing Healthcare.

Unit-I

2. Discuss the salient features of National Health Policy 2002. 10

3. Mention the roles of private groups in Healthcare management. 3

Unit-II

4. Define characteristics and goals of Healthcare system in India. 10

5. Discuss the potential of health system research in private and public sector giving suitable examples. 10

Unit-III

6. Discuss the major issues and methods to improve the low public health expenditure of India. 10

7. Write short notes on:

(*a*) Budgeting

(*b*) Efficiency in case of Healthcare Management. 5x2=10

Unit IV

8. Discuss the role and potential of hospital administration in current scenario. 10

9. Define the features of Healthcare communications for social causes of anti-smoking. 10

B.B.A. (Vth Semester) Examination, 2009

Healthcare Management

(BBA-503)

Note : Answer *Five* questions in all, including Question No. 1, which is compulsory In addition attempt *one* question from each, of the four Units.

1. Write short notes on the following.:

(*i*) Healthcare services

• For answer see Q. 3 on page 32.

(*ii*) Healthcare and social development

• For answer see Q. 17 on page 11.

(*iii*) NGO and Healthcare

• For answer see Q. 2 on page 106.

(*iv*) Need assessment activity

• For answer see Q. 3 on page 107.

(*v*) Quality feature of Healthcare professional

• For answer see Q. 1 on page 27.

(*vi*) Hospital's classification in connection to health education.

• For answer see Q. 4(d) on page 91.

Unit I

2. Define primary Healthcare and elaborate the role of P.H.C.

• For answer see Q. 1 on page 107.

3. Role of UNICEF and WHO in Healthcare delivery system in India.

• For answer see Q. 2 on page 108.

Unit II

4. Discuss the role of Managers in Healthcare system.

• For answer see Q. 3 on page 109.

5. Discuss in brief the National Rural Health Mission.

• For answer see Q. 4 on page 112.

Unit III

6. Discuss the role of private sector in Healthcare management in India.

• For answer see Q. 5 on page 115.

7. Discuss the budgeting activity and its importance in Healthcare planning and implementation.

• For answer see Q. 6 on page 118.

Unit IV

8. Describe hospital's role in rural health education.

• For answer see Q, 7 on page 120.

9. Define communication and its role in sexually transmitted disease (STD), citing the example of HIV/AIDS.

• For answer see Q. 7 on page 96.

B.B.A. (Vth Semester) Examination, 2010
Healthcare Management
(BBA-503)

Time Allowed : Three Hours **Maximum Marks : 70**

Note: Answer *Five* questions in all, including Question No. 1, which is compulsory. In addition attempt *one* question from each of the four Units.

1. Write short notes on the following: 3x10=30
   (*a*) Distribution of health services in India
   (*b*) Role of voluntary groups in Healthcare
   (*c*) Healthcare decision making
   (*d*) Contemporary trends in Healthcare
   (*e*) Health service financing
   (*f*) Classification of hospitals
   (*g*) Statutory control of hospitals
   (*h*) Role of hospital administrator
   (*i*) Distribution of health services in India
   (*j*) National Health Policy

Unit I

2. Define Primary Healthcare and elaborate role of Primary Health Center. 10
3. Write an essay on Healthcare and social development in India. 10

Unit II

4. Explain the characteristics, goals and functions of Healthcare system in India 10
5. What is Health System Research ? Explain its uses and applications 10

Unit III

6. Write in detail about pricing in Healthcare services 10
7. What is budgeting ? Discuss in detail its significance in Healthcare economics. 10

Unit IV

8. What is hospital ? Discuss in detail its classification, organization and function. 10
9. Write in detail about Healthcare communication for social causes like AIDS, anti-smoking etc. 10